Four Central Theories of the Market Economy

This highly original work offers an intellectual history of four central theories underlying the market economic system, focusing on their conception, evolution, and applications.

Four Central Theories of the Market Economy traces the root of the theories, their conception and articulation, as well as their evolutions to the present time. It focuses on the four theories that are generally recognized as fundamental to the discipline of economics: the invisible hand, comparative advantage, the law of markets, and the quantity theory of money. These theories have profoundly influenced the world. Chapters explore their rich intellectual history from classical Greece to today, drawing on the original works of the great economic minds of the classical era and other thinkers who prepared the path for them, as well as those who refined their works or challenged them. This volume will leave the reader with a deep understanding of these pillars of the market economic system in the context of their historical development.

This book will be of great interest to all scholars and students of economics who are interested in the intellectual history of their discipline as well as scholars and students of intellectual history who are interested in economics.

Farhad Rassekh is a Professor of Economics at the University of Hartford, USA.

Routledge Studies in the History of Economics

For a full list of titles in this series, please visit www.routledge.com/series/SE0341

167 Revisiting Classical Economics
Studies in long-period analysis
Heinz Kurz and Neri Salvadori

168 The Development of Economics in Japan
From the inter-war period to the 2000s
Edited by Toichiro Asada

169 Real Business Cycle Models in Economics
Warren Young

170 Hayek and Popper
On rationality, economism, and democracy
Mark Amadeus Notturno

171 The Political and Economic Thought of the Young Keynes
Liberalism, markets and empire
Carlo Cristiano

172 Richard Cantillon's Essay on the Nature of Trade in General
A variorum edition
Richard Cantillon, Edited by Richard van den Berg

173 Value and Prices in Russian Economic Thought
A journey inside the Russian synthesis, 1890–1920
François Allisson

174 Economics and Capitalism in the Ottoman Empire
Deniz T. Kilinçoğlu

175 The Idea of History in Constructing Economics
Michael H. Turk

176 The German Historical School and European Economic Thought
Edited by José Luís Cardoso and Michalis Psalidopoulos

177 Economic Theory and its History
Edited by Giuseppe Freni, Heinz D. Kurz, Andrea Lavezzi and Rodolfo Signorino

178 Great Economic Thinkers from Antiquity to the Historical School
Translations from the series Klassiker der Nationalökonomie
Bertram Schefold

179 On the Foundations of Happiness in Economics
Reinterpreting Tibor Scitovsky
Mauizio Pugno

180 A Historical Political Economy of Capitalism
After metaphysics
Andrea Micocci

181 Comparisons in Economic Thought
Economic interdependency reconsidered
Stavros A. Drakopoulos

182 Four Central Theories of the Market Economy
Conception, evolution and application
Farhad Rassekh

Four Central Theories of the Market Economy

Conception, evolution and application

Farhad Rassekh

LONDON AND NEW YORK

First published 2017
by Routledge

2 Park Square, Milton Park, Abingdon, Oxfordshire OX14 4RN
52 Vanderbilt Avenue, New York, NY 10017

Routledge is an imprint of the Taylor & Francis Group, an informa business

First issued in paperback 2019

British Library Cataloguing in Publication Data
A catalogue record for this book is available from the British Library

Library of Congress Cataloging in Publication Data
Names: Rassekh, Farhad, author.
Title: Four central theories of the market economy : conception, evolution and application / Farhad Rassekh.
Description: Abingdon, Oxon ; New York, NY : Routledge, 2016.
Identifiers: LCCN 2016003138| ISBN 9780415622028 (hardback) | ISBN 9781315543109 (ebook)
Subjects: LCSH: Capitalism. | Economics.
Classification: LCC HB501 .R278 2016 | DDC 330.12/2—dc23
LC record available at http://lccn.loc.gov/2016003138

ISBN: 978-0-415-62202-8 (hbk)
ISBN: 978-0-367-86719-5 (pbk)

Typeset in Times New Roman PS
by diacriTech, Chennai

For my wife Shoreh; our children Norah, Monah, and Leilah; and our grandchildren Hannah, Raya, and Mina.

Contents

Detailed contents

Illustrations

Figures

Tables

Acknowledgments

I am deeply grateful to the following individuals who in many ways greatly improved my work on the present book. Of course they are not responsible for the content of the book. All errors are mine.

The late Warren Samuels, Michael Panik, Roy Ruffin, and Jonathan Wight made constructive comments on an early draft of chapter one. A number of individuals responded to my queries on various parts of the chapter. I have thanked them in the relevant places within the text. Andrea Maneschi, Jorge Morales Meoqui, and Henry Thompson offered valuable comments on an early draft of chapter two. Alan Deardorff's responses to my numerous questions clarified the intricacies of the comparative advantage theory. Similarly, Steven Kates' answers to my questions explicated several issues regarding Say's law. David Laidler's comments on chapter four substantially improved the work. My colleagues, particularly Bharat Kolluri and Michael Panik, were a source of encouragement while I was writing the book. Larry Gould, a physicist with a keen interest in economics, read my book proposal early on and ever since has encouraged me to continue the work.

The University of Hartford helped me in many ways. It granted me two sabbaticals without which this project would have been either impossible or would have taken much longer. The University's financial support made it possible for me to attend conferences, acquire numerous books, and subscribe to journals which were essential for the completion of the project. The staff at the library, especially Christine Bird, were quite helpful. Christy always responded promptly to my requests for books and articles. The book club at the University of Hartford stimulated my curiosity over many subjects related to the theme of the book. I have cited and quoted from many books that my fellow club members have chosen over the past 15 years. Their insightful discussions are priceless. My research assistant Jonathan Francois diligently and efficiently checked the accuracy and consistency of the references.

The editors of *History of Economic Ideas* kindly gave me permission to incorporate certain parts of my papers on the invisible hand and comparative advantage into the book. Laura Johnson, Editorial Assistant at Routledge, always answered my questions promptly. She discharged her duties with professionalism and efficiency.

Introduction

> "No idea or theory in economics, physics, chemistry, biology, philosophy and even mathematics is ever thoroughly understood except as the end-product of a slice of history, the result of some previous intellectual development." (Mark Blaug, 2001, p. 156)
>
> "… no sensible rational appraisal can be made of any doctrine without a rich knowledge of its historical development." (Larry Laudan, 1977, p. 193)

During the classical era of economics – roughly from the mid-eighteenth century to the mid-nineteenth century – David Hume, Adam Smith, Jean-Baptiste Say, and David Ricardo articulated the central theories of economics while many other thinkers, above all John Stuart Mill, explicated and expounded these theories. But the fundamental contributions of classical economists depended on the intellectual efforts of the preceding generations of scholars. The path dependency of economic theories – that came to fruition in the classical era and have continued to evolve ever since – constitutes the core of the present book. In particular, we will focus on the intellectual history of the following theories: the invisible hand, comparative advantage, the law of markets, and the quantity theory of money.

Historians of thought have often tried to identify the discoverer of a seminal idea. This is evident, for example, from the extensive writings on the discovery of the theory of comparative advantage and Say's law. In this regard William Baumol (1999, p. 202) writes, "Jacob Viner taught me long ago the dangers of asserting that a doctrine was first enunciated by any particular writer. Such claims only encourage scholars to turn up earlier writers who asserted something related to the proposition in question." Hence, the present book emphasizes the articulation (rather than discovery) of theories. This means we identify thinkers who articulated a particular theory in a way that, in the words of Francis Darwin, "convinced the world" of its veracity.

Below I will provide a brief definition of each of the four theories, but there are other definitions and interpretations that are also presented in the book.

The invisible-hand proposition

According to this proposition, a viable economic order cannot be contrived and imposed; rather, such order arises and evolves from interactions of individuals who seek to achieve their own economic ends. This is the most fundamental and paradoxical proposition in economics, which leads to questions such as: how does order emerge and survive without central direction? And why is it impossible to design an economic order? Chapter one attempts to answer these and many other related questions.

The invisible-hand proposition is an ancient insight. A contemporary of Aristotle, Chuang Tzu (369–286 BCE) observed, "Good order results spontaneously when things are left alone" (quoted in Murray Rothbard, 1999, p. 25). But it was Adam Smith who, by drawing on the intellectual legacy of his predecessors, articulated the essence of this proposition with utmost clarity and lucidity in a lecture in 1749, and spent a substantial portion of his scholarly career (until his death in 1790) to explicate it. The invisible hand has been highly controversial, and will certainly continue to engage the minds of many scholars in the foreseeable future. But this is a hallmark of a fundamental idea. Kenneth Arrow and Frank Hahn, despite being critical of the invisible-hand proposition, have characterized it as "surely the most important intellectual contribution that economic thought has made to the general understanding of social processes" (1971, p. 1).

The theory of comparative advantage

This theory demonstrates that all countries regardless of their circumstances can beneficially participate in the world economy. Accordingly, every economy (rich or poor, large or small, well-endowed or meagerly-endowed, and so on) has the opportunity to produce some good that other economies would be willing to purchase. While this proposition results from a seemingly simple model that David Ricardo crafted in 1817, sophisticated theoretical works in the twentieth century showed that, except in a few cases, the theory remains valid under a large number of conditions and assumptions. The theory of comparative advantage has served as the basis for supporting free trade among all countries.

Many people find the theory of comparative advantage too paradoxical to accept, or at least oppose its policy implication. If economy A is superior to economy B in every respect and able to produce *all* goods with fewer resources, then how can A gain from trading with B? Furthermore, if A has a comparative advantage in industries whose productivities rise faster than those in industries where B has a comparative advantage, will not free trade cause B to remain less advanced and never catch up with A? Several years ago, following an analysis of the theory in class a student asked me, "What can Ethiopia possibly produce that the U.S. cannot make more efficiently? Why should we buy anything from that country?" Such questions and doubts cross the minds of not only young students but also mature scholars. In reference to the theory of comparative advantage, the renowned historian Fernand Braudel (1984, pp. 47–48) has observed that "simple-minded tautologies" such as "a poor country is poor because it is poor" and "growth breeds more growth" make more sense "than the so-called 'irrefutable' pseudo theorem of David Ricardo." Those unfamiliar with the intricacies and subtleties of the theory of comparative advantage may be forgiven if they express doubts about its veracity. Indeed the paradoxical nature of Ricardo's theory and its deceptive simplicity mask its complexity and profundity. As the trade theorist Paul Krugman (1998, p. 35) has noted, "Ricardo's idea is truly, madly, deeply difficult" as well as being "utterly true, immensely sophisticated – and extremely relevant to the modern world." Chapter two demonstrates how Ricardo developed this difficult and sophisticated theory based on the insights of his intellectual predecessors.

The law of markets

The law of markets (or Say's law) regards production as the primary economic activity. It operates on the premise that human beings have an innate and insatiable desire for consumption of goods and services. Hence, what an economy needs is "the power to purchase," which only production can provide. The obvious implication is that public policy should aim at encouraging the aggregate supply rather than the demand. While the seeds of the law of markets, for the most part, were sown in the eighteenth century, Jean-Baptiste Say and James Mill articulated it (in separate publications) in the first decade of the nineteenth century.

Of the four theories covered in this book, the law of markets is the most controversial. In chapter three I have expressed my own objections to certain statements by the founders of the law. Nonetheless, it is a central economic theory because it launched the systematic study of business cycles, and the insights it imparts remain relevant to market economies. While periodic macroeconomic fluctuations had been occurring for a century or two prior to the advent of classical economics, the early economic thinkers in the classical era (Adam Smith and to some extent David Hume) focused their intellectual energy not on explaining the fluctuations, but exposing the errors of mercantilism and creating the new discipline of economics. By the early nineteenth century, however, the time was ripe for the economic minds to tackle questions such as: why do commercial crises occur and how can they be mitigated? Since then a great deal of theoretical and empirical works have attempted to answer these questions.

Students of economics generally think of Say's law as "supply creates its own demand," which is the definition John Maynard Keynes gave in the *General Theory*. But as William Baumol (1999, p. 199), who happens to be a Keynesian, has convincingly argued, "Keynes, at best, didn't get it quite right." Baumol (2003, p. 35) even goes as far as writing that Keynes' definition of Say's law is "a very bad caricature that only marginally resembles any of the original and certainly leaves out the bulk of its substance." Chapter three attempts to present "the bulk of its substance."

The quantity theory of money

According to this theory, the volume of money is of no consequence to the economy in the long run because prices ultimately adjust to whatever that volume may be. But the theory also maintains that a *change* in the quantity of money will have a short-run effect on the economy's output. Thus the quantity theorists maintain that fluctuations in the supply of money play a significant role in the economy.

Many observers throughout history have noted the positive correlation between the quantity of the medium of exchange (in any shape or form) and the price level. In fact according to Mark Blaug (1995, p. 27) the quantity theory is "the oldest surviving theory in economics." But it assumed a new dimension when the mercantilist writers in the sixteenth and seventeenth centuries argued for exports expansion and import restriction in order to cause gold and silver to flow into the country. In the framework of the quantity theory, David Hume showed why the mercantilist policy position is unsustainable. He introduced his theory first in a letter to Montesquieu in 1749 (the same year as Smith's lecture) and then elaborated on his theory in several essays in 1752. Hume's essays launched the field of monetary economics.

The quantity theory of money was debated intensely among the economists in the nineteenth century. Their debates over the role of money in the economy and whether money should be supplied exogenously or should be allowed to adjust passively to market activities prepared the path for the creation of central banks such as the Federal Reserve System in 1913. To a significant degree, central banks operate within the framework of, and guided by, the quantity theory of money. Here history is important. In 1929–1930 the Federal Reserve System ignored the basic implication of the quantity theory and adhered to the "Real Bill Doctrine." This means the Federal Reserve expanded the money supply when the economy was growing and reduced it (or let it fall) when the economy was shrinking. This policy contributed to, if not caused, the Great Depression. Chapter four, while presenting the evolution of the quantity theory, reviews the history of this episode as well as the Great Recession of 2008–2009.

Further reflections on the four theories

To a considerable extent, the theories described above were developed in order to refute and replace the mercantilist dogmas. In the nineteenth century, almost all economists accepted the basic idea of the invisible hand and attempted, within its framework, to build upon the works of their predecessors and further advance the theory of comparative advantage, the law of markets, and the quantity theory. Of course there were objections to all four theories. But the classical paradigm was quite triumphant until the onset of the Great Depression and the advent of Keynesian economics. John Maynard Keynes challenged what he called "the classical theory" and attacked its tenets, in particular, Say's law and the quantity theory. He had more success in marginalizing Say's law than the quantity theory. He also attacked certain corollaries of the invisible-hand proposition, and his views on free trade evolved from support into opposition.

Keynesian economics achieved much success in the 1950s and 1960s but lost its luster in the 1970s when the concurrent existence of unemployment and inflation contradicted its prediction that there is a tradeoff between the two macroeconomic phenomena. The 1980s and 1990s witnessed a mild revival of classical economics but the Financial Crisis and the Great Recession of 2008–2009, in the minds of many people, raised serious questions about the tenets of classical economics – reminiscent of the Great Depression. A recent and notable example is Jeff Madrick's *Seven Bad Ideas*, published in 2014 in the aftermath of the Great Recession, reviewed in the *New York Times* by Paul Krugman in September 2014, and in the *New York Review of Books* by Alan Blinder in December 2014. Madrick's beginning sentence is, "Economists' most fundamental ideas contributed centrally to the financial crisis of 2008 and the Great Recession that followed – the worst economic calamity since the Great Recession" (2014, p. 3). The first fundamental "bad" idea he attacks is the invisible hand and the second one is Say's law. His chapter four criticizes Milton Friedman's dictum that inflation is a monetary phenomenon – a dictum that results from the quantity theory of money. Madrick's chapter seven attempts to discredit the theory of comparative advantage and refute free trade.

The publication of Madrick's book as well many other books, articles, and newspaper columns in recent years – that hold the tenets of classical economics responsible for all economic maladies – indicate that the intellectual discourse regarding the desirable economic system and the optimum mix of the public and private sectors will continue in the foreseeable future. I hope the present book has made a contribution to this process by delineating the intricacies of the central economics theories while presenting and analyzing their conception, evolution, and application.

Bibliography

Arrow, Kenneth and Frank Hahn (1971), *General Competitive Analysis*, San Francisco, CA: Holden-Day, Inc.

Baumol, William (1999), "Say's Law," *Journal of Economic Perspectives* 13, 1, pp. 195–204.

Baumol, William J. (2003), "Say's Law and More Recent Macro Literature: Some Afterthoughts," in *Two Hundred Years of Say's Law*, ed. by Steven Kates, Cheltenham, UK: Edward Elgar, pp. 34–38.

Blaug, Mark (2001), "No History of Ideas, Please, We're Economists," *The Journal of Economic Perspectives* 15, 1, Winter, pp. 145–164.

Blaug, Mark (1995), "Why Is the Quantity Theory of Money the Oldest Surviving Theory in Economics?" in *The Quantity Theory of Money: From Locke to Keynes and Friedman*, ed. by Mark Blaug, Brookfield, VT: Edward Edgar, pp. 27–49.

Braudel, Fernand (1984), *Civilization and Capitalism, 15th–18th Century*, New York, NY: Harper & Row.

Krugman, Paul (1998), "Ricardo's Difficult Idea," in *The Economics and Politics of International Trade*, ed. by Gary Cook, London, UK and New York, NY: Routledge, pp. 22–41.

Laudan, Larry (1977), *Progress and Its Problems: Towards a Theory of Scientific Growth*, London, UK: Routledge and Kegan Paul.

Madrick, Jeff (2014), *Seven Bad Ideas: How Mainstream Economists Have Damaged America and the World*, New York, NY: Alfred A. Knopf.

Rothbard, Murray N. (1999), *Economic Thought before Adam Smith: An Austrian Perspective on the History of Economic Thought*, Volume I, Cheltenham, UK: Edward Elgar.

1 The invisible-hand proposition

"A common man marvels at uncommon things. A wise man marvels at the commonplace." (Confucius)

Chapter contents

1. Introduction

The phrase "invisible hand" serves as a metaphor for the proposition that market order arises and evolves from interactions of economic agents pursuing their own ends. More specifically, households and business firms engage in micro-planning that – although decentralized and dispersed throughout the economy – creates a macro-order which is neither designed (arguably, cannot be designed) nor intended. According to the invisible-hand proposition, the micro-plans, like the pieces of a puzzle, fall into place and produce the macro-order. Expressed in this way, the invisible hand constitutes *the* most fundamental proposition underlying the market economic system, for the utility and even the viability of the system rest on the validity of this proposition. If the invisible hand did not hold true – that is, if the voluntary actions and interactions of individuals did not produce a stable and beneficent, although not necessarily a perfect, economic order – the whole edifice of the market system would collapse.

This chapter delves into the fascinating intellectual history of the invisible-hand proposition and presents its conception, articulation, evolution, interpretations, and applications. Adam Smith (1723–1790), a leading figure of the Scottish Enlightenment, deserves the central place in this intellectual odyssey, for, although the phrase "invisible hand" predates him, and many other scholars have contributed to its elucidation, he is the first thinker who invoked it in economic discourse, and – more importantly – provided a systematic analysis of the market economy to which the workings of the invisible hand are fundamental. In a later section we will thoroughly review and analyze the use of the phrase "invisible hand" in Smith's writings; here, it suffices to note that Smith invoked it for the first time in a non-economic context in an essay in the early 1750s. He then used it once in *The Theory of Moral Sentiments* (1759/1984, p. 184) and once in *The Wealth of Nations* (1776/1981, p. 456). In both books he invoked it while explaining that self-interested economic behavior – unintentionally and unbeknown to the agents – promotes society's interest.

Although economists generally invoke the invisible hand as a metaphor for the market order, no consensus exists among the historians of economic thought on what Smith meant by the phrase or why he used it. In fact the invisible hand remains remarkably controversial and even elusive.[1] Peter Minowitz (2004, p. 411) writes, "Centuries after Smith's death, we are still struggling to fathom a two-word phrase that stands out in a thousand-page book." However, the invisible-hand *proposition* pervades Smith's writings and plays a fundamental role in his scholarly project. In an influential analysis of the invisible hand, Emma Rothschild (2001, p. 121) argues that Smith "used *words* which were to him slightly comical, or slightly unpleasant – the words 'invisible hand' – to describe an *idea* which was of profound importance to his theoretical system. The idea of the invisible hand can thus be distinguished, as far as it is possible, from the words in which it is described" (italics in original). The present chapter focuses on the *concept* of the invisible hand and uses the phrase only as a reference for the concept.

But the concept has also been subject to controversy. Gerard Debreu (1987, p. 216) notes that Smith had wondered "why a large number of agents motivated by self-interest and making independent decisions do not create social chaos in a private ownership economy." Similarly, Amos Witztum (2010, p. 159) – while noting that interdependence among individuals arises from specialization and trade – argues, "the question whether this interdependence leads to a continuous conflict or to some order that may or may not be beneficial is paramount to Smith's overall agenda." The views of many prominent scholars on the invisible hand range from praise to suspicion and even ridicule. James Tobin (1992, p. 117) refers to the invisible hand as "one of the great ideas of history and one of the most influential" and Friedrich Hayek (1967a, p. 99) hails the invisible hand as a "profound insight into the object of all social theory." But Frank Hahn (1982, p. 16) argues, "both on purely logical considerations as well as on the basis of quite simple observations, the invisible hand is likely to be unsure in its operations and occasionally downright arthritic" and Joseph Stiglitz (2002, p. 460) confidently asserts, "the reason the hand is invisible is that it is simply not there – or at least if it is there, it is palsied." We shall return to such views on the invisible hand.

Although the invisible hand embodies unintended consequences, human actions and public policy often produce unintended consequences with no relation whatsoever to the invisible-hand proposition. For an unintended consequence to count as the outcome of the invisible-hand process several conditions must hold. First, it must gradually arise and evolve from the interactions of individuals who pursue their own ends and are oblivious to the unintended outcome of their actions. Second, the emergent outcome should embody the contributions of interacting individuals in the process. Third, the interactions must lead to an order that Hayek (1973, p. 36) has described as "a state of affairs in which a multiplicity of elements of various kinds are so related to each other that we may learn from our acquaintance with some spatial or temporal part of the whole to form correct expectations concerning the rest, or at least expectations which have a good chance of proving correct." Finally, the structure of the emergent order must be different from the sum of its parts. (The last condition is called the principle of organic unity, to which we will return in a later section.)

Thus, as Amartya Sen (1999, p. 254) has pointed out, "the discovery of penicillin from a leftover dish not intended for that purpose" and "the destruction of the Nazi party caused by – but not intended in – Hitler's military overconfidence" constitute examples of unintended consequences but not of the invisible hand. Unintended consequences can be reprehensible, such as China's "one-child family" policy that has resulted in "sex-specific abortions" (Ibid., p. 258).[2] As an example of unintended consequences of public policy, consider the Three-Strikes Law passed in 1994 in California that had intended to reduce crime. Radha Iyengar (2008, p. 25) has documented that this law "imposed 50,000 crimes on other states due to the migration of criminals out of California." This unintended consequence does *not* qualify as an example of the invisible hand because it did not result from an evolutionary process involving interactions that produce an order in the Hayekian sense (noted above) and most importantly, it does not satisfy the principle of organic unity.

Examples of emergent phenomena that do qualify as the outcome of the invisible-hand process, as Hayek (1988, p. 24) has noted, include law, language, money, morals, markets, and even biological evolution.[3] But the extent of the invisible hand has gone beyond Hayek's list. Craig Smith (2006, p. 1), in his book *The Invisible Hand and Spontaneous Order*, writes, "spontaneous order-inspired arguments can be found in the fields of biology, science, epistemology, language, economics, history, law, theology, sociology, anthropology and even recently in management studies and computing."

There are only few and sporadic references to the phrase "invisible hand" in the nineteenth century's economics literature.[4] Since the early twentieth century, however (especially after the Second World War), the phrase has become quite popular, often invoked by economists and even non-economists in diverse settings.[5] Focusing on the concept, and not so much on the phrase, Hayek made the self-formation (his phrase) of social institutions the centerpiece of his scholarly project and gave a new life to the invisible-hand proposition. Contributions to general equilibrium theory (originating with Leon Walras in 1874), which – as we shall see later – attempts to model the workings of the invisible hand, also played an important role in reviving the proposition. More recently many scholars have turned to the insights and tools of the science of complexity – which focuses on self-organization in a number of natural and social phenomena – in order to understand the invisible-hand process. Similarly, evolutionary game theory – which studies the endogenous emergence of social institutions – has also attracted the attention of many scholars to the operation of the market.

Two intellectual developments gave birth to the invisible-hand proposition: first, contributions to the theory of market which originated in classical Greece and Rome; second, a controversy over human nature, launched by Thomas Hobbes' *Leviathan* in 1651. The next two sections present the contributions of these developments to the conception of the invisible-hand proposition.[6]

2. The theory of market before Adam Smith

The theory of market evolved throughout history as numerous thinkers, not all in favor of commercial activities, analyzed the consequences of market transactions. This section presents the main ideas that contributed to a general theory of market, culminating in a number of path-breaking and influential writings in the eighteenth century.

2.1. From antiquity to the sixteenth century

Western civilization (broadly defined) is profoundly influenced by the Greco-Roman intellectual legacies as well as the Judeo-Christian teachings. Hence the views of the seminal thinkers in these traditions on commerce, although largely unfavorable, have played a critical role in shaping the theory of market.[7] For example, the influential Greek philosophers (above all Socrates, Plato, and Aristotle) loathed commercial activities because they viewed them as inimical to the acquisition and practice of virtues. Socrates (469–399 BCE) believed that the pursuit of financial gain is incompatible with living a virtuous life. Plato (427–347 BCE) argued for the abolition of private property and advocated some form of communism. Aristotle (384–322 BCE) equated virtuous behavior with practicing moderation in all things, which, he argued, merchants do not observe because of their insatiable desire for wealth. Nonetheless, Aristotle believed in private property on the grounds that people have an interest to preserve their own belongings. He argued, "What is common to the greatest number has the least care bestowed upon it. Everyone thinks chiefly of his own, hardly at all of the common interest" (quoted in Elinor Ostrom, 1990, p. 2). Despite his support for private property, Aristotle never valued commercial activities. Rodney Stark (2005, p. 74) points out, "Aristotle's was not a voice in the wilderness; his was the conventional view in Greece. Labor was for slaves and commerce was for noncitizens."

But not all thinkers at the time were against commerce. Barry Gordon (1975, p. 14) in *Economic Analysis before Adam Smith, Hesiod to Lessius* notes that the philosopher Democritus (460–370 BCE) advocated freedom in economic activity on the grounds that "a society organised in terms of private ownership of resources will enjoy economic superiority over one where communal ownership prevails." The historian Xenophon (427–355 BCE), to whom we shall return in chapter two, realized that merchants' desire for profits leads to beneficial commodity arbitrage. Another Greek historian, Plutarch (45–125 CE), highly praised trade, for it had "brought the Greeks the wine from India, from Greece transmitted the use of grain across the sea, from Phoenicia imported letters as a memorial against forgetfulness, thus preventing the greater part of mankind from being wineless, grainless, and unlettered" (1927, p. 299). Plutarch's views, along with those of Democritus and Xenophon, constitute the early steps towards formulating the theory of market. But they were overshadowed for centuries by their influential contemporary philosophers who disdained commercial pursuits. The adverse views of Greek philosophers were reinforced by Roman thinkers such as Cicero (126–47 BCE) and Seneca (5 BCE–65 CE). Cicero praised agricultural work but denounced most other professions. He was "concerned with the respectability of various occupations, not with their productiveness" (Gray, 1931, p. 35). Seneca had little respect for commerce and declared that "money is the root of all evils."[8]

Christianity's view of commerce over the past two millennia has evolved from rejection to qualified acceptance and eventually to embracing and even nurturing the market system. Certain passages in the Bible disparage wealth and (apparently) commerce as well. The Gospel of Matthew (21:12–13) records the well-known parable that "Jesus entered the temple of God and drove out all who sold and bought in the temple, and he overturned the tables of the moneychangers and the seats of those who sold pigeons. He said to them, 'It is written, "My house shall be called a house of prayers"; but you make it a den of robbers.'"[9]

Although Jesus may not have meant to dissuade people from commercial activities, Jerry Muller (2002, p. 6) writes, "Referring to these verses, the early *Ejiciens Dominus* declared that the profession of merchant was scarcely ever agreeable to God." Muller further notes (Ibid.) that Gratian, a twelfth-century jurist who compiled canon law, "condemned trade and its profits absolutely," utterly rejected the act of arbitrage, and declared that those who engage in it "are cast forth from God's temple."

For centuries, religious teachings condemned commercial activities because they ostensibly rest on personal gains. Man was supposed to seek salvation, not self-interest. Jacob Viner (1960/1991, p. 203) explains:

> Early Christian thought held temporal matters as of only trivial and transitory significance, regarded commercial activity as almost inevitably motivated by avarice and permeated by cheating and exploitation, and insisted that the only true valuable freedom in temporal matters was the subjective freedom which could be won by the suppression of desire for temporal goods not unqualifiedly necessary for survival. The slave who had disciplined his passions was declared authoritatively to be in all that really mattered freer than his master who eagerly pursued worldly goods.

The influential theologian Augustine of Hippo (354–430) endorsed the prevailing view in his time that economic transactions are a zero-sum game.[10] Remarkably, a contemporary of Augustine, Libanius of Antioch, a pagan teacher, considered commerce to be a creation of God for the enjoyment of people because through commerce the fruits of earth can be brought to all people.[11] Libanius influenced the early Church Fathers St. Basil and John Chrysostom, who were his students and espoused the same sentiment. Such a view, however, "was fleeting and soon forgotten" (Muller, 2002, p. 7).

Drawing on recent translation of non-Western texts, Harry Landreth and David Colander (2002) introduce the economic writings of Al-Ghazali (1058–1111), an influential Islamic scholar. They (2002, p. 33) note that Al-Ghazali wrote about voluntary exchange, coordination of markets, and division of labor. Al-Ghazali's writings likely contributed to the later development of the theory of market because scholars in medieval Europe such as St. Thomas Aquinas (1225–1274), who wrote on commercial activities, had read the writings of Islamic philosophers.[12] Aquinas lent a qualified support to commerce and even agreed that merchants could serve a useful function.[13] Aquinas' views on two major economic issues of the time, namely, the "just price" and "usury," were regarded as authoritative in the medieval period (1988, p. 65).[14] Albertus Magnus (1193?–1280), Aquinas' teacher, defined the just price as the market price and wrote, "goods are worth according to the estimation of the market at the time of the sale" (quoted in Stark, 2005, p. 65). David Freidman (1987, p. 1043), writing on the medieval theologians, points out, "for many, including Aquinas, the just price of a good was normally its market price or where price control existed, its legal price." Aquinas may have accepted the market price as "just," but he disdained profit-seeking and, under the influence of the Greek philosophers, viewed commerce as inimical to the pursuit of virtues.[15] According to Joseph Schumpeter (1954, p. 91), Aquinas believed there was "'something base' about commerce."

Plato, Aristotle, Augustine, and Aquinas failed to appreciate the complexity of the market economy because they never delved deeply into the workings of commerce.[16] The understanding and articulation of this complexity lies at the heart of the theory of market which came to fruition in the eighteenth century, but numerous thinkers paved the way. For example, one of Aquinas' contemporary theologians, Richard of Middleton (1249–1360) taught "the social usefulness of the practice of buying in a cheaper market and selling in a dearer one" (Schumpeter, 1954, p. 91). Although Middleton's approval of commodity arbitrage is similar to that of Xenephon, he went further and explained that it benefits the producers as well as the consumers while the arbitrageurs themselves profit from the transaction. Middleton remarkably realized that the social utility of commercial transactions does not depend upon the motive of the merchants. This realization qualifies as a paradigm shift in judging the moral desirability of commerce, for it redirected the focus of scholars from the motives of economic agents towards the consequences of their actions. The desire for profit and the pursuit of self-interest in the market could no longer be easily invoked to condemn commerce.

Other scholastic doctors who analyzed the operation of the market include Duns Scouts (1266–1308), Luis de Molina (1535–1600), and Diego de Covarrabis (1512–1572). The contributions of these thinkers helped transform the perception of commerce from a necessary evil to a beneficial occupation.

2.2. From the sixteenth to the eighteenth century

Economic theories in the two centuries before the publication of the *Wealth of Nations* largely reflected the political reality of nation-building and the desire for strengthening the state. International conflicts during this period were a constant in continental Europe. Leonard Gomes (2003, p. 6) notes:

> Warfare was almost a normal relationship among European superpowers – England, Spain, France, and the Dutch Republic – as they engaged in geopolitical and dynastic struggles throughout most of the period. There was complete peace in only a single year during the period 1600–1667. Commercial rivalry – "jealousy of trade" as it was called – was a frequent cause of open conflict in sixteenth- and seventeenth-century Europe.

The economic policies associated with "jealousy of trade" were embodied in the writings of certain mercantilists and represented the economic thinking of the time.[17] Mercantilism is generally defined as a system that regards money as wealth, views foreign trade as a zero-sum game, and advocates policies that generate trade surplus. To the extent that mercantilist writers espoused such views (not all of them did), they slowed down the progress in the development of a general theory of market. Lars Magnusson (1995), however, has argued that mercantilist writers are often misinterpreted and misrepresented in the literature. Magnusson believes that beginning with two major figures of mercantilism, Thomas Mun (1571–1641) and Edward Misselden (d. 1654), "there was an increased recognition of the importance of the market mechanism. In both consumers and factor markets it was stressed that the forces of supply and demand create cheapness or dearness" (Magnusson, 1995, p. 16).

Nevertheless, many mercantilist writers including Mun espoused views that fairly or unfairly appear as protectionist. For example, he (1664/1959, p. 5) argued, "The ordinary means … to increase our wealth and treasure is by foraign trade, wherein wee must ever observe this rule: to sell more to strangers yearly than we consume of theirs in value." Magnusson (2007, p. 55) has noted that such a view reflected "a main concern" over a shortage of money in the economy. He (Ibid.) further notes, since England "had no silver or gold mines of its own," the mercantilists argued, "The only solution to this dilemma was to import money from abroad." According to this view, the mercantilist writers did not confuse money with wealth, nor did they necessarily intend to protect domestic industries, rather they aimed to increase the supply of money through foreign trade.

The mercantilists' focus on "practical political and economic policy issues" with "an overall objective … to achieve national wealth and power" clashed with the cosmopolitan views of thinkers who favored free trade (Magnusson, 2007, p. 49). Quite crucially for our purpose, the clash inadvertently contributed to the conception of the invisible hand. Consider, for example, Dudley North (1641–1691), Charles Davenant (1656–1714), and Henry Martyn (d. 1712) who argued that the pursuit of free trade promotes the general welfare. Of these, North consistently and clearly equated the individual interest with the public interest in a free-trade system. In 1691, he wrote: "there can be no trade unprofitable to the public; for if any prove so, men leave it off; and wherever the traders thrive, the public, of which they are a part, thrives also" (quoted in Gomes, 2003, p. 21). Similarly, Charles Davenant in an essay in 1696 argued: "Trade is in its Nature Free, finds its own Channel and best directeth its own Course; and all Laws to give it Rules and Directions, and to Limit, and Circumscribe it, may serve the Particular Ends of Private Men, but seldom Advantageous to the Publick" (quoted in Hont, 2005, p. 216).[18] As the seventeenth century drew to a close, all the elements for the conception of a solid theory of market were coming together.

3. Self-love and the invisible hand

The preceding section briefly surveyed the contributions of thinkers who tilled the intellectual landscape and sowed the seeds of a theory of market – a necessary development for the invisible-hand proposition. The controversy over human nature, launched with the publication of Thomas Hobbes' *Leviathan* in 1651, also made a decisive contribution, albeit indirectly and unintentionally, towards the conception of the invisible hand.

3.1. Hobbes' challenge

In his seminal work *Leviathan*, Thomas Hobbes paints a gloomy picture of human nature. He (1651/1946, p. 82) writes,

> in the nature of man, we find three principal causes of quarrel. First, competition; secondly, diffidence; thirdly, glory. The first maketh men invade for gain; the second, for safety; and the third, for reputation. The first use violence, to make themselves masters of other men's persons, wives, children, and cattle; the second, to defend them; the third, for trifles, as a word, a smile, a different opinion, and any other sign of undervalue … during the time men live without a common power to keep them all in awe, they are in the condition which is called war; and such a war, as is of every man, against every man.

Hobbes defines "war" not necessarily as "actual fighting; but in the known disposition thereto, during all the time there is no assurance to the contrary" (Ibid.). Human's natural impulse, he argues, for self-preservation leads to destructive behavior because it clashes with the desire for conquest. Consequently, a condition will emerge in which

> there is no place for Industry, because the fruit thereof is uncertain: and consequently no culture of the earth; no navigation, nor use of commodities that may be imported by sea; no commodious building; no instruments of moving and removing such things as require much force; no knowledge of the face of the earth; no account of time; no arts; no letters; no society; and which worst of all, continual fear, and danger of violent death; and the life of man, solitary, poor, nasty, brutish, and short. (Ibid.)

In such an arena of strife and conflict, Hobbes regards force and fraud as "the two cardinal virtues" (Ibid., p. 83). To avoid this abyss, he argues, all must surrender to an absolutely powerful sovereign through a contract.

Hobbes' portrait of human nature and condition led to intense debates on the role of self-love in society and resulted in several responses, one of which, known as the "economic response," (explained below) contributed to the conception and formulation of the invisible-hand proposition. Hobbes' own views, however, were contrary to the invisible hand. In fact, Hayek (1967b, p. 131) has placed Hobbes – as well as Descartes and Leibniz – in the category of rationalists whose work for "the understanding of social processes … was simply disastrous." In general, rationalists, socialists, and many utilitarians – to varying degrees – believe in directing the economy and society while the proponents of the invisible-hand proposition regard such a top-down approach as counter-productive and even destructive. We will return to this issue in a later section.

3.2. Early responses to Hobbes[19]

Hobbes' thoroughly materialistic philosophy outraged many of his contemporary ecclesiastics, theologians, and other thinkers who attempted to refute him. The first set of responses came from Richard Cumberland (1631–1718), Bishop of Peterborough; Anthony Ashley Cooper (1671–1713), the third Earl of Shaftesbury; and most importantly Joseph Butler (1692–1752), Bishop of Bristol and Durham. While each of these thinkers analyzed Hobbes' philosophy in a specific way, they all shared a deep conviction in the principle of design according to which since God has crafted the order of the universe and everything in it including human nature, self-love cannot be inherently evil and must be harmonious with social interests.[20] The design principle was quite popular at the time because the discoveries of scientists, such as Johannes Kepler (1571–1630), Galileo Galilei (1564–1642), and above all Isaac Newton (1642–1727), had presented the universe as an orderly place, operating according to certain mathematical and mechanical laws. To most thinkers in the seventeenth and eighteenth centuries, the universe appeared to be the work of a divine "watch-maker."

In response to Hobbes, Cumberland argued that since the interest of each individual is connected to the interest of others, private interests must be harmonious with public interest. Shaftesbury saw many impulses in human psyche of which self-interest is one and balanced by innate virtues such as benevolence as well as a sense of right and wrong. In a sermon in 1726 Butler prepared the path for Smith's invisible-hand passage in the *Wealth of Nations* when he (1726/1965, vol. 1, p. 201) said, "by acting merely from regard (suppose) to reputation, without any consideration of the good of others, men often contribute to public good. In both these instances … [men] carry on ends, the preservation of the individual and good of society, which they themselves have not in their view or intention." Although Butler clearly discerned the harmony between self-interest and the public interest, more analytical work was needed to lay out the workings of the invisible hand.

In the arguments against Hobbes, the design principle played another important role. The jewel of all scientific achievements at the time was the formulation of the law of gravity, which Newton had shown holds the universe together and serves as the source of order in the physical world. Inspired by Newton's discovery, several thinkers, whose most influential figure was Francis Hutcheson (1694–1746), Adam Smith's teacher, argued that the cohesion of the moral and social universe would require a similar force. They held that self-interest plays the same role in society as the force of gravity does in the universe.[21] These sentiments deeply influenced contemporary intellectuals and scholars including Alexander Pope (1688–1744) and Bernard Mandeville (1670–1733) whose works are presented next.

3.3. A tale of two literary works

In the early decades of the eighteenth century, the literary works of Pope and Mandeville reached a large audience. Pope, the most widely read poet in the eighteenth century, like many other thinkers of his time, embraced the design principle and its brainchild "optimistic deism," which he eloquently expressed in the following poem:

> Safe in the hands of one disposing Power,
> Or in the natal, or the mortal hour.
> All Nature is but Art, unknown to thee;
> All chance, direction, which thou canst not see;
> All discord, harmony not understood,
> All partial evil, universal Good:
> And spite of Pride, in erring Reason's spite,
> One truth is clear, *Whatever is, is right.*
> ("An Essay on Man," 1734/1931,
> p. 141, italics in original)

If "*Whatever is, is right*" then self-love cannot (at least has the potential not to) be evil, nor should the pursuit of self-interest conflict with the public interest.[22] Pope ended his poem by reaffirming that self-love and social good are identical:

> From sounds to things, from fancy to the heart:
> For Wit's false mirror held up Nature's light,
> Show'd erring pride, *Whatever is, is right*;
> That Reason, Passion answer one great aim;
> That true Self-love and Social are the same;
> That Virtue only makes our bliss below,
> And all our knowledge is, *ourselves to know*.
> (Ibid., p. 155, italics in original)

One can sense the dramatic intellectual transformation that was under way by the time this poem reached the public in 1734. Self-love, generally perceived as a destructive impulse, was morphing into a constructive force. Albert Hirschman (1977, p. 42) regards this transformation as a paradigm shift (á la Thomas Kuhn). But the process was not yet complete; more analytical work was needed. Let us now turn to the other literary work.

Mandeville published his poem *The Grumbling Hive, Or Knaves Turn'd Honest* in 1705. He republished the poem in 1714 along with a prose commentary and called it *The Fable of Bees OR Private Vices, Publick Benefits*. Mandeville argued human vices (fraud, deception, hypocrisy, theft, and so on) are socially beneficial. Here are a few examples:

> Such were the Blessings of that State;
> Their Crimes conspir'd to make them Great:

And Virtue, who from Politicks
Had learn'd a Thousand Cunning Tricks,
Was, by their happy Influence,
Made Friends with Vice: And ever since,
The Worst of all the Multitude
Did Something for the Common Good.
(1714/1924, p. 24)

THE Root of Evil, Avarice,
That damn'd ill-natur'd baneful Vice,
Was Slave to Prodigality,
That noble Sin; whilst Luxury
Employ'd a Million of the Poor,
And odious Pride a Million more;
Envy it self, and Vanity,
Were ministers of Industry;
Their darling Folly, Fickleness,
In Diet, Furniture and dress,
That strange ridic'lous Vice, was made
The very Wheel that turn'd the Trade.
(Ibid., p. 25)

Mandeville ended his poem with "The Moral," in which he included the following:

Without great Vices, is a vain
EUTOPIA *seated in the Brain.*
Fraud, Luxury and Pride must live,
While we the Benefits receive.
(Ibid., p. 36, italics in original)

With the assertion that human vices actually benefit the public, the *Fable* outraged the intellectual community that was already embroiled in the controversy over the role of self-love in society.[23] Hutcheson repeatedly criticized Mandeville to the point that F. B. Kay (1924, p. cxli), the editor of Mandeville's book, notes: "Mandeville was an obsession with Hutcheson. He could hardly write a book without devoting much of it attacking the Fable." Although Smith (1759/1984, p. 309) reaffirmed a Mandevillian notion that "self-love may frequently be a virtuous motive of action," he rejected the thesis that private vices such as fraud, deception, hypocrisy, and theft benefit the public. In fact Smith (1759/1984, p. 315) believed that "Virtue is the great support, and vice the great disturber of human society." He characterized "the system of Dr. Mandeville" as "wholly pernicious" because it takes "away altogether the distinction between vice and virtue" (1759/1984, p. 308).

In an extensive commentary on his own poem, Mandeville devoted several pages to the last couplet, quoted above, "The Worst of all the Multitude Did

Something for the Common Good" (Mandeville 1714/1924, p. 24). He anticipated that he would "be ask'd what Benefit the Publick receives from Thieves and House-Breakers." He responded, "if all People were strictly honest, and no body would meddle with or pry into any thing but his own, half the Smiths of the Nation would want Employment" (Ibid., p. 86). He went on to say that "Pilferer and Robbers" benefit the society by creating jobs for the police. He also argued quite seriously that since "Thieves and Pick-pockets steal for a Livelihood" and spend it, they benefit the public.[24] Mandeville went as far saying that the Fire of London (which happened on September 2, 1666) had actually benefited the Londoners because it had provided jobs for all those who reconstructed the city.[25]

Mandeville's economic argument fits the "Broken Window" fallacy of Frederic Bastiat (1801–1850), who pointed out that some people regard a destructive act, such as breaking a window or commencing a war, as beneficial because it increases the sales in some businesses (e.g., the glazier).[26] The fallacy lies in the fact that the money paid to the glazier is a diversion from some other businesses. Mandeville confused the creation of wealth with the distribution of wealth and apparently did not realize that stealing money only redistributes wealth. He also confused wealth with money by espousing mercantilist views (Viner, 1991, p. 184).[27] More importantly, Mandeville dismissed the harm to the economy due to the erosion of trust resulting from committing vices.[28] Adam Smith (1759/1984, p. 86) advanced a devastating refutation of the Mandevillian argument:

> Society … cannot subsist among those who are at all times ready to hurt and injure one another. The moment that injury begins, the moment that mutual resentment and animosity takes place, all the bands of it broke asunder, and the different members of which it consisted are, as it were, dissipated and scattered abroad by the violence and opposition of their discordant affections. *If there is any society among robbers and murderers, they must at least, according to the trite observation, abstain from robbing and murdering one another.* Beneficence, therefore, is less essential to the existence of society than justice. Society may subsist, though not in the most comfortable state, without beneficence; but the prevalence of injustice must utterly destroy it. (Italics added)

Social orders crumble without what Smith, as we shall see, elsewhere calls "a tolerable administration of justice." We will analyze the concept of justice in Smith's writings in a later section.

Nonetheless, whatever one may think of Mandeville's views on economics or ethics, he did exhibit an insight into the endogenous emergence of order in a free society, which he regarded superior to any contrived order. He (1714/1924, p. 353) wrote:

> In the Compound of all Nations, the different Degrees of Men ought to bear a certain Proportion to each other, as to Numbers, in order to render the whole

> a well-proportion'd Mixture. And as this due Proportion is the Result and natural Consequence of the difference there is in the Qualifications of Men, and the Vicissitudes that happen among them, so it is never better attained to, or preserv'd, than when no body meddles with it. Hence we may learn, how the short-sighted Wisdom, of perhaps well-meaning People, may rob us of a Felicity, that would flow spontaneously from the Nature of every large Society, if none were to divert or interrupt the Stream.

This passage advances a core aspect of the invisible-hand proposition; that is (paraphrasing Mandeville), felicity flows naturally in a free society. Hayek (1967b, p. 251) speculates that Mandeville "probably never fully understood what was his main discovery." He regards Mandeville as a precursor of the invisible hand and the spontaneous order theory, and writes (1967b, p. 253) that Mandeville's

> main contention became simply that in the complex order of society the results of men's actions were very different from what they had intended, and that the individuals, in pursuing their own ends, whether selfish or altruistic, produced useful results for others which they did not anticipate or perhaps even know; and, finally, that the whole order of society, and even all that we call culture, was the result of individual strivings which had no such end in view, but which were channeled to serve such ends by institutions, practices, and rules which they had never been deliberately invented but had grown up by the survival of what proved successful.

How can one explain the apparent contradiction in Mandeville? How could he embrace faulty economic views and simultaneously espouse the invisible-hand proposition? A likely answer lies in the fact Mandeville wrote the *Fable* almost half a century before David Hume and Adam Smith would effectively demolish much of the erroneous economic thinking to which Mandeville had been exposed. As a keen observer of society, however, he saw the shadow of the invisible hand even though he failed to recognize its economic implications.

3.4. The economic response

As we saw above, in the late 1600s and early 1700s many scholars in response to Hobbes had expressed the idea that private interest and social interest are (or at least have the potential to be) harmonious. But they did not explicate the mechanism or the process that generates the harmony. Thus the question remained: how does the pursuit of self-interest promote the public interest? Mandeville had attempted to provide an answer but his economic reasoning was flawed and his ethical argument repugnant. In the early decades of the eighteenth century, several thinkers finally provided an answer within the framework of the market, known as the economic response.[29] In 1713, a year before Mandeville republished his poem, William Derham (1657–1735), a vicar at Upminster, Essex argued that we naturally pursue our "genius" and gravitate towards the employment we enjoy. Since each person is endowed with a unique talent, division of labor ensues. John Maxwell, a contemporary scholar of Derham, espoused the same view and added that our happiness and even our survival depends on social cooperation, which markets facilitate as people perform what they do best and then exchange the fruits of their labor. A younger contemporary, James Harris (1709–1780), argued that since no one can master all the sciences and arts, each of us specializes in a certain profession, resulting in a surplus of what we produce. The exchange of surpluses benefits people and connects them together. He, too, noted that division of labor and commerce forge the critical link between self-interest and the public interest in the market. Another contributor to this line of reasoning was the natural philosopher Joseph Priestley (1733–1804) who published his political views in 1768 and again in 1774. Priestley held that the multiplicity of talents and the pursuit of self-interest lead to specialization and the consequent efficiency in the production of knowledge. As a result, Priestly argued, human beings gain mastery over nature and improve life indefinitely.

To recap: Derham, Maxwell, Harris, and Priestly argued that to improve our lives we specialize and engage in market transactions that necessarily promote the interests of all people involved because of the voluntary character of the market. The outcome of this process (the promotion of other people's interests) is not a part of any one's intention, and it does not matter that it is not.[30] The articulation of the economic response, inspired by the Hobbesian dilemma, made a fundamental contribution to the conception of the invisible hand.[31] Smith elaborated on this process and advanced it to a higher level where the market order emerges.

4. Smith's method of inquiry

Isaac Newton, well-known for his path-breaking advances in physics and mathematics, made an influential contribution to the scientific method. In Book Three of his masterpiece *Mathematical Principles of Natural Philosophy* (1686), Newton laid down four "Rules of Reasoning in Philosophy." The fourth rule reads,

> *In Experimental philosophy we are to look upon propositions inferred by general induction from phenomena as accurately or very nearly true, notwithstanding any contrary hypotheses that may be imagined, till such time as other phenomena occur, by which they may either be made more accurate, or liable to exceptions*. This rule we must follow, that the argument of induction may not be evaded by hypotheses. (1686/1954, p. 271, italics in original)

In his later work *Optics* (1704) Newton further described his scientific method, which he called "Analysis and Synthesis":

> the method of analysis … consists in making experiments and observations, and in drawing general conclusions, but such as are taken from induction, and admitting of no objections against the conclusions, but such as are taken

> from experiments, or other certain truths.... And if no exception occur from phenomena, the conclusion may be pronounced generally.... By this way of analysis we may proceed from compounds to ingredients ... from effects to their causes, and from particular causes to more general ones, till the argument end in the most general.... And if natural philosophy in all its parts, by pursuing this method, shall at length be perfected, the bounds of moral philosophy will also be enlarged. (1704/1954, p. 543)

By extending his scientific method to moral philosophy, Newton profoundly influenced scholars in all intellectual disciplines.[32] Leonidas Montes (2008, p. 566) has noted that "it was Newton's methodological influence, epitomized by his analytic-synthetic method, and his acknowledgment of scientific progress as an open-ended process that contributed to the development of Scottish moral philosophy."

Newton's discoveries – in particular, the universal law of gravitation – gave birth to a new philosophy that viewed the universe as "rational and intelligible through and through, and capable, therefore, of being subdued to the uses of men" (Becker, 1932, p. 60). For the new generation of philosophers, nature replaced God. Becker (Ibid., p. 63) describes this transformation eloquently: "the disciples of the Newtonian philosophy had not ceased to worship. They had only given another form and a new name to the object of their worship: having denatured God, they deified nature." This new philosophy regarded nature and society as a theater in which man (guided by reason and passion rather than religion and revelation) plays the central role and has the capability to discover natural and social laws to the benefit of mankind.

Virtually all thinkers in the eighteenth-century, including David Hume and Adam Smith, deeply admired Newton and attempted to apply his method to their own work. They set out to understand the operation of the moral and social universe just as Newton had done for the physical universe; that is, they attempted to discover the laws of *human* nature and of society. Consider David Hume's remarks in *A Treatise of Human Nature*, where he says, "It is evident, that all the sciences have a relation, greater or less, to human nature" (1739/1951, p. 4). He then describes his project, which he poignantly calls, "the science of man":

> And, as the science of man is the only solid foundation for the other sciences, so, the only solid foundation we can give to this science itself must be laid on *experience and observation*. It is no astonishing reflection to consider ... the application of experimental philosophy to moral subjects... (1739/1951, p. 5, italics in original)

In a section on "Justice and Injustice" in *A Treatise of Human Nature*, Hume identifies "three fundamental laws of nature, *that of the stability of possession, of its transference by consent, and the performance of promises*" (1739/1951, part II, p. 228, italics in original). Hume writes of "the fundamental laws of nature" even though the subject matter pertains to morality and society.[33]

As for Smith, in a lecture in 1763, he argued that "the Newtonian method" is superior to the Aristotelian approach and applicable to every branch of science including moral philosophy (Smith, 1985, pp. 145–6). Smith shared Newton's belief that the proper investigation of both natural and moral philosophy rests on empirical approach. As D. D. Raphael has noted, Smith "began with experienced fact and then produced a hypothesis to explain the facts" (1997, p. 68). This approach enabled Smith to advance a number of testable propositions in *The Wealth of Nations* and *The Theory of Moral Sentiments* – propositions that have been and continue to be subjected to empirical scrutiny.[34]

The influence of Newton on Smith was noted early on by John Millar (1735–1801) who attended Smith's university lectures on the "History of Civil Society." Millar referred to Smith as "the Newton of the study of civil society" (Campbell, 1971, p. 55) and noted, "The Great Montesquieu pointed out the road. He was the Lord Bacon in this branch of philosophy. Dr. Smith is the Newton" (cited by Dugald Stewart 1793/1982, p. 275). Indeed, for the generation of classical economists who followed Smith the *Wealth of Nations* served as a source of inspiration and guidance just as Newton's *Principia* did for the physicists.[35]

Mark Blaug (1992, p. 52) notes, "Given the pivotal role of sympathy for other human beings in *The Theory of Moral Sentiments* and that of self-interested behavior in *The Wealth of Nations*, both of these books must be regarded as deliberate attempts by Smith to apply the Newtonian method first to ethics and then to economics." Similarly, T. D. Campbell (1971, p. 55) has observed, "There are direct parallels between [Smith's] use of sympathy, self-interest and even, to some extent, following Hutcheson, benevolence, and the place of gravity in Newton's system." Norriss Hetherington (1983, p. 497) has argued that "Adam Smith's efforts to discover the general laws of economics were directly inspired and shaped by the example of Newton's success in discovering the natural laws of motion." Hetherington (Ibid., p. 504) further argues that "there are important similarities of structure between Smith's *Wealth of Nations* and Newton's *Principia*. The method of moving by induction from phenomena to the framing of principles, and then deducing the phenomena from the principles is found in both Newton and Smith."

5. Smith's contribution to the economic response

Consistent with the scientific method laid out above, Smith began his inquiry into the wealth of nations with observing people's economic behavior and the motives that drive market transactions. His inquiry led him to discern "a certain propensity" in human nature that gives rise to division of labor. He (1776/1981, p. 25) wrote,

> The division of labor … is not originally the effect of any human wisdom, which foresees and intends that general opulence to which it gives occasion. It is the necessary, though very slow and gradual consequence of a certain propensity in human nature which has in view no such extensive utility; the propensity to truck, barter, and exchange of one thing for another.

Smith applied the economic response to the Hobbesian problem and argued that (as several thinkers had already done) self-interest leads to specialization and the exchange of surpluses – a process that increases productivity and the living standards (1776/1981, pp. 27–28). But Smith went beyond his predecessors and argued that division of labor entails far reaching unintended consequences including the rise of commercial societies:

> When division of labour has been once thoroughly established, it is but a very small part of a man's wants which the produce of his own labour can supply. He supplies the far greater part of them over and above his own consumption, for such parts of the produce of other men's labour as he has occasion for. Every man thus lives by exchanging, or become in some measure a merchant, and the society itself grows to be what is properly a commercial society. (1776/1981, p. 37)

Commerce and division of labor are inseparable through a feedback mechanism in that commerce both requires and sustains division of labor. Smith argued that commerce has made three contributions to "the improvements of the country." The first is the development of markets, the second is the creation of wealth, and

> Thirdly, and lastly, commerce and manufactures *gradually* introduced *order and good government, and with them, the liberty and security of individuals*, among the inhabitants of the country, who had before lived almost in a continual state of war with their neighbors, and of servile dependency upon their superiors. This, though it has been the least observed, is *by far the most important of all their effects*. Mr. Hume is the only writer who, so far as I know, has hitherto taken notice of it. (1776/1981, p. 412, italics added)

Here, the invisible hand pervades the whole process: the outcomes of commerce – order, good government, liberty, and security – all emerge without any one's intention and knowledge. Further, commerce is linked to liberty and security through a *gradual* introduction of order and good government, implying an evolutionary process involving human actions but not human design, a core aspect of the invisible hand.[36]

Smith's study of human nature led him to the observation that "Every man is, no doubt, by nature, first and principally recommended to his own care; and as he is fitter to take care of himself than of any other person, it is fit and right that it should be so" (1759/1984, p. 82). Moreover, "the principle, which prompts us to expence, is the passion for the present enjoyment.… But the principle which prompts us to save, is the desire of bettering our condition, a desire which, though generally calm and dispassionate, comes with us from the womb, and never leaves us till we go into grave" (1776/1981, p. 341).[37] These natural impulses in the market lead to paradoxical and unintended outcomes:

> Every individual is continually exerting himself to find out the most advantageous employment for whatever capital he can command. It is his

> own advantage, indeed, and not that of the society, which he has in view. But *the study of his own advantage naturally, or rather necessarily leads him to prefer that employment which is most advantageous to the society.* (1776/1981, p. 454, italics added)

Although Smith made this observation (the italicized sentence) in the context of investment in the home country versus investment abroad, he imparted a general proposition: if an economy needs a larger number of workers in a certain sector, wages in that sector will rise and attract more people. Those who enter this sector may be seeking their own advantage, but they necessarily advance society's interests because they satisfy the needs of the economy. Moreover,

> the private interests and passions of individuals naturally dispose them to turn their stock towards the employment which in ordinary cases are most advantageous to the society. But if from this natural preference they should turn too much of it towards those employments, the fall of profit in them and the rise in all others immediately dispose them to alter this faulty distribution. Without any intervention of law, therefore, the private interests and passions of men naturally lead them to divide and distribute the stock of every society, among all the different employments carried on in it, as nearly as possible in the proportion which is most agreeable to the interest of the whole of society. (1776/1981, p. 630)

The foregoing analysis harks back to a question at the heart of the invisible-hand proposition: how does order arise from countless transactions in the economy? Since any transaction consists of the exchange of surpluses between individuals, the market order hinges on the coordination of these exchanges. The process becomes exponentially complex as "the social distance increases and people specialize" (Witztum, 2010, p. 180). In Smith's account, the price mechanism serves as the coordinating device. In chapter seven of Book II of the *Wealth of Nations* Smith writes, "The natural price … is, as it were, the central price, to which the prices of all commodities are continually gravitating" (1776/1981, p. 75). Smith further observes that "When the quantity of any commodity which is brought to market falls short of the effectual demand … the market price will rise. … When the quantity brought to market exceeds the effectual demand … the market price will sink more or less below the natural price" (1776/1981, pp. 73–74). Moreover,

> The quantity of every commodity brought to market suits itself to the effectual demand. It is the interest of all those who employ their land, labour, or stock, in bringing any commodity to market, that the quantity never should exceed the effectual demand; and it is interests of all other people that it never should fall short of that demand. (1776/1981, p. 74)

Witztum (2010, pp. 184–185) describes the process as follows: "when prices are at their natural rates, markets successfully distribute life's necessities and in so doing, ensures that people do not cease to specialize and trade. Moreover … there would be coincidence of wants." Here, the price mechanism is credited with much accomplishment. Kenneth Arrow and Frank Hahn (1971, p. vii) put it this way:

> There is by now a long and a fairly imposing line of economists from Adam Smith to the present who have sought to show that a decentralized economy motivated by self-interest and guided by price signals would be compatible with a coherent disposition of economic resources that could be regarded, in a well-defined sense, as superior to a large class of possible alternative dispositions. Moreover, the price signals operate in a way to establish this degree of coherence.

A related function of a commercial society is the facilitation of cooperation among countless economic agents. Smith (1776/1981, p. 26) writes,

> In civilized society he [man] stands at all times in need of the cooperation and assistance of great multitudes, while his whole life is scarce sufficient to gain the friendship of a few persons ... man has almost constant occasion for the help of his brethren, and it is in vain for him to expect it from their benevolence only. He will more likely to prevail if he can interest their self-love in his favour, and shew them that it is for their advantage to do for him what he requires of them.

Paradoxically, Smith observes that "cooperation," "assistance," and "help" result from the pursuit of self-love in the market. He assigns as much importance to cooperation as to competition in the market paradigm. Competition takes place at the micro level, while cooperation is an activity at the macro level. A baker may compete with other bakers in town but needs the cooperation and assistance of a very large number of agents including suppliers, workers, distributors, bankers, insurance companies, and so on. And they all cooperate and contribute to the production of a loaf of bread because it is in their interest to do so. This process is precisely what Hayek (1988) has called "the extended order of human cooperation." Smith's analysis of the price mechanism as the coordinating and harmonizing device, which also facilitates cooperation, replaced the alleged providential design of the market.[38]

Smith's conviction in the harmonious outcome in decentralized economies is deeply rooted in the natural-law philosophy. D. P. O'Brian in his book *The Classical Economists Revisited* (2004, p. 27) notes that Smith came under many influences including pre-classical economic writers, historical events, and institutional settings. O'Brian (Ibid.) then writes, "Of these by far the most important, at least for Adam Smith (and through him for Classical economics in general), was the influence of the natural-law philosophers." The tradition of natural-law maintains that "there is an underlying order in material phenomenon" and that man is capable of discovering it. Moreover,

> natural laws are productive of immutable forces which man cannot deflect or impede ... that if freedom is accorded, then society will progress

> harmoniously to a better state … and that therefore the operation of natural laws requires a great degree of freedom to achieve their ends – … called the doctrine of *natural liberty*. (O'Brian, 2004, p. 27, italics in original)[39]

Given Smith's deep conviction in the natural-law philosophy, he advanced a powerful and influential case for a society which allows "every man to pursue his own interest in his own way, upon the liberal plan of equality, liberty, and justice" (1776/1981, p. 664).

6. Smith and his contemporary philosophers on the invisible hand[40]

Shortly before the centenary of the publication of *The Wealth of Nations*, the historian Henry Thomas Buckle (1873, v. 1, p. 154) noted, "In the year 1776, Adam Smith published his *Wealth of Nations*; which, looking at its ultimate results, is probably the most important book that has ever been written, and is certainly the most valuable contribution ever made by a single man towards establishing the principles on which government should be based." Indeed, Smith's tome ranks as one of the most influential books in history. Alec Macfie (1955/2009, p. 391) believes that "Book I of the *Wealth of Nations* is now a part of world thought, as is the *Origin of Species* or *Principia Mathematica*." The noted historian Arnold Toynbee credits the *Wealth of Nations* and the steam engine with having "destroyed the old world and built a new one" (cited in Mark Skousen, 2001, p. 20).

Nonetheless, well before 1776, Smith had already presented in his writings and lectures most if not all of the theories, propositions, and policy recommendations that later he included in *The Wealth of Nations*.[41] Consider a lecture Smith delivered in 1749 (at the age of twenty-six) in which he threw light on a critical aspect of the invisible-hand proposition. He observed:

> Man is generally considered by statesmen and projectors as the materials of a sort of political mechanics. Projectors disturb nature in the course of her operations on human affairs, and it requires no more than to leave her alone and give her fair play in the pursuit of her ends that she may establish her own designs. (Quoted in Dugald Stewart, 1793/1982, p. 322)[42]

This passage expresses a seminal intellectual legacy of the Scottish Enlightenment, the brainchild of a number of thinkers, above all, David Hume and Smith. The rest of Smith's lecture throws more light on the Scottish legacy:

> Little else is requisite to carry a state to the highest degree of affluence from the lowest barbarism but peace, easy taxes, and a tolerable administration of justice; all the rest being brought about by the natural course of things. All governments which thwart this natural course, which force things into another channel, or which endeavour to arrest the progress of society at a particular point, are unnatural, and, to support themselves, are obliged to be oppressive and tyrannical. (Ibid., p. 322)[43]

This passage embodies several critical points. First, the market economic system serves as a natural mechanism for the creation of affluence;[44] second, it sets the necessary and sufficient conditions (peace, low taxes, and justice) for the attainment of affluence; and third, governments that ignore these two points become oppressive and tyrannical. Smith does not mention the political system, natural resources or anything else as prerequisites for economic growth in his list because, perhaps, he regards them insufficiently important or even irrelevant.[45,46]

The administration of justice, noted in the lecture, plays a central role in Smith's theoretical system. In a lecture in 1766, he said: "The end of justice is to secure from injury. … As a man, he may be injured in his body, reputation, or estate" (Smith 1982b, p. 399). In *The Theory of Moral Sentiments*, he noted, "the violation of justice is injury: it does real and positive hurt to some particular person, from motives which are naturally disapproved of" (1759/1984, p. 79). Viner (1968/1991, p. 252) elaborates on this point:

> Smith's treatment of "justice" in the *Theory of Moral Sentiments* is especially important for a proper interpretation of the *Wealth of Nations*. Smith always used the word to mean substantially what Aristotle and the Schoolmen meant by "commutative justice." Justice is a negative virtue; it consists of refraining from injury to another person and from taking or withholding from another what belongs to him. It is distinct from benevolence, friendship, or charity. Smith considered justice, so understood, to be the necessary foundation of a viable society.

Smith famously advocated "the simple system of natural liberty," which as the following passage shows, depends on justice. In this system

> Every man, as long as he does not violate the laws of justice, is left perfectly free to pursue his own interest his own way, and to bring both his industry and capital into competition with those of any man, or order of men. The sovereign is completely discharged from a duty, in the attempting to perform which he must always be exposed to innumerable delusions, and for the proper performance of which no human wisdom or knowledge could ever be sufficient; the duty of superintending the industry of private people, and of directing it towards the employments most suitable to the interest of society. (1776/1981, p. 687)

The proposition – "Every man, as long as he does not violate the laws of justice, is left perfectly free to pursue his own interest his own way" – is actually quite restrictive in choosing the means by which one pursues one's ends.[47] Further, Smith's argument – that "no human wisdom or knowledge could ever be sufficient" for "superintending the industry of private people" – lies at the heart of the invisible-hand proposition. Smith elaborates on this point in the paragraph following the invisible-hand passage in the *Wealth of Nations*:

> What is the species of domestick industry which his capital can employ, and of which the produce is likely to be of the greatest value, every individual,

> it is evident, can, in his local situation, judge much better than any statesman or lawgiver can do for him. The statesman, who should attempt to direct private people in what manner they ought to employ their capitals, would not only load himself with a most unnecessary attention, but assume an authority which could safely be trusted, not only to no single person, but to no council or senate whatever, and which would nowhere be so dangerous as in the hands of a man who had the folly and presumption enough to fancy himself fit to exercise it. (1776/1981, p. 456)

Smith's argument against directing "private people in what manner they ought to employ their capitals" serves as a potent affirmation for the simple system of natural liberty.

Smith is well aware of human vulnerability to committing errors in economic decisions, but from this fact it does not follow that some authority should control human decisions. He observes that "The man who employs either his labour or his stock in a greater variety of ways than his situation renders necessary … may hurt himself, and he generally does so. … But the law ought always to trust people with the care of their own interest, as in their local situations they must generally be able to judge better of it than the legislator can do" (1776/1981, p. 530–531).

The following passage from *The Theory of Moral Sentiments* – with utmost clarity and lucidity – sums up Smith's explication and articulation of the proposition that the invisible-hand metaphor represents:

> The man of system, on the contrary, is apt to be very wise in his own conceit; and is often so enamoured with the supposed beauty of his own ideal plan of government, that he cannot suffer the smallest deviation from any part of it.… He seems to imagine that he can arrange the different members of a great society with as much ease as the hand arranges the different pieces upon a chess-board. He does not consider that the pieces upon the chess-board have no other principle of motion besides that which the hand impresses upon them; but that, in the great chess-board of human society, every single piece has a principle of motion of its own, altogether different from that which the legislature might chuse to impress upon it. If those two principles coincide and act in the same direction, the game of human society will go on easily and harmoniously, and is very likely to be happy and successful. If they are opposite or different, the game will go on miserably, and the society must be at all times in the highest degree of disorder. (1759/1984, pp. 233–234)[48]

David Hume exhibits the same conviction as Smith that social and economic orders cannot be contrived. He (1777/1987, p. 124) writes, "To balance a large state or society, whether monarchical or republican on general laws, is a work of so great difficulty, that no human genius, however comprehensive, is able, by the mere dint of reason and reflection, to effect it." Hume argues that we owe our social institutions to an evolutionary process in which our sentiments, passions, and interests (not reason) are the driving forces. On Hume's influence, Arthur Herman (2001, p. 199) notes:

> For more than two thousand years, Western philosophers had praised the primacy of reason as the guide to all human action and virtue. Plato, Aristotle, Augustine, Aquinas, Descartes, Locke, Hobbes, and even Hutcheson could all agree with the great time-honored consensus, that the job of reason was to master our emotions and appetites. With one earth-shaking book [*A Treatise of Human Nature*], his first, Hume reversed this. "Reason is," he wrote, "and ought to be, the slave of passions."[49]

Hume poignantly, although perhaps with some exaggeration, says, "it is not contrary to reason to prefer the destruction of the world to the scratching of my finger." Moreover, he (1739/1951: II, p. 167) writes,

> Since morals ... have an influence on the actions and affections, it follows that they cannot be derived from reason alone.... Morals excite passions, and produce or prevent actions. Reason of itself is utterly impotent.... The rules of morality, therefore, are not conclusions of our reason.[50]

In Hume's (and Smith's) account both the intelligence and the character of central planners ("men of system" as Smith calls them) are irrelevant to designing an economic order, for regardless of their mental aptitude and moral rectitude, they necessarily lack the requisite knowledge about the economy and people whose lives they wish to direct. The next section will elaborate on this issue.

Adam Ferguson is generally regarded as a seminal thinker in the tradition of the invisible hand and spontaneous order.[51] In *An Essay on the History of Civil Society* (1767/1995) Ferguson argues that human actions and interactions have far reaching and unforeseen consequences. On the emergence of the institution of property rights, he (1767/1995, p. 119) writes:

> Mankind, in following the present sense of their minds, in striving to remove inconveniences, or to gain apparent and contiguous advantages, arrive at ends which even their imagination could not anticipate, and pass on, like other animals, in the track of their nature, without perceiving its end. He who first said 'I will appropriate this field: I will leave it to my heirs' did not perceive that he was laying the foundation of civil laws and political establishments.

Ferguson's analysis led to the following oft-quoted passage:

> Mankind in following the present sense of their minds, in striving to remove inconveniencies, or to gain apparent and contiguous advantages, arrive at ends which even their imagination could not anticipate.... Every step and every movement of the multitude, even in what are called enlightened ages,

> are made with equal blindness to the future; and *nations stumble upon establishments, which are indeed the result of human actions but not the execution of any human design*. (Ibid., pp. 119, 122, italics added)

The last (italicized) part of this passage was popularized by Hayek (1967a) as the *locus classicus* of the spontaneous order theory.[52] Later in the *Essay*, Ferguson (1767/1995, p. 182) adds:

> Those establishments arose from successive improvements that were made, without any sense of their general effect; and they bring human affairs to a state of complications, which the greatest reach of capacity with which human nature was ever adorned, could not have projected; nor even when the whole is carried into execution, can it be comprehended in its full extent.

In a later work Ferguson (1792, volume 1, p. 43) argued that language has evolved "without the intervention of uncommon genius … in a succession of ages." As we shall see, Carl Menger (1840–1921) applied this argument to the emergence of money as the product of an evolutionary process over a long period of time.

7. Self-interest versus benevolence

Smith holds benevolence in such high regards that he (1759/1984, p. 25) says, "to retrain our selfish, and to indulge our benevolent affections, constitutes the perfection of human nature." But he (1759/1984, p. 305) argues that benevolence cannot drive all human actions:

> Benevolence may, perhaps, be the sole principle of action in the Deity.… But whatever may be the case with the Deity, so imperfect a creature as man, the support of whose existence requires so many things external to him, must often act from many other motives.

One of the "many other motives," according to Smith, is self-interest that dominates economic behavior. He argues that benevolence plays a limited and unreliable role in the market because "man has almost constant occasion for the help of his brethren, and it is in vain to expect it from their benevolence only. He will be more likely to prevail if he can interest their self-love in his favour, and shew them it is for their own advantage to do for him what he requires of them" (1776/1981, p. 26). Moreover, "Nobody but a beggar" Smith points out, "chuses to depend chiefly upon the benevolence of his fellow-citizens" (1776/1981, p. 27). In the following analysis, Viner (1959/1991, p. 74) sheds considerable light on why Smith thinks self-interest dominates economic behavior:

> for his … theory of society outside the market-place, for the explanation of man's behavior in his family, towards his friends and neighbors, and as a citizen of his country, Adam Smith stressed the Shaftesburian

> "moral sentiments," sympathy, benevolence, propriety, desire for public approval and for self-approval ... in the market-place social relations were basically mechanical or "anonymous," so that the social sentiments were insufficiently strong as a disciplinary force, and self-interest, moderated by an inner sense of justice as well as by politically-enforced justice, would be the dominant psychological force.

Indeed the practice of benevolence is inversely correlated with social distance although people do exhibit generosity towards strangers.[53]

On the role of self-interest and benevolence in economic decisions, the writings of Hayek are particularly illuminating. In a classic essay, titled "The Use of Knowledge in Society," Hayek (1945, p. 519) lays down vividly the central function of the market:

> The peculiar character of the problem of a rational economic order is determined precisely by the fact that the knowledge of the circumstances of which we must make use never exists in concentrated or integrated form but solely as the dispersed bits of incomplete and frequently contradictory knowledge which all the separate individuals possess. The economic problem of society is ... how to secure the best use of resources known to any of the members of society, for ends whose relative importance only these individuals know. Or, to put it briefly, it is a problem of the utilization of knowledge which is not given to anyone in its totality.[54]

Hayek's analysis is a restatement and elaboration of Smith's observation that "no human wisdom or knowledge could ever be sufficient" for "superintending the industry of private people" (1776/1981, p. 687). Hayek also explicates the coordination of economic activities and the communication of knowledge by the market process. What lies at the heart of the market is the invisible-hand paradox: the system operates *as if* "someone" deliberately coordinates economic activities. What is even more paradoxical is that the economy would eventually be thrown into chaos if the coordination were centrally directed. Hayek (1976/1978, p. 237) argues this point as follows:

> That we have been able to achieve a reasonably high degree of order in our economic lives despite modern complexities is *only* because our affairs have been guided, not by central direction, but by the operations of the market and competition in securing the mutual adjustment of separate efforts. The market system functions because it is able to take account of millions of separate facts and desires, because it reaches with thousands of sensitive feelers into every nook and cranny of the economic world and feeds back the information acquired in coded form to a "public information board."... the complexity of the structure required to produce the real income we are now able to provide for the masses of the

> Western World – which exceeds anything we can survey or picture in detail – could develop *only because we did not attempt to plan it or subject it to any central direction, but left it to be guided by a spontaneous ordering mechanism*, or a self-generating order… (Italics added)

Hayek (1945, p. 527) notes that if the price mechanism "were the result of deliberate human design, and if the people guided by the price changes understood that their decisions have significance far beyond their immediate aim, this mechanism would have been acclaimed as one of the greatest triumphs of the human mind."[55]

Hayek (1988) applies his analysis of the market to the issue of self-interest versus benevolence. He (1988, p. 81) argues,

> In an order taking advantage of the higher productivity of extensive division of labour, the individual can no longer know whose needs his efforts do or ought to serve, or what will be the effects of his actions on those unknown persons who do consume his products or products to which he has contributed. Directing his productive efforts altruistically thus becomes literally impossible for him. In so far as we can still call his motives altruistic in that they eventually redound to the benefit of others, they will do this not because he aims at or intends to serve the concrete needs of others, but because he observes abstract rules…. Observing these rules, while bending most of our efforts towards earning a living, enables us to confer benefits beyond the range of our concrete knowledge (yet at the same time hardly prevents us from using whatever extra we can earn also to gratify our instinctive longing to do visible good).

Hayek's argument implies that when the necessary knowledge is available people can and do act altruistically, which explains why in market societies, as documented in a footnote above, altruistic actions such as charitable donations of money and time are quite common.[56]

8. The invisible-hand passages in Smith's writings

Warren Samuels (2011, pp. 21–29) presents numerous references to the phrase "invisible hand" in theological and literary works predating the writings of Smith by well over two millennia. Gavin Kennedy (2009, p. 242) has also assembled many references to the word "hand" as a metaphor in phrases such as "mighty hand," "God's hand," and "invisible hand" as early as 720 BCE in Homer's *Iliad*. Emma Rothschild (2001, p. 119), too, cites several references to "invisible hand" in Anglo-Scottish literature including *Macbeth* and Ovid's *Metamorphoses*. Smith was quite familiar with this literature. Ian Ross (1995, p. 167) speculates that the *Meditations of Emperor Marcus Antonius* had served as the source of the phrase for Smith.[57]

Smith's first use of the phrase appeared in an essay titled, "The History of Astronomy" in the early 1750s. Here he notes that believers in polytheism and superstition ascribed irregular natural events such as "thunder and lightning, storms and sunshine" to "the favor or displeasure of intelligent, though invisible beings, to gods, daemons, witches, genii, fairies." But for the regular events such as "water refreshes; heavy bodies descend…" never "was the invisible hand of Jupiter … apprehended to be employed in those matters" (Smith, 1982a, pp. 49–50).[58] While Alec Macfie (1971, pp. 597–598) has argued that we cannot draw any firm conclusion from the phrase in the essay, Smith places the invisible hand in the same category as non-existent entities such as "gods, daemons, witches…" which polytheists invoked whenever the cause of an event such as thunder was unknown or inexplicable.

In a paragraph leading up to the invisible hand passage in *The Theory of Moral Sentiments*, Smith focuses narrowly on the landlord whom he characterizes as "proud and unfeeling … without a thought for the wants of his brethren" whose "capacity of his stomach bears no proportion to the immensity of his desires, and will receive no more than that of the meanest peasant" (1759/1984, p. 184). This natural restriction on the landlord obliges him

> to distribute among those, who prepare … that little which he himself makes use of, among those who fit up the palace in which this little is to be consumed, among those who provide and keep in order all the different baubles and trinkets … all of whom thus derive from his luxury and caprice, that share of the necessaries of life, which they would in vain have expected from his humanity or his justice. (1759/1984, p. 184)

Anthony Brewer (2009, p. 521) has argued that Smith in this passage "was responding to a debate over 'luxury' that went back (literally) thousands of years." From the time of Plato to the Enlightenment many thinkers had regarded the possession of luxurious items as morally wrong. Against this entrenched view, Smith argues that luxuries actually benefit the society because the money that the rich spend on themselves becomes income for other people.[59] It is in connection with this process that Smith invokes the invisible hand:

> The rich … consume little more than the poor, and in spite of their natural selfishness and rapacity, though they mean only their own conveniency, though the sole end which they propose from the labours of all the thousands whom they employ, be the gratification of their own vain and insatiable desires, they divide with the poor the produce of their improvements. They are led by an invisible hand to make nearly the same distribution of the necessaries of life, which would have been made, had the earth been divided into equal portion among its inhabitants, and thus without intending it, without knowing it, advance the interest of the society, and afford means to the multiplications of the species. When Providence divided the earth among a few masters,

> it neither forgot nor abandoned those who seemed to have been left out in the partition. These last too enjoy their share of all that it produces. (1759/1984, pp. 184–185)

The first part of the passage is conveyed in the *Wealth of Nations* as well (but without invoking the invisible hand): "The rich man consumes no more food than his poor neighbor" (1776/1981, p. 180) because "The desire of food is limited in every man by the narrow capacity of the human stomach" (1776/1981, p. 181). But Smith points out that the "quality may be very different" (1776/1981, p. 180).

Some scholars have read in the invisible-hand passage more than what one sees at the first glance. For example, Witztum (2010, p. 182) has argued,

> The invisible hand in the *Theory of Moral Sentiments* represents a concept of equilibrium in the sense of coordinating some desires across interdependent individuals. However, the desires it coordinates are confined to the fulfillment of basic needs and they are not necessarily coordinated throughout the market.... In other words, the invisible hand is the equilibrium of needs that makes the division of labor a sustainable order.

It remains an open question whether by the invisible hand Smith meant such grand achievements as coordination and fulfillment of basic needs and the creation of a viable order. What is quite clear from the passage is that the advancement of society's interests and the multiplication of the species are unintended, self-generating, and self-sustaining processes. As presented in Appendix III, the term "Providence," which Smith capitalized, has led some scholars to suggest the invisible hand is the hand of the Deity.[60]

The invisible-hand passage in the *The Wealth of Nations* embodies the same process as that in *The Theory of Moral Sentiments* but the context is different. In the early part of chapter two of Book Four of *The Wealth of Nations*, Smith advances a powerful case against regulating international trade (1776/1981, p. 453) and then turns to the issue of investing at home versus investing abroad. What propels an individual to invest at home is self-interest, which unintentionally promotes the public interest:

> By preferring the support of domestick to that of foreign industry, he intends only his own security; and by directing that industry in such a manner as its produce may be of the greatest value, he intends only his own gain, and he is in this, as in many other cases, led by an invisible hand to promote an end which was no part of his intention. Nor is it always the worse for the society that it was no part of it. By pursuing his own interest he frequently promotes that of the society more effectually than when he really intends to promote it. I have never known much good done by those who affected to trade for the publick good. (1776/1981, p. 456)

This passage embodies two properties of the invisible hand. The first one is the same as that in *The Theory of Moral Sentiments* where the pursuit of one's interest unintentionally and unknowingly promotes the public interest. The second one maintains that the unintended market outcome (i.e., public interest) is often achieved more effectively when it is *not* deliberately pursued. William Grampp (2000) has argued that the invisible hand in the *Wealth of Nations* is "simply the inducement a merchant has to keep his capital at home, thereby increasing the domestic capital stock and enhancing military power, both of which are in the public interest and neither of which he intended" (p. 441). He bases his argument on the fact that Smith approved of trade restriction for the sake of building a defense industry.[61] Grampp's argument, however, is unconvincing because the proposition that markets unintentionally generate beneficial outcomes is not limited to this passage; it pervades almost the whole of the *Wealth of Nations*.[62]

Abstracted from the rest of Smith's writings, neither the invisible-hand passage in the *The Wealth of Nations* nor the one in *The Theory of Moral Sentiments* convey or imply the grand proposition that social and economic orders arise from free interactions of people. To put forth this proposition, one must resort to the entire writings of Smith as well as those of several other philosophers of the eighteenth century. We will return to this point later.

9. Interpretations, qualifications, and objections

This section presents and analyzes various interpretations and criticisms of the invisible-hand theory.

9.1. The classical interpretation

In this interpretation the invisible hand metaphorically represents the mechanism or the process that transforms economic self-interests into the public interests. This transformation hinges on four critical qualifications. First, the beneficence of the invisible hand is limited to market transactions; that is, for interactions outside the marketplace Smith stressed motives other than self-interest. Second, even in the marketplace, Smith argued, in many instances self-interest and public interest are incompatible. Third, the harmony between private and public interests require proper institutions. Fourth, as noted above, market transactions are beneficial only if they are subject to the observation and administration of justice, which Smith defines as avoiding harm to others. We shall explain these qualifications below.

Since the publication of *The Wealth of Nations*, selective and incomplete reading of Smith at times have led to certain misapplication of the invisible hand with tragic consequences. Amartya Sen (1987, p. 27) in his book, *On Ethics & Economics*, notes, "While Smith was often cited by imperial administration for justification of refusing to intervene in famines in such diverse places as Ireland, India and China, there is nothing to indicate that Smith's ethical approach to public policy would have precluded intervention in support of the entitlement of the poor." In particular, the Irish famine of 1845–1850 provides a vivid example. Edward O'Boyle (2006) has noted that the English government could have lessened the horror of the tragedy, but influential economists of the time by invoking Adam Smith and the tenets of classical economics urged the government to pursue a hands-off policy. O'Boyle (2006, p. 45) poignantly notes, "If Smith's Moral Sentiments had taken hold among classical economists, surely sympathy, generosity, and benevolence would have been evident in public statements and policy recommendations during the Famine and afterwards."

Indeed in crises such as natural disasters not only are benevolent actions of individuals compatible with the system of natural liberty but also government initiatives in helping the victims. In this system according to Smith, the government has three main duties: national defense; the establishment of "an exact administration of justice"; and the provision of "certain publick works and certain publick institutions, which it can never be for the interest of any individual, or a small number of individuals, to erect and maintain" (1776/1981, pp. 687–688). Arguably, "certain publick institutions" should include an agency assisting distressed people in a crisis if no individual can undertake the task.[63] At the time of the Irish famine, no sufficiently large and capable private institution existed to provide food for the starving masses. Would Smith have approved of the government assistance to the victims of the Irish famine? The following passage suggests an answer:

> Man, according to the Stoics, ought to regard himself, not as something separated and detached, but as a citizen of the world, a member of the vast commonwealth of nature. To the interest of this great community, he ought at all times to be willing that his own little interest should be sacrificed. Whatever concerns himself, ought to affect him no more than whatever concerns any other equally important part of this immense system. *We should view ourselves, not in the light in which our own selfish passions are apt to place us, but in the light in which any other citizen of the world would view us*. (1759/1984, pp. 140–141, italics added)

Quite importantly, Smith identified significant exceptions and deviations from the classical interpretation of the invisible hand. For example, merchants and manufacturers seek monopolistic advantages and strive "to narrow the competition" that "must always be against" the public interest (1776/1981, p. 267). They constitute "an order of men whose interest is never exactly the same with that of the publick, who have generally an interest to deceive and even to oppress the publick, and who have, upon many occasions, both deceived and oppressed it" (1776/1981, p. 267). Hence "The proposal of any new law or regulation of commerce which comes from this order [merchants and manufacturers] … ought never to be adopted" (1776/1981, p. 267).

Smith argues that certain laws have contributed to the formation of monopolies by facilitating the meeting of unscrupulous merchants. He (1776/1981, p. 145) writes,

> though the law cannot hinder people of the same trade from sometimes assembling together, it ought to do nothing to facilitate such assemblies, much less to render them necessary.

> A regulation which obliges all those of the same trade in a particular town to enter their names and places of abode in a publick register, facilitates such assemblies. It connects individuals who might never otherwise be known to one another, and gives every man of the trade a direction where to find every other man of it.

Moreover, the government should resist pressure from industries demanding restrictions on imports precisely because such regulations are against the public interest. Instead, capital must be allowed "to follow its natural course"; otherwise, "The industry of the country … is … turned away from a more, to a less advantageous employment, and the exchangeable value of its annual produce, instead of being increased, according to the intention of the lawgiver, must necessarily be diminished by every such regulation" (1776/1981, p. 457). Viner (1927/1991, p. 99) points out that in *The Wealth of Nations*,

> Masters and workmen have a conflict of interest with respect to wages, and the weakness in bargaining power of the latter ordinarily gives the advantage in any dispute to the former. Master, traders, and apprentices, on the one hand, and the public on the other, have divergent interests with respect to apprenticeship rules.… The corn-dealer, on the whole, performs a useful service, but because of his 'excessive avarice' he does not perform it perfectly. The merchant exporter sometimes finds it to his interest, when dearth prevails both at home and abroad, 'very much [to] aggravate the calamities of the dearth' at home by exporting corn. Men commonly overestimate their chances of success in risky ventures, with the consequence that too great a share of the nation's stock of capital goes into such ventures.[64]

Smith identified so many exceptions to the harmony between private and public interest that some scholars have questioned his conviction in the classical interpretation. For example, Arthur C. Pigou (1877–1959) observes, "the doctrine of the invisible hand evolving social benefit out of private selfishness has never been held by economists – certainly it was not held by Adam Smith – in that absolute and rigid form in which popular writers conceive it" (1936, p. 115). Further, in his important book *The Economics of Welfare* (1952, p. 195) Pigou notes:

> It is as idle to expect a well-planned town to result from independent activities of isolated speculators as it would be to expect a satisfactory picture to result if each separate square inch were painted by an independent artist. No "invisible hand" can be relied on to produce a good arrangement of the whole from a combination of separate treatment of the part.

The harmony between self-interest and the public interest, the Enlightenment philosophers argued, requires social institutions that would channel human passions towards the common good. In 1755, Josiah Tucker (1713–1799), an Anglican divine wrote, “The main point to be aimed at is neither to extinguish nor enfeeble self-love, but to give it such a direction, that it may promote the public interest by pursuing its own” (quoted in Muller, 2002, p. 51).[65] Mark Blaug (1978, p. 65) has noted that according to Smith “the market mechanism would foster harmony but not unless it was surrounded by an appropriate legal and institutional framework.”[66] Jerry Muller (1993, pp. 6–7) has argued that in the Smithian system it is the

> social institutions which draw the passions toward socially and morally beneficial behavior. This is the thread that runs through all his works: how the market can be structured to make the pursuit of self-interest benefit consumers; how the passion for the approval of others can make us act more selflessly; how public institutions can be structured to ensure that they deliver the services they are mandated to provide; how our desires for sex and for progeny can be structured by the law to create family institutions that foster self-control; how institutions concerned with defense and taxation can be structured to avoid unnecessary wars …

Equally crucial for the workings of the invisible hand is the abolition of institutions that infringe upon individual liberty. In particular, Smith targeted colonialism and slavery. He branded the colonial policies of Great Britain as “unjust” and “a manifest violation of the most sacred rights of mankind,” for such policies prohibit people “from making all that they can of every part of their own produce, or from employing their stock and industry in the way that they judge most advantageous to themselves” (1776/1981, p. 582). He chastised the British government for granting privileges to the East India Company, the colonial tool of Great Britain in India. He (1776/1981, p. 641) wrote, “I mean not … to throw any odious imputation upon the general character of the servants of the East India Company.… It is the system of the government, the situation in which they are placed, that I mean to censure.” Smith argued that the colonial policies have sacrificed “the interest of the colonies” as well as “the interest of the mother country” “to the interests of … merchants” (1776/1981, p. 584).[67]

Smith’s condemnation of slavery rests on both moral and economic grounds. For example, he (1759/1984, pp. 206–207) noted:

> There is not a negro from the coast of Africa who does not … possess a degree of magnanimity which the soul of his sordid master is too often scarce capable of conceiving. Fortune never exerted more cruelly her empire over mankind, than when she subjected those nations of heroes to the refuse of the jails of Europe, to wretches who possess the virtues neither of the countries which they come from, nor of those which they go to, and whose levity, brutality, and baseness, so justly expose them to the contempt of the vanquished.

In several lectures in the 1760s Smith spoke against slavery and in one occasion he (1982b, p. 185) said,

> Opulence and freedom, the two greatest blessings men can possess, tend greatly to the misery of this body of men [slaves], which in most countries where slavery is allowed makes up by far the greatest part. A humane man would wish therefore if slavery has to be generally established that these greatest blessing(s), being incompatible with the happiness of the greatest part of mankind, were never to take place.

On economic ground, Smith argued that slave labor is more expensive than free labor. He (1776/1981, p. 99) noted, "from the experience of all ages and nations, I believe, the work done by freemen comes cheaper in the end than that performed by slaves. It is found to do so at Boston, New York, and Philadelphia, where the wages of common labour are so very high." He (1776/1981, p. 684) argued that "Slaves … are very seldom inventive" because

> Should a slave propose any improvement of this kind, his master would be very apt to consider the proposal as the suggestion of laziness, and a desire to save his own labour at the master's expence. The poor slave, instead of reward, would probably meet with much abuse, perhaps with some punishment. In the manufactures carried on by slaves, therefore, more labour must generally have been employed to execute the same quantity of work than in those carried on by freemen. The work of the former must, upon that account, generally have been dearer than that of the latter.

Moreover, "Hungarian mines" operated by freemen cost less than the Turkish mines "wrought by slaves" (1776/1981, p. 684).[68]

Justice, law, and certain regulations are central for the workings of the invisible hand. This is clear from the following lecture that Smith delivered in 1762:

> In the age of commerce, as the subjects of property are greatly increased the laws must be proportionally multiplied. The more improved any society is and the greater length the severall means of supporting the inhabitants are carried, the greater will be the number of their laws and regulations necessary to maintain justice, and prevent infringements of the right of property. (Smith 1982b, p. 16)

Smith (1776/1981, p. 324) argues that certain

> regulations may, no doubt, be considered as in some respects a violation of natural liberty. But those exertions of the natural liberty of a few individuals, which might endanger the security of the whole society, are, and ought to be, restrained by the laws of all governments, of the most free as well as of the

most despotical. The obligation of building party walls, in order to prevent the communication of fire, is a violation of natural liberty exactly of the same kind with the regulations of the banking trade which are here proposed.[69]

The classical economists in general adopted Smith's position on the beneficence of the market while advocating regulations and interventions in certain sectors of the economy.[70] For example, in the following passage David Ricardo unequivocally accepts the classical interpretation of the invisible hand:

> The pursuit of individual advantage is admirably connected with the universal good of the whole. By stimulating industry, by rewarding ingenuity, and by using most efficaciously the peculiar powers bestowed by nature, it distributes labor most effectively and most economically: while by increasing the general mass of productions, it diffuses general benefit … (1817/1996, p. 93)

Nonetheless, Ricardo identified certain exceptions to this general principle. In a pamphlet titled, "Proposals for an Economical and Secure Currency" he wrote, "Advantageous, however, as the liberty of trade would prove, it must be admitted that there are a few, and a very few exceptions to it, where the interference of government may be beneficially exerted" (*Works*, Vol. IV, 1816/2004, p. 71). Just like Smith, Ricardo argued for certain regulation of financial markets. In particular, he (Ibid., pp. 72–73) focused on "country banks" and noted,

> What objection can there be against requiring of those who take upon themselves the office of furnishing the public with a circulating medium, to deposit with the government an adequate security for the due performance of their engagement? In the use of money, every one is a trader; those whose habits and pursuits are little suited to explore the mechanism of trade are obliged to make use of money, and are no way qualified to ascertain the solidity of the difference between banks whose paper is in circulation; accordingly we find that men living on limited incomes, women, labourers, and mechanics of all descriptions, are often severe sufferers by the failures of the country banks, which they have lately become frequent beyond all former example. …
>
> Against this inconvenience the public should be protected by requiring of every country bank to deposit with government, or with commissioners appointed for that purpose, funded property or other government security, in some proportion to the amount of their issues. …

The regulation that Ricardo put forward was intended to benefit not only the "men living on limited incomes, women, labourers, and mechanics of all descriptions" but also, as the last paragraph shows, the banks themselves. According to Lionel Robbins (1953, pp. 31–32) Ricardo supported "strict regulation of note issues, holding that, in the possibility of over-issue, there lay a major danger of over-trading and financial crisis...." Smith and other classical liberal thinkers aimed to promote institutions that facilitate (and abolish institutions that hinder) the workings of the invisible hand.

9.2. The neoclassical interpretation

In 1874 Leon Walras (1834–1910) published his landmark book, *Elements of Pure Economics*, in which he set out to solve a problem that a generation earlier Antoine Augustin Cournot (1801–1877) had posed. Cournot had argued that a single market can reach equilibrium by the interactions of demand and supply (i.e., partial equilibrium) but it is unclear whether and how all markets simultaneously can move towards equilibrium (i.e., general equilibrium). Walras' attempt to resolve this problem led to the development of the field of general equilibrium, and paved the way for the advent of neoclassical economics.[71] Since (at least in theory) the price mechanism plays the central role in the emergence of both partial and general equilibrium, in the neoclassical interpretation, the invisible hand serves as a metaphor for this mechanism. As we explained in section five, Smith had already identified the price mechanism as the harmonizing device in the market.

The work of Walras inspired the contributions of several scholars to general equilibrium, reaching its pinnacle in the mathematical models of Gerald Debreu, Kenneth Arrow, and Lionel McKenzie.[72] Some economists believe the general equilibrium model "has finally proved mathematically what Smith argued two centuries ago" (Andreu Mas-Colell *et al.*, 1995, p. 549). More specifically, the invisible hand is interpreted as the First Welfare Theorem, which holds competitive markets are Pareto optimal.[73] Andreu Mas-Colell *et al.* (1995, p. 549) argue that the First Welfare Theorem constitutes "a formal and very general confirmation of Adam Smith's asserted 'invisible hand' property of the market." Some other economists, however, are skeptical of the utility of general equilibrium models. Bruna Ingrao and Giorgio Israel (1990) in their book, *The Invisible Hand, Economic Equilibrium in the History of Science*, explain the accomplishments as well as the shortcomings of general equilibrium. They (1990, pp. 360–361) note:

> from its very beginning right up to the present, general economic equilibrium theory has retained an *invariant paradigmatic core* constituted by its aim to demonstrate three fundamental results: that a state of compatibility of the actions of economic agents in a competitive market is possible (*existence of equilibrium*); that only one such state is possible (*uniqueness of equilibrium*); and that the "forces" of the market inevitably lead to this state of compatibility (*stability of equilibrium*)...
>
> With regard to the existence of equilibrium, the situation is quite satisfactory...

> The question of uniqueness presents a very different picture. It is clear that uniqueness theorems can only be obtained on assumptions so restrictive as to appear unacceptable.... However, opinions vary...
>
> While no agreement has yet been reached as to the implications of the results concerning uniqueness, those concerning global stability (i.e., the market ability to attain equilibrium) are unquestionably negative. (Italics in original)

Mark Blaug (2007, p. 188) has argued that it "is a historical invention; indeed, it is a historical travesty" to equate the First Welfare Theorem with the invisible hand because this theorem is premised on perfect competition that Smith never had in mind. Blaug (Ibid.) points out that "Augustin Cournot invented the concept of perfect competition in 1838 – perhaps the one time in the history of economic thought that a fundamental idea was invented *de novo* without any predecessors ..." Further, Blaug (1992, chapter eight) argues that Adam Smith regarded the market as a dynamic process and in continuous motion whereas general equilibrium theory focuses on static efficiency and equilibrium. Elsewhere, Blaug (2001, p. 160) notes that "the most rigorous solution of the existence problem by Arrow and Debreu turns general equilibrium theory into a mathematical puzzle applied to a virtual economy that can be imagined but could not possibly exist."[74] Even the leading architects of general equilibrium, Kenneth Arrow and Frank Hahn (1971, p. vii) in their influential book *General Competitive Analysis* note:

> It is not sufficient to assert that, while it is possible to *invent* a world in which the claims made on behalf of the "invisible hand" are true, these claims fail in the actual world. It must be shown just how the features of the world regarded as essential in any description of it also make it impossible to substantiate the claims. In attempting to answer the question "Could it be true?", we learn a good deal about why it might not be true.

Accordingly, the main contribution of general equilibrium model lies in explicating why in the real world the invisible hand might fail rather than succeed.

In neoclassical economics, the efficient allocation of resources requires that markets be sufficiently competitive, externality be absent, and market participants be fully informed about the products.[75] As noted above, Smith addresses the issue of competition when he argues that merchants and manufacturers have an incentive to gain market power through political means. But under certain conditions monopolies can emerge endogenously. For example, if a firm's unit cost falls as production rises (i.e., in the presence of internal increasing returns to scale) then the firm might become a monopolist by simply producing more. Such a condition will likely result in misallocation of resource and socially sub-optimal outcome. In this regard, Paul Krugman (2006, p. 14) has expressed the neoclassical view as follows: "for the invisible hand to work properly, there must be many competitors in each industry, so that nobody is in a position to exert monopoly power." This condition, Krugman (Ibid.) notes, "depends on the assumption that returns to scale are diminishing, not increasing."[76]

W. Brian Arthur (1989, p. 116) has argued that under increasing returns, the market outcomes may be inflexible and non-ergodic. Non-flexibility means, "once an outcome (a dominant technology) begins to emerge it becomes progressively more 'locked in.'" Hence, "a technology that by chance gains an early lead in adoption may eventually 'corner the market' of potential adopters, with the other technologies becoming locked out." Non-ergodicity means "historical 'small events' are not averaged away and 'forgotten' by the dynamics – they may decide the outcome" (Ibid., p. 117). Arthur provides several examples of inferior technologies that have prevailed in the market. The "US nuclear industry is practically 100% dominated by high-water reactors," Arthur (Ibid., p. 126) points out, even though scientists believe that "the gas-cooled reactors would have been superior." In a similar vein but in the context of international trade theory, Ralph Gomory and William Baumol (2000, p. 97) argue,

> in a world of scale economies market forces can be relied on to drive the economy toward a local maximum of profits and even of welfare. But these forces have no power to free the world economy from that local optimum and move it toward one that is unambiguously better. That is why, under scale economies, decidedly inferior equilibria can nevertheless be locally stable. The invisible hand can indeed, by the happenstance of history, find itself stuck at an equilibrium that is locally optimal but globally far inferior to others, even inferior to the autarky equilibrium for at least one of the trading countries.

David Colander (2000, p. 31) casts a serious doubt on the ability of neoclassical economics to provide an accurate or even a reasonable description of the economy because "Important elements of economic processes – path dependency, increasing returns, multiple equilibria, and technology are downplayed, and the importance of institutional structure is almost lost." Nonetheless, neoclassical paradigm has dominated economics education and policy.

Another challenge to the workings of the invisible hand comes from the presence of externalities, defined as benefits or costs not reflected in the price. Pigou (1952), a leading theorist of externality, argues that in the presence of externality "marginal social net product" would diverge from "marginal private net product" and such divergence would cause resource misallocation and suboptimal levels of output. Since in neoclassical economics such outcomes may arise endogenously and there is no automatic mechanism to correct the problem, Pigou and economists in general call for government intervention through taxation and regulation. But, is the invisible hand of the market hopelessly paralyzed in the presence of externality? Is government intervention the only solution to the problem of externality? In a classic paper, Ronald Coase (1960) argued that if property rights are well-defined and the transaction costs are zero, the parties involved in an externality can negotiate and arrive at a mutually acceptable and efficient solution. Coase showed – to the astonishment of economists and legal scholars – that the efficient solution emerges regardless of the initial assignment of property rights. Medema (2009, p. 111) has noted that "the implications here are stunning: If market transactions are costless, court decisions assigning liability for damages will have no effect on the allocation of resources."[77]

The Coase theorem is an elegant and intriguing proposition, but its applicability is limited because the transaction costs are rarely, if ever, zero. Medema (Ibid., p. 178) has pointed that if market transactions are not costless but "low enough to make bargaining cost-effective" then the resource allocation will depend on the property rights assignments.[78] Blaug (2007, p. 200) has sharply criticized the Coase theorem, arguing that it "is nothing but the first fundamental theorem of welfare economics in disguise … a truth confined to the logical fiction of a world without transactions costs." But Medema (2009, p. 187) has pointed that the Coase theorem "is better understood … as a *useful* fiction" (italics added). Indeed the Coase theorem, rather than asserting that markets alone can always solve the problem of externalities, calls attention to the centrality of property rights protection in the workings of the market.[79]

A related phenomenon, known as "the tragedy of the commons," is noted by some authors as an example of a "subversive invisible hand" in that the pursuit of self-interest harms the public.[80] Garrett Hardin (1968) introduced the phrase "the tragedy of the commons," to argue that if a property is commonly (rather than privately) owned, self-interest would lead to its overuse and even its destruction. Although Hardin has rightly received much credit, the concept had been known to economists long before Hardin wrote his article. For example, in 1907 Irving Fisher published an essay in which he noted, "Where individuals in the community are allowed to seek their own interests the destruction of forests in some regions inevitably follows" (1907, p. 23).[81]

What should be done to avoid the tragedy? In her important book, *Governing the Commons*, Elinor Ostrom (1990) notes that many scholars generally propose either state regulation (including government ownership) or privatization of the commons (consistent with the Coase theorem). Ostrom, however, rejects such an either-or solution and argues that alternative remedies to the commons problem have existed across time and place, as communities facing the possibility of the tragedy of the commons have found ingenious and effective solutions without the state regulation or privatization. Nevertheless, the logic of the tragedy of the commons reinforces the point that the beneficence of the market depends on well-defined and effectively enforced property rights.

The tragedy of the commons can be explained in the framework of the Nash equilibrium and the prisoners' dilemma in that the dominant strategy entices everyone to exploit the commons as much as possible. For an application, consider a model introduced by Harvey Leibenstein (1982) in which the employees of a firm can pursue their own private interests or adopt "a 'Golden Rule' effort option." In the "Golden Rule" case, the employees work in the firm's best interests while in the alternative case they exert very little effort. Similarly, the firm faces two options: a "Golden Rule" option in which the firm maximizes the employees' interests (salary, security, etc.) while in the alternative option, the firm minimizes its costs by providing as little for the employees as possible. Leibenstein presents the payoffs for a typical employee and the firm in the four corners of Table 1.1.

Although the pursuit of the Golden Rule option (W_1 and π_1) offers the highest joint payoff (15 and 15) it is not a viable option, for if the employees practice the Golden Rule (π_1), the firm can increase its payoff (from 15 to 20) by seeking its own interest, resulting in payoff W_3 and π_1. But in this case the employees, too, can increase their payoff (from 3 to 5) by seeking their own interests, leading to the outcome W_3 and π_3. Since this logic applies symmetrically to both players, the payoff W_3 and π_3 emerges as the dominant outcome as well as Nash equilibrium in that any deviation from it by either player would produce a lower payoff. Leibenstein (1982, p. 93) argues that in reality the firm and the employees gravitate towards a middle ground (W_2 and π_2) in which "employees consider the average effort level in terms of pace, quality, and choice of activities, and perform (as a group) according to the established average level." Similarly, the firm "recognizes the existing peer group effort standard, and provides wages and working conditions in accordance with the average peer group effort" (Ibid., p. 93). Since this middle option is inferior to the Golden Rule option, Leibenstein (Ibid., p. 96) suggests:

> the invisible hand theory has to be reconsidered. Even if we assume decreasing returns to scale, and no externalities, we can still end up with non-traditional conclusions. The invisible hand theorem which leads to an optimal exchange situation no longer represents an unalloyed optimum in the sense that the *produced* commodities exchanged could have been produced under an infinity of different conventions some of which are very much inferior to others. (Italics in original)

Table 1.1 Leibenstein's Model

		Firm Options		
		W_1	W_2	W_3
	Employee Options	Golden Rule	Peer Group Standard	Indiv. Maxi
π_1	Golden Rule	15 / 15	17 / 6	20 / 3
π_2	Peer Group Standard	6 / 17	10 / 10	12 / 4
π_3	Indiv. Maxi	3 / 20	4 / 12	5 / 5

Source: Harvey Leibenstein (1982)

Leibenstein criticizes "the invisible hand theory" on the grounds that the pursuit of self-interest does not generate the optimum result (W_1 and π_1). But the payoff W_1 and π_1 unrealistically requires that everyone practice the Golden Rule. As noted above, Adam Smith and his contemporary philosophers based their projects on how human beings actually behave, and not on how they ought to behave. Indeed, Leibenstein's conclusion – the emergence of the middle outcome – illustrates that, despite human frailty and tendency to free ride, the market entices both players to moderate their behavior. For, if the firm acted selfishly, it would lose its most productive employees, and if the employees exerted little effort, they would risk losing their jobs.[82] Given the reality of human nature, the emergence of the middle outcome is consistent with Smith's vision of the invisible hand. A lofty but unrealistic goal is not relevant to the workings of the market.

Irving Fisher, whom we cited above in relation to the tragedy of the commons, carries his argument further and says, "it is not true that each man can be trusted to pursue his own best interests"; hence, he rejects the proposition that "each individual is the best judge of what sub-serves his own interest, and the motive of self-interest leads him to secure the maximum of well-being for himself." For Fisher, "Not only is it false that men, when let alone, will always follow their best interests, but it is false that when they do, they will always thereby best serve society" (1907, p. 21). From this argument Fisher deduces that the pursuit of self-interest does not lead to "the maximum well-being for society as a whole" (Ibid., p. 19). Similarly, John Maynard Keynes (1883–1946) in his Sidney Ball lecture, titled "The End of Laissez-Faire" (1924, p. 8) argued, "It is *not* a correct deduction from the principle of economics that enlightened self-interest always operates in the public interest. Nor is it true that self-interest generally *is* enlightened; more often individuals acting separately to promote their own ends are too ignorant or too weak to attain even these" (italics in original).[83]

As noted before, Smith was well aware of human propensity to commit errors. He spoke of "so imperfect a creature as man" (1759/1984, p. 305) and even made statements that clearly point to human folly in understanding the economic consequences of one's own actions. For example, he (1776/1981, p. 266) wrote,

> though the interest of the labourer is strictly connected with that of the society, he is incapable of either comprehending that interest, or of understanding its connection with his own. His condition leaves him no time to receive the necessary information, and his education and habits are commonly such as to render him unfit to judge even though he was fully informed.

However, there exists a profound difference between the views of thinkers such as Fisher and Keynes on the one hand and those of Smith and Hayek on the other. Fisher's views, for example, led him to the conviction that "The world consists of two classes – the educated and the ignorant – and it is essential for progress that the former should be allowed to dominate the latter" (1907, p. 20).[84] But Smith in the tradition of the Scottish Enlightenment rejected such elitist and condescending thinking, a theme on which Hayek elaborated in the twentieth century. As quoted above, Smith (1776/1981, pp. 530–531) noted that "The man who employs either his labour or his stock in a greater variety of ways than his situation renders necessary … may hurt himself, and he generally does so.… But the law ought always to trust people with the care of their own interest, as in their local situations they must generally be able to judge better of it than the legislator can do."

Finally, Joseph Stiglitz in his Nobel lecture (2002) argues strongly against the notion that "free markets lead to efficient outcomes." To the extent that information is unavailable or distributed asymmetrically (between buyers and sellers, the insured and insurers, borrowers and lenders, and so on) the invisible hand cannot deliver efficient outcomes, and thus Stiglitz finds a necessary role for the state in the economy. From the neoclassical perspective, Stiglitz is right. But not everyone accepts the idea that the economy is a static system that can be modeled mathematically. In fact, as noted above, it was this neoclassical orthodoxy that Mark Blaug seriously challenged. We shall return to this issue in the next section.

Hayek developed his theory of market on the fact that people face ignorance and uncertainty in the market, and argued that the price mechanism constitutes the most effective and reliable (although not necessarily a perfect) tool to reveal and transmit the knowledge necessary for its operation. Whether one agrees with Stiglitz or Hayek largely depends on whether one regards the market as a static and equilibrating force or a dynamic and evolving process. There is a deeper issue involved here. Stiglitz (2002) and Arrow (1994) do not distinguish between information and knowledge. But information is simply organized data whereas, in the words of Daniel Klein (2012, p. 79) which we quoted before, "knowledge entails information, interpretation, and judgment." Klein (Ibid., p. 144) points out that scholars such as Arrow "flatten knowledge down to information." But as Hayek stressed, the market operates on the division of *knowledge*.[85] This analysis relates to the next interpretation of the invisible hand.

9.3. The evolutionary interpretation

Many scholars reject the neoclassical interpretation with its emphasis on equilibrium and static efficiency. Some have gone as far saying that "the invisible hand … consists of forces that push individuals to seize entrepreneurial opportunities, and that foster economic progress. In this sense the invisible hand may play a disequilibrating role …"[86] (Holcombe, 1999, p. 233). Such remarks views the invisible hand in an evolutionary light, articulated most influentially by Smith and, among others, by Hayek.

Brian Arthur (1999, p. 109), a leading contributor to complexity economics, also adopts a dynamic perspective and argues that we should "portray the economy not as deterministic, predictable and mechanistic; but as process-dependent, organic, and always evolving." A dynamic perspective would maintain that oligopolies and even monopolies are not immune from competitive pressures because exerting market power and enjoying abnormal profits would ultimately attract rivals. Viewed in this light, business firms are inherently and inevitably contestable. In such a setting, as in the Schumpeterian creative-destruction process, the utility of the market is measured by the introduction of new products and ideas, rather than by criteria such as returns to scale, market structure, or the size of excess capacity – which are commonly taught in economics. James Buchanan and Viktor Vanberg (1991) describe the market economy as "an open-ended creative process" and to Hayek (1968/2002) "competition" is "a discovery procedure." The proponents of the evolutionary perspective regard the economy as too complex and too dynamic to be expressed in precise mathematical models. Interestingly, this was the view of certain leading physicists of the twentieth century including Neils Bohr and Max Planck.[87] If the macro-economy can be successfully modeled in mathematical terms, then it can be controlled because policymakers can change an independent variable to generate a desired outcome. But it is far from clear that the knowledge required for modeling the economy is available.

Further, recall Smith's lecture in 1749 (quoted earlier) in which he referred to any attempt to impose a social order as "unnatural … oppressive and tyrannical." Over two centuries later, Hayek in his Nobel lecture in 1974 echoed Smith:

> The recognition of the insuperable limits to his [man's] knowledge ought indeed to teach the student of society a lesson of humility which should guard him against becoming an accomplice in men's fatal striving to control society – a striving which makes him not only tyrant over his fellows, but which may well make him the destroyer of a civilization which no brain has designed but which has grown from the free efforts of millions of individuals. (1974/1989, p. 7)

Indeed the free efforts of countless individuals continue to advance civilization. In the earlier times, money (by facilitating division of labor) and language (by allowing transmission of knowledge) played the fundamental roles in advancing civilization. But both money and language emerged through an invisible-hand process. Carl Menger (1840–1921) argued that money "is not an invention of the state. It is not the product of a legislative act.… Certain commodities came to be money quite naturally, as the result of economic relationships that were independent of the state" (1871/1976). Menger (Ibid., p. 260) further wrote,

> As *each* economizing individual becomes increasingly aware of his economic interest, he is led by *this interest, without any agreement, without legislative compulsion, and even without regard to the public interest,* to give his commodities in exchange for other, more saleable, commodities, even if he does not need them for any immediate consumption purpose. (Italics in original)

Menger in essence reiterated Adam Ferguson (noted in section 6) by describing how social institutions emerge as the product of human actions, but not of human design.[88] However, Warren Samuels (2011), in his extensive and diligent study of the invisible hand, argues that according to Menger social institutions are the products of non-deliberate as well as deliberate processes. Samuels (2011, p. 212) writes,

> as Menger maintained, each generation in every society has as its calling the evaluation and revision of received institutions. These institutions may have grown up organically, spontaneously and non-deliberatively. Each institution arguably comprises elements of both wisdom and folly, and the task is to identify them, retain the former and correct or extirpate the latter. Thus, although institutions have grown up organically, spontaneously, and non-deliberatively, they are to be made subject to deliberative critique and revision/reform.

Samuels (Ibid., p. 214) further argues that interactions among individuals and the aggregation of their actions

> occur within and are structured and channeled by social system and structure – in short, institutions. So, we have a fundamental dualism: Institutions are the evolving result of deliberative and non-deliberative (spontaneous) elements, and the operation of the deliberative and non-deliberative (spontaneous) elements is a result of institutions.

The Constitution of the United Sates provides a vivid example of Samuels' dualism. The Founding Fathers of the United States crafted a set of political, economic, and legal institutions based on certain historical precedents, especially those of the classical Greece and Rome. But they also deliberated long and hard on the idiosyncrasies of the institutions suitable for the new Republic. Consequently, the Constitution embodies the wisdom of the past as well as the deliberations of those involved in its creation. The newly established constitutional framework allowed (and continues to allow) for a bottom-up emergence of economic and political outcomes.

The rest of this chapter focuses on the applications of the invisible hand, especially those outside economics. The next section analyzes the interplay between the invisible hand and the science of complexity. Appendix I presents the views of many scholars who have argued that the articulation of the invisible-hand concept by Smith and other Scottish philosophers influenced Charles Darwin's discovery of natural selection as the mechanism of the evolution of species. Appendix II focuses on the application of the invisible hand to the philosophy of science. Appendix III presents additional interpretations of the invisible hand.

10. The invisible hand and the science of complexity

The philosopher Robert Nozick (1974, p. 18) coined the phrase "invisible-hand explanation" as a reference to "some overall pattern or design, which one would have thought had to be produced by an individual's or group's successful attempt to realize the pattern, instead was produced and maintained by a process that in no way had the overall pattern or design in 'mind.'"[89] Nozick presents sixteen examples of "invisible-hand explanation," one of which is Thomas Schelling's segregation model. Schelling (1978, p. 147) demonstrates that in a racially integrated neighborhood if every member of one group wants "at least half its neighbors to be" his or her type and every member of the other group desires only "a third of its neighbors to be" like him or her, then integration will be unstable and ultimately complete segregation will emerge as the residents move in and out of the neighborhood. As H. Peyton Young (1998, p. 10) points out – given those preferences – "completely segregated neighborhoods are more likely to emerge than any other pattern. In fact, this remains true even if everyone *prefers* to live in a mixed neighborhood (where one neighbor is similar and the other is different)" (italics in original). The undesigned and unintended social outcome in Schelling's model serves as an example of self-organization in society.[90]

Self-organization is a characteristic of complex systems, which the physicist Sunny Auyang (1998, p. 13) defines as "systems that have many components and many characteristic aspects, exhibit many structures in various scales, undergo many processes in various rates, and have the capabilities to change abruptly and adapt to external environments." Additionally, complex systems have a characteristic that the philosopher George Edward Moore (1902, p. 36) dubbed "organic unity" and defined as follows: "a whole has an intrinsic value different from the sum of the values of its parts."[91] The principle of organic unity implies that in complex systems "macroscopic properties cannot be formally or analytically deduced from the properties of its parts" (Markose, 2005, p. F161). Auyang (1998, p. 3) further notes:

> The subject matters of economics, evolutionary biology, and statistical physics are all complex systems made up of many interacting constituents: national economies made up of millions of consumers and producers bargaining and trading; evolving species comprising billions of organisms competing for resources; solids constituted by septillions of electrons and ions attracting and repelling each other.

A key question in the science of complexity concerns the origin of order. How does a system self-organize? How can an orderly pattern emerge without a designer? In some instances the process of self-organization is explicable. For example, Schelling himself as well as Edna Ullmann-Margalit (1978) and Aydinonat (2008) have shown how in Schelling's model complete segregation emerges. But not all self-organized systems are comprehensible or explainable. For example, the relationship between the size and rank of cities (in terms of population) can be presented by the power law equation, $R = AS^{-\alpha}$ where A is a constant, R denotes rank, S represents size, and α is a parameter, which in this particular example is not significantly different from 1. This relationship is also known as Zipf's law. Andrew Rose (2006) has found that this mathematical realtionship holds almost perfectly for the 50 largest cities in the United States as well as for the 50 largest countries. Figures 1.1 and 1.2 depict the stunning relationship between the logarithm of R (rank) and the logarithm of S (size) for the year 2000.

Whence the inverse relationship between R and S? Rose (2006) surveys several scholarly works on the city rank–size correlation, and finds no satisfactory theory or explanation. It is a mysterious and, as Krugman (1996) puts it, a "spooky" phenomenon. Equally puzzling is Robert Axtell's (2001, p. 1818) finding that "Using data on the entire population of tax-paying firms in the United States … the Zipf distribution characterizes firm sizes …" and the "results hold for data from multiple years and for various definitions of firm size." Moreover, the Zipf "distribution describes surprisingly diverse natural and social phenomena, including population processes, immune system response, frequency of word usage, city sizes,

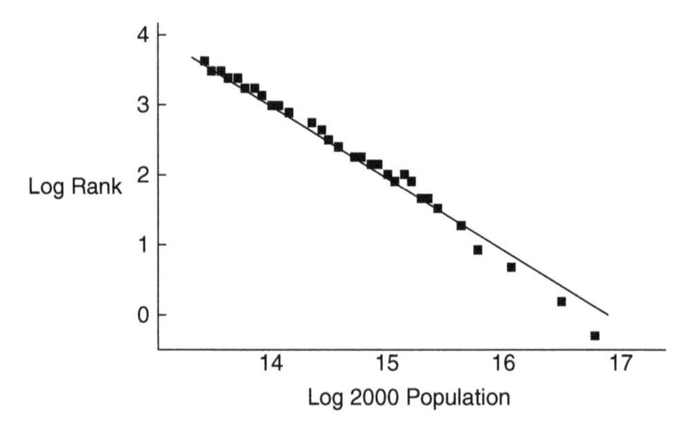

Figure 1.1 Rank–size relationship for 50 largest US cities, 2000.
Source: Andrew Rose (2006)

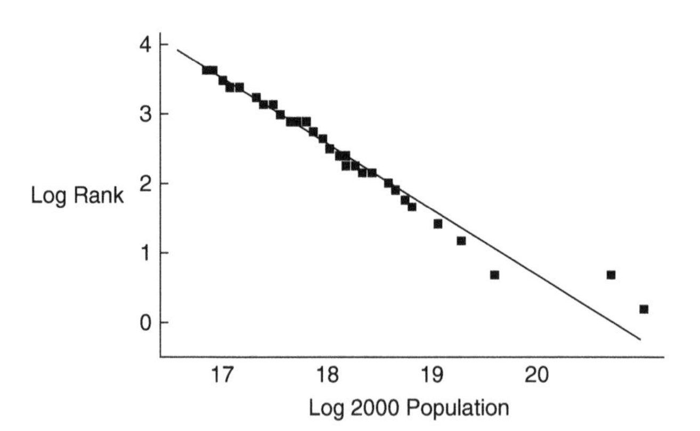

Figure 1.2 Rank–size relationship for 50 largest countries, 2000.
Source: Andrew Rose (2006)

and aspects of internet traffic" (Ibid., p. 1819). Xavier Gabaix (2009, p. 281), who provides a detailed and mathematical analysis of Zipf's law in a number of phenomena, notes that even in international trade "the Balassa index of revealed comparative advantage satisfies Zipf's law." The ubiquity of Zipf's distribution (an expression of self-organization) in so many phenomena remains unexplained.[92, 93]

The affinity between the evolutionary interpretation of the invisible hand in economics and the science of complexity is remarkably clear. In fact Markose (2005, p. F160) has identified the Scottish Enlightenment philosophers as the progenitors of the idea of complexity. She further notes that complexity is expressed in "the Adam Smith metaphor of the invisible hand" which "premises a disjunction between system-wide outcomes and the design capabilities of individuals at a micro level and the distinct absence of an external organizing force."[94] The science of complexity considers nature and market economy to be continuously evolving and dynamically adaptive. John Holland (1988, p. 118), a leading complexity theorist, refers to the global economy as "an example, par excellence" of complex systems.[95] Accordingly, markets are self-organizing processes in which order arises endogenously as Smith, Hayek, and others have argued. But whence the market order? Does the price mechanism sufficiently explain the emergence of the market order?

Daniel Klein (1997) has called attention to two types of self-organizing processes, which he calls "coordination" and "metacoordination."[96] Schelling's segregation model is an example of coordination in which the emergent order is explicable. The market order is an example of metacoordination, which is much more complex, and exceedingly difficult, if not impossible, to explicate. In fact a number of complexity scholars (economists and non-economists) are not satisfied with the argument that the price mechanism generates the market order – they long to know exactly *how* the order emerges. Two scholars have emphatically argued:

> More than two centuries after the publication of Smith's masterpiece, economists still do not know how, why, and when the invisible hand works in a truly decentralized system of interacting individual agents. In other words, even more basic questions underlie such questions as when should one expect stability, booms, or slumps in a decentralized economy. (Kochugovindan and Vriend, 1998, p. 55)

Similarly, in an interview with *Challenge*, Mark Blaug (1998) said: "We in economics know a hell of a lot about equilibrium, but we really don't know how markets actually get to equilibrium." And Alex Leijonhufvud (2006, p. 1930) laments that "economists don't know much about how markets work." These views reflect the fact that it is unclear how exactly the price mechanism operates; consequently, some scholars have applied non-traditional approaches to the market. For example, many researchers have employed the theory and tools of complexity in order to shed light on the invisible-hand process. David Colander (2000, pp. 33–34) notes,

> The complexity approach to economics … sees the economy as a complex system that follows the same laws as all complex systems … many economists

> may have had a complexity perspective, but did not follow up on it in their formal work because they did not have the tools to do so.

Colander further notes that recent advancements in mathematics and high powered computers have enabled economists "to get numerical solutions to complicated non-linear equations and to see the implications of iterative processes involving non-linear equations that it changes the way it is reasonable to look for patterns in data" (Ibid., p. 34).[97] A noteworthy work in this area is Nicolaas Vriend (1995). He (1995, p. 95, italics in original) set out to find an answer to the following question: "How, why, and when does the '*invisible hand*' work?" He conducted a market simulation involving "50 firms and 5000 consumers" and "more than 14 million transactions." His simulation shows that market order does arise endogenously, and supports Hayek's (1946/1980, p. 106) contention that "Competition is essentially a process of the formation of opinion: by spreading information, it creates that unity and coherence of the economic system which we presuppose when we think of it as one market." According to Vriend's (1995, p. 224) simulation, "competition appears to lead to coordination of economic activities, communication by firms and patronage by consumers play an important role therein."

Another line of research, closely related to complexity, has focused on the application of evolutionary game theory to the market. For example, Peyton Young (1998, p. 4) notes that "a great variety of social and economic institutions – language, codes of dress, forms of money and credit, pattern of courtship and marriage, accounting standards, rules of the road … no one willed them into being: they are what they are due to the accumulation of precedent; they emerged from experimentation and historical accident." Young's application of evolutionary game theory to the emergence of these institutions leads him to the following observation:

> complex economic and social structure can emerge from the simple, uncoordinated actions of many individuals. When an interaction occurs over and over again and involves a changing cast of characters, a feedback loop is established whereby past experiences of some agents shape the current expectations of other agents. This process yields predictable patterns of equilibrium and disequilibrium behavior that can be construed as social and economic "institutions," that is, established customs, usages, norms, and forms of organization. (1998, p. 144)

Young's further work (2001, p. 140), using evolutionary game theory, "shows how a kind of 'spontaneous social order' can arise from the decentralized, purely self-interested decisions of many individuals."[98]

The empirical works cited above, based on complexity and evolutionary game theory, amply confirm the insight of Smith, Hayek, and other thinkers concerning the endogenous emergence of the market order. These works, however, do not tell us *how* the order arises.

11. A final note

In a market economy consumers as well as producers of goods and services along with their suppliers, distributors, creditors, and employees generally seek their own interests. These agents have different and, quite likely, even opposing interests. Since in this process there is no apparent arbiter or planner in charge, one wonders whether such a system can be trusted and expected to produce an orderly outcome. Adam Smith's answer to this question consists of four observations. First, individuals seeking their own economic interests, unintentionally and unknowingly, frequently (Smith's word) promote the interests of other people. Second, self-interested economic behavior involves competition at the micro level but cooperation at the macro level. Third, market order arises endogenously from the twin processes of competition and cooperation. Here, the price mechanism performs the pivotal function by conveying the necessary and relevant knowledge to economic agents while coordinating all economic decisions including division of labor. The fourth observation, the flip side of the third, is that any attempt to design and impose an order would inevitably lead to chaos and tyranny.

Notwithstanding Smith's masterful exposition of the market operation and the subsequent analytical and empirical works by numerous brilliant minds, the emergence of the market order remains a mystery. Robert Clower (1994, p. 806) has observed that what "economists have yet to explain is the working of the *fingers* of the invisible hand" (italics in original). Even Hayek, who wrote voluminously about the operation of the market, admitted that "How the production of the tens of thousands of different things which are needed to produce a much smaller but still very large number of final products is determined by the market process is a matter of infinite complexity; and how order is brought about by a spontaneous mechanism … we do not fully understand" (1976/1978, p. 242). As long as "the working of the *fingers*" remains unexplained and "we do not fully understand" how order emerges in the market, "the invisible hand" will serve as an apt metaphor in economic discourse on the market.

Appendix I: the invisible hand and the theory of natural selection

In his autobiography, Charles Darwin (1887/1958, p. 120) describes how Malthus' population theory helped him formulate the theory of natural selection.[99]

> In October 1838, I happened to read for amusement Malthus on *Population*, and being well prepared to appreciate the struggle for existence which everywhere goes on from long-continued observation of the habits of animals and plants, it at once struck me that under these circumstances favourable variations would tend to be preserved, and unfavourable ones to be destroyed.[100]

But Malthus was not the only economist who influenced Darwin. A number of historians of ideas have shown that Darwin received inspiration from the thinkers associated with the Scottish Enlightenment, above all Adam Smith. In a detailed analysis of Darwin's work and its application to social and economic evolution, Geoffrey Hodgson and Thorbjorn Knudsen (2010, p. 109) note, "It is no accident that Darwin's theory of natural selection was inspired by economists such as Adam Smith and Thomas Robert Malthus as we observe selection in the business world when some firms are eliminated through bankruptcy and successful forms are copied by new entrants." In comparison with Malthus' influence, "Adam Smith's influence" Stephen Jay Gould (1993, p. 148) writes, "was more indirect, but also more pervasive." Gould (Ibid., p. 149) regards natural selection and laissez-faire economics as "'isomorphic' – that is, structurally similar point for point, even though the subject matter differs." Elsewhere, Gould (1980, pp. 67–68) writes, "I believe that the theory of natural selection should be viewed as an extended analogy – whether conscious or unconscious on Darwin's part I do not know – to the laissez-faire economics of Adam Smith."[101] What are their similarities? Gould (1993, p. 149) invokes the invisible hand to answer the question:

> To achieve the goal of a maximally ordered economy in the laissez-faire system, you do not regulate from above by passing explicit laws for order. You do something that, at first glance, seems utterly opposed to your goal: You simply allow individuals to struggle in an unfettered way for personal profit. In this struggle, the inefficient are weeded out and the best balance each other to form an equilibrium to everyone's benefit.
>
> Darwin's system works in exactly the same manner, only more relentlessly.... Individuals are struggling for reproductive success, the natural analog of profit.... Adam Smith embodied the guts of his theory – his core insight – in a wonderful metaphor.... The 'invisible hand' that produces order, but does not really exist at all, at least not in any direct way.

The scientist and science historian Silvan Schweber in several essays focuses on the influence of political economists, especially Adam Smith, on Darwin. Schweber (1980, p. 276) points out that prior to formulating his theory of evolution, "Darwin had immersed himself in that literature, and more particularly in the Scottish attempts to account for the evolution and stability of moral and economic order." Schweber (1977, p. 233) writes that according to Darwin's notes, "by August 1830, [Darwin] came to study among others, Hume, Burke, Dugald Stewart and Adam Smith which reinforced his focus on the individual as the central element and unit in his theory and led him to adopt the Scottish view of trying to understand the whole in terms of the individual parts and their interactions." In his notebooks Darwin wrote that in 1830 he read *The Theory of Moral Sentiments* and Smith's *Essays on Philosophical Subjects*, which includes Dugald Stewart's "Account of the Life and Writings of Adam Smith."[102]

Many passages in *The Theory of Moral Sentiments* including the invisible hand passage seem relevant to Darwin's work because of the numerous references to the functioning of organisms in nature. For example, Smith expresses his wonder at the natural instincts in human beings and animals that have far reaching and unforeseen consequences. He presents nature as a holistic entity where species instinctively produce "beneficial ends" including "self-preservation and propagation" (1759/1984, pp. 77–78).

Schweber (1977, p. 233) points to a "parallel between the role freedom of choice and free will play in Scottish economic and moral science and the role played by random variations in the theory of evolution." He (Ibid., p. 283) further notes:

> The fact that variations are chance elements (stochastic, to use an anachronistic term) made Darwin look at Adam Smith and other Scottish economists and moral economists and moral philosophers to see how a theory (that is, an explanation) with random elements can account for the stability of the social and economic order. In the moral and economic sphere the chance element is introduced by the assumption that the individual actors have free will. Yet there is an ensuing order (as if each individual were 'led by an invisible hand').[103]

The "ensuing order" plays the central role in both the Scottish Enlightenment and Darwin's evolutionary biology. In this regard, according to Craig Smith (2006, p. 6), "Hayek believed that Darwin picked up these ideas through the medium of the Scots geologist James Hutton (1726–1797), a member of the broader Scottish Enlightenment, and through the influence of Hume upon his grandfather Erasmus Darwin, and then applied the approach to nature."[104]

Appendix II: the invisible hand of science

Michael Polanyi (1891–1976), in an influential essay titled "The Republic of Science" (1962/1969), argues that science advances through a self-coordination process similar to the coordination of economic activities in the market. He (Ibid., pp. 50–51) writes, the "co-ordination is guided as by 'an invisible hand' towards the joint discovery of a hidden system of things … such co-ordination assures the most efficient possible organization of scientific progress." More importantly, just as Smith and Hayek argued that any attempt to plan and direct the economy would be impossible and would even destroy them, Polanyi (Ibid., p. 59) notes, "any authority which would undertake to direct the work of the scientist centrally would bring the progress of science virtually to a standstill" (p. 52). "You can kill or mutilate the advance of science," Polanyi writes, "you cannot shape it."

David Hull (1988), in his book *Science as a Process*, also invokes the invisible hand to explain the progress of science, but in a different light from Polanyi's application of the term. He (Ibid., p. 357) argues that in scientific circles the pursuit of credit for one's achievement bestows unintended benefits on society and "promotes the greater good." While Polanyi stresses the evolutionary aspect of the invisible hand in science, Hull focuses on the transformation of self-interest into the public interest. The mechanism for this transformation lies "in the social organization of science" leading to "the frequent coincidence in science of individual 'selfish' goals and the greater good."

The invisible hand of science argument has gained adherents as well as detractors. For example, Philip Mirowski (1997, p. S131) objects to Polanyi's use of the market metaphor in science and argues that the "comparison of the social structure of science to the operation of a market … bears no necessary content or implications in and of itself." Mirowski also points out that the price mechanism, which coordinates markets, operates very differently from "the act of formal acknowledgment of published results of other scientists" (Ibid., p. S132). Although Mirowski raises a valid point, Polanyi's use of the invisible hand metaphor in science helps him make the crucial observation that scientific progress, just like the market process, cannot be directed and planned. Indeed, Polanyi's observation and the application of the invisible-hand paradigm to science further supports the thesis that in any sphere of human activity in which the individual members interact with each other (as in the economy and science), central direction and macro-planning would fail and ultimately result in stagnation, retrogression, and even destruction.

As in Mirowski (1997), Petri Ylikoski (1995) also raises some objection to the use of the invisible hand metaphor in science.[105] In particular, he points out that no one has spelled out the social organization of science within which the invisible hand is presumed to work. In an essay, entitled "Reflection on Rules in Science: An Invisible-Hand Perspective," Thomas Leonard (2002) attempts to fill the void. He (Ibid., p. 142) seeks to find out "under what circumstances can a real community of fallible, 'epistemically sullied' … inquirers achieve the good outcomes traditionally thought to require ideal inquirers." He (Ibid., p. 143) then argues, "Scientific rules, and the means for their enforcement, constitutes the invisible hand mechanism, by which I mean: scientific rules induce (partly) interested scientific actors with worldly goals to make choices that (sometimes) lead to epistemically good scientific outcomes." Leonard goes on to say that just as Adam Smith's invisible hand works well under proper "institutional structure" (as, for example, when property rights are well-defined and enforced), the invisible hand of science works well when the rules of scientific investigation are observed.

The views of Polanyi, Hull, Leonard, and others on the invisible hand of science imply that the progress of science largely (if not entirely) depends on the organization of scientific inquiry. And the organization most conducive to the advancement of science resembles the market in that scientists pursue their own goals while adhering to the rules of scientific inquiry. While it would be an exaggeration to claim that science advances in the same way economies advance, the progress of both requires a bottom-up (as opposed to top-down) approach.[106]

Appendix III: other interpretations of the invisible hand

Many scholars including Jacob Viner believe the phrase "invisible hand" has a deistic connotation in Smith's principal works. William Baumol (1978, p. 121), while analyzing the invisible hand, notes that for Smith the market represents "… an instrument of the Deity designed to curb the frailty of humanity.… It is a device adopted by a very practical Providence to deal with the … very weakness of human character."[107]

Jerry Evensky (2005, p. 3) invites us to

> Imagine that there is an order to the universe, an order that is the work of a deity as designer. Imagine further that somewhere beyond our sight that deity has a drafting table and on that table are the blueprints for that design. Those imagined blueprints are invisible to us, and so too the hand that drew them.[108]

The deistic interpretation arguably rests on Smith's invocation of the deity in numerous places in *The Theory of Moral Sentiments* including in the invisible-hand passage. Following the sentence where Smith says the rich "are led by an invisible hand to make nearly the same distribution of the necessaries of life," he writes, "When Providence divided the earth among a few masters, it neither forgot nor abandoned those who seemed to have been left out in the partition." (1759/1984, pp. 184–185). However, as Anthony Brewer (2009) has suggested, "Providence" in the passage may well be a figure of speech rather than the personal God of the Bible in whom Smith as a deist did not believe.[109]

As noted earlier, decades before Smith wrote his books, several scholars including Derham, Maxwell, and Harris had described how the market transforms self-interest into the public interest, and to varying degrees they had attributed the transformation to super- natural powers. Perhaps, under the influence of these scholars, Smith used the invisible hand phrase with a deistic connotation in mind. In fact the physiocrat Victor de Riqueti Mirabeau (1715–1789), in a 1763 publication entitled *La Philosophie Rurale*, described the natural harmony of the economy as a process that conceptually is similar to Smith's invisible-hand passages. Quite explicitly, Mirabeau attributed the natural harmony and the market process to the Biblical God. He wrote:

> The whole magic of well-ordered society is that each man works for others, while believing that he is working for himself. This magic, the general character and effects of which are revealed by the subject we are studying, shows us that the Supreme Being bestowed upon us as a father the principles of economic harmony, when condescended to announce and prescribe them to us, as God, in the form of religious laws. (Translated and quoted by Ronald Meek, 1963, p. 70)[110]

Lionel Robbins (1953, p. 56) introduced an entirely different interpretation of the invisible hand. He first wrote that the "pursuit of self-interest, unrestrained by suitable institutions, carries no guarantee of anything except chaos." He (Ibid.) then wrote, the "invisible hand which guides men to promote ends which were no part of their intention, is not the hand of some god or some natural agency independent of human efforts; it is the hand of the lawgiver, the hand which withdraws from the sphere of the pursuit of self-interest those possibilities which do not harmonize with the public good." Equating Smith's invisible hand with "the hand of the lawgiver," seemingly turns the invisible-hand proposition on its head.

However, to the extent that the workings of the invisible hand rest on the state (lawgiver) performing its proper functions such as the administration of justice, Robbins has a point.

Rothschild (2001) has argued that the invisible hand, as we know it today, is a twentieth century "invention." She points out that neither Smith's contemporaries nor the nineteenth century scholars invoked the phrase. Nor was it even mentioned at the centenary celebration of the *Wealth of Nations* in 1876. It is true that Smith's contemporaries who contributed to the development of the invisible-hand concept did not use the phrase. Adam Ferguson (1792, vol. 1, p. 201) could have invoked the invisible hand in the following passage: "The bulk of mankind are … subjected to the law of their nature, and, without knowing it, are led to accomplish its purpose." Similarly, Thomas Reid (1710–1796), who succeeded Smith at the University of Glasgow, wrote: "By instinct and habit, man, without deliberation or will, is led to many actions, necessary for his preservation and well-being, which without those principles, all his skill and wisdom would not have been able to accomplish" (1788, vol. 2, p. 558). The fact that Ferguson and Reid did not use the phrase "the invisible hand" in the foregoing quotes – even though they resemble Smith's invisible-hand passages – suggests that Smith's contemporary scholars did not attach much significance to the phrase or perhaps they wished to avoid the possible deistic connotation of the phrase in the increasingly secular European intellectual environment. The fact that none of the Smith's contemporaries asked him why he used the phrase or what he meant by it lends credence to Gavin Kennedy's (2009) argument that the invisible hand was a well-known metaphor in the eighteenth century.[111]

Finally, Samuels (2011, p. 281) has argued that the phrase invisible hand "does not add anything" to our knowledge. Delete the phrase from the invisible-hand passages in Smith's two books, and the content will remain intact just as the passages by Ferguson and Reid quoted above are perfectly clear without the phrase. But, one wonders, why would Smith, a careful writer and deep thinker, invoke a useless phrase? Smith described himself as "a very slow workman, who do and undo everything I write at least half a dozen times before I can be tolerably pleased with it" (1987, p. 311). In addition to rewriting his books "half a dozen times" before publication, Smith revised them several times after publication. He had ample opportunity to remove the phrase but he chose to keep it. Why? A possible answer is that the phrase bestows a linguistic beauty and an aura of mystery that captures and even captivates the reader's attention.[112] It is no wonder that Arrow and Hahn (1971, p. 1) refer to the invisible hand as a "poetic expression of the most fundamental of economic balance relations."

Notes

1 See the exchanges between Gavin Kennedy (2009) and Daniel Klein (2009).

2 Spencer Pack (1994, p. 182) has also stressed the distinction between the invisible hand and unintended consequences. See also Deepak Lal's *Unintended Consequences* (1998).

3 Hayek was not the first thinker to mention law, language, money, and morals have arisen and evolved without a conscious design. However, under the influence of Darwinian natural selection (explained in appendix 1), he added biological evolution to the list.
4 For these references see Daniel Klein (2009, pp. 271–272).
5 Gavin Kennedy (2010) has argued that Paul Samuelson's 1948 introductory textbook was highly influential in the ubiquitous usage of the invisible hand in economics literature. Philip Mirowski (2013, p. 9) presents a graph showing the "Number of articles mentioning 'invisible hand' in JSTOR, by year." The usage peaked at 250 in the year 2000, but it has since been falling.
6 The present study, however, is *not* concerned with the development of markets. Markets, in one form or another, almost always have been an integral part of human society. As Adam Smith (1776/1981, p. 25) noted, "the propensity to truck, barter, and exchange of one thing for another" is a principle of human nature. For a thorough coverage of the contribution of markets to the development of the modern world, see Kenneth Pomeranz and Steven Topik (1999).
7 For an analysis of the Greco-Roman and Christian views, see chapters one and two in Joseph Schumpeter (1954), chapter one in Mark Perlman and Charles McCann Jr. (2001), and the first five chapters in Murray Rothbard (1999).
8 Murray Rothbard (1999, p. 21) attributes the dictum "money is the root of all evils" to Diogenes (412–323 BCE). The Biblical pronouncement "the *love* of money is the root of all evils" (italics added) might have been a response to this dictum. The reference to the quote in the Bible is 1 Timothy, 6:10.
9 This passage with some variation is recorded in the Gospel of John and of Mark as well.
10 Augustine wrote, "If one does not lose, the other does not gain" (quoted in Muller, 2002, p. 6). Similarly, St. Jermoe (340–420), a contemporary of Augustine, believed that "man does not accumulate money except through the loss of and injury suffered by another" (quoted in Barry Gordon, 1975, p. 101). Augustin, however, acknowledged the utility of commerce. See Rudi Verburg (2012).
11 See Douglas Irwin (2006, p. 16).
12 For a survey on the writings of Muslim scholars on economics, see Hamid Hosseini (2007).
13 For a thorough and detailed coverage of economic thought of the Scholastic period, see Odd Langholm (2006). See also a survey article by S. Todd Lowry (2007) and Barry Gordon (1975) on the writings of Aquinas on economics.
14 The Scholastic doctors had inherited the concept of the "just price" from Aristotle. For analysis of "just price," see David Freidman (1987). On Aquinas' view on money-lending at interest, which he condemned, see his *Summa Theologiae*, edited by Paul Sigmund (1988, p. 74).
15 See Muller, 2002 (pp. 7–8).
16 The dismissive attitude of the Greek philosophers towards economics does not mean they did not write on economics. Indeed a substantial literature on Greek economic thought has developed. This literature includes Albert Augustus Trever (1916/1978), Scott Meikle (1995), Barry Gordon (1975), and in particular S. Todd Lowry (1979). See also the first three LSE lectures of Lionel Robbins (1998).
17 In the next chapter on the theory of comparative advantage we will thoroughly present the controversy as well as the literature on "jealousy of trade." Here, it suffices to note that in 1758 David Hume wrote an essay titled, "Of the Jealousy of Trade" in which he argued, among other things, the economic advancement of a country spills over to other countries and benefits its trading partners. See Hume (1758/1955).
18 Chapter two presents the ideas of Henry Martyn on trade because they relate to the theory of comparative advantage.
19 Perlman and McCann Jr. (2001, pp. 48–54) include the philosophy of John Locke (1632–1704) as a devastating response to Hobbes' challenge. However, Locke is not included in this section because his response had no direct bearing on the development

of the invisible-hand argument. But his philosophy did provide a firm foundation for classical liberalism whose cornerstone is the market system.

20 The design argument led to a philosophical viewpoint known as "optimistic deism," a version of which is expressed in "all is the best in the best of all possible worlds" attributed to Leibnitz and mocked by Voltaire in *Candide*. Ivar Ekeland (2006), in his book titled *The Best of All Possible Worlds*, fully explores the intellectual history of the idea associated with Leibnitz and other thinkers.

21 On the philosophical evolution of self-love, see Milton Myers (1983), Albert Hirschman (1977), and Pierre Force (2003). Force presents the views of a number of French philosophers on self-love and its role in society.

22 The historian of ideas Carl Becker (1932, p. 67) comments on this poem, "Pope was merely repeating St. Thomas, who had written twenty volumes to reassure a world on the verge of doubt – twenty volumes to say that it was really right that things should be wrong, God only knows why."

23 In late seventeenth century several writers expressed similar views but none of them became as influential and as (in)famous as Mandeville. See Jerry Muller (1993, pp. 50–51) for a few examples of such writers.

24 In a commentary on the *Fable*, Marina Bianchi (1993, p. 212), a scholar of Mandeville, notes: "fraud and deception stimulates creative ways to increase profits; self-love, pride, and luxury excite the desire for new wants and the search for new ways of satisfying them. Avarice, envy, and greed elicit accumulation and growth..."

25 John Maynard Keynes (1936, p. 129) expressed a similar view when he wrote, "Pyramid-building, earthquakes, and even wars may serve to increase wealth..." We will study Keynes in chapters three and four of the present book.

26 Deidre McCloskey (2010, p. 147) also argues that Mandeville's "economics was false." See also Murray Rothbard (1999). The broken window fallacy is explained in Henry Hazlitt (1946/1979).

27 In the early draft of *The Wealth of Nations*, Smith notes that Mandeville confused wealth with money by following the erroneous economics of Thomas Mun.

28 A vast literature has appeared on the significance of trust or social capital to economic prosperity. For a non-technical work, see Francis Fukuyama (1995). For a rigorous analysis, see Helmut Rainer and Thomas Siedler (2006).

29 The following section draws on Milton Myers, 1983, chapter seven.

30 To varying degrees, Derham, Maxwell, Harris, and Priestley attributed the transformation of self-interest into the public interest to a providential design.

31 In a private communication, Jerry Evensky pointed out to me that the economic response does not solve the Hobbesian problem. My only contention is that the economic response contributed to the conception of the invisible-hand process, not that it solved the problem.

32 Newton introduced his scientific method after Francis Bacon (1561–1626) and Galileo Galilei (1564–1642) had already established their own influential method of inquiry in science. Bacon had stressed the importance of inductive (as opposed to deductive) reasoning in science while Galileo had argued for quantitative (as opposed to qualitative) approach to science. He famously declared that "the universe" is a "grand book ... written in the language of mathematics, and its characters are triangles, circles, and other geometric figures without which it is humanly impossible to understand a word of it" (quoted in Martin Seymour-Smith, p. 200).

33 Although Hume endorsed a scientific method based on "experience and observation" (see the quote above), he identified a fundamental problem with induction in that experience and observation can never establish certainty and causality. In *An Enquiry Concerning Human Understanding* (1748/2000), Hume argued, "The contrary of every matter of fact is still possible.... That the sun will not rise tomorrow is no less intelligible a proposition, and implies no more contradiction than the affirmation, that it will

rise." In this regard, Laurence Boland (2003, p. 13) comments, "we cannot provide an inductive proof that 'the sun will rise tomorrow.'" In addition to Boland (chapter one), see Mark Blaug, 1992, pp. 15–17.

34 Since *The Wealth of Nations* is the founding document of modern economics, to a significant degree, theoretical and empirical economics since 1776 have rested on this book. Nava Ashraf, Colin Camerer, and George Loewenstein (2005) present the results of a number of empirical studies that vindicate several predictions of Smith's psychological propositions in *The Theory of Moral Sentiments*. They (2005, p. 138) note, "Considerable modern research backs up Smith's contentions."

35 See Murray Milgate and Shannon Stimson, 2009, p. 130.

36 See Hayek (1967a).

37 Smith refers to "bettering our condition" as "the great purpose of human life" (1759/1984, p. 50). For a detailed analysis, see Maria Pia Paganelli (2009).

38 This explains why there are no references to any super-natural entity (God, deity, author of nature, etc.) in *The Wealth of Nations* while such references are easily found in *The Theory of Moral Sentiments*. But as we shall see, some scholars believe that the invisible hand has a deistic connotation.

39 See also Jacob Viner (1927/1991) and Henry Bitterman (1940) on the ideas and thinkers who influenced Smith.

40 For an extensive coverage of the views of many thinkers on the invisible hand, especially in the eighteenth and twentieth centuries, see Craig Smith (2006). The present section moderately overlaps with this book.

41 Schumpeter (1954) considers it to be a "fact" that "*The Wealth of Nations* does not contain a single *analytic* idea, principle, or method that was entirely new in 1776" (p. 184, italics in original). Here, we are concerned, not with the originality of Smith's works, but with their significance and influence. But see the next footnote.

42 In his "Account of the Life and Writings of Adam Smith, LL. D." Stewart presented the passage (quoted above) to defend Smith against the charges that his ideas were not original. Stewart pointed out that the French economists such as Turgot who expounded the same views as Smith's prior to the publication of *The Wealth of Nations* could not have influenced Smith because Smith's lecture predates his French counterparts who published their views in the 1760s.

43 Stewart attributed the source of this passage to a manuscript that Smith had written in 1755 (Stewart, 1793/1982, p. 321). Jacob Viner (1927, p. 87) mentions this 1755 publication, but notes that Smith in his manuscript "cited a lecture, delivered in 1749" as the source of the passage. Viner attributes his source to John Rae's 1895 book on Adam Smith. Regardless of the date, the fact remains that Smith had conceived the invisible-hand idea well before he would write *The Theory of Moral Sentiments* and *The Wealth of Nations*.

44 Vaclav Havel, the Czech playwright and president of his country, has referred to the market economy "as the only natural economy, the only kind that makes sense, the only one that leads to prosperity, because it is the only one that reflects the nature of life itself. The essence of life is multiform, and therefore it cannot be contained or planned for, in its fullness and variability, by any central intelligence" (quoted in John McMillan, 2002, p. 7).

45 Empirical studies on economic growth vindicate Smith on the irrelevancy of the political system to economic growth. See, for example, Barro and Sala-i-Martin (1995) as well as Deepak Lal and Hla Myint (1996). However, Acemoglu and Robison (2012) extensively analyze the central role of political and economic institutions in economic growth.

46 Although Smith did not mention the role of geography in economic growth in this lecture, in his later writings he did. On this point see Jeffrey Sachs (1997). Many scholars believe that geography is important for economic prosperity but its adverse (or favorable) effects can be overcome by the right (or wrong) economic

policies. David Landes (1998) has extensively described the role of geography in the wealth and poverty of nations. Acemoglu and Robison (2012) reject the role of geography as the primary determinant of economic growth. Jared Diamond critiqued their book in *The New York Review of Books* (June 7, 2012) and disagreed with them on the role of geography. See also the subsequent exchange between them in the August 16, 2012 issue of the *Review*.

47 Milton Friedman (1962 and 1970), too, has placed restrictions on business conduct in the pursuit of profits. Friedman's restrictions are: no fraud or deception, obeying the law, observing ethical customs, and not impeding competition by political means for one's own gains. For an elaboration on the restrictions that both Smith and Freidman place on "free markets," see Harvey James and Farhad Rassekh (2000).

48 William Easterly (2009), a leading development economist, cites this passage to argue why the efforts by western countries to "save" Africa in the last several decades have failed and will likely continue to fail.

49 Recent empirical research in moral psychology has amply supported Hume's argument that passion, not reason, drives human actions. On this point, see Jonathan Haidt (2012).

50 Smith shared Hume's view on reason. He (1759/1984, p. 320) wrote, "it is altogether absurd and unintelligible to suppose that the first perceptions of right and wrong can be derived from reason." He (1759/1984, p. 77) also noted, "Though man … be naturally endowed with a desire of the welfare and preservation of society, yet the Author of nature has not entrusted it to his reason to find out that a certain application of punishments is the proper means of attaining this end; but has endowed him with an immediate and instinctive approbation of that very application which is most proper to attain it." See also Spence Pack (1993).

51 For an extensive coverage of Ferguson's views on this point, see Craig Smith (2006).

52 Murray Milgate and Shannon Stimson (2009, p. 45) take issue with Hayek's presentation of Ferguson as a thinker in the tradition of spontaneous order theory. But they do not elaborate on their disagreement with Hayek, nor do they cite any passage from Ferguson's writings to refute Hayek's argument.

53 Duncan Foley (2006) has argued that Smith was wrong in separating "an economic sphere of life, in which the pursuit of self-interest is guided by objective laws to socially beneficent outcome, from the rest of social life, in which the pursuit of self-interest is morally problematic and has to be weighed against other ends" (p. xiii). He calls this separation "Adam's Fallacy." Foley's argument, however, is contradicted by the fact that in market economies the same people who act out of self-interest in economic decisions, donate time and money to charitable causes. The site www.cnbc.com/2015/06/16/americans-gave-a-record-358-billion-to-charity-in-2014.html reports that in 2014 the financial donations in the United States amounted to $358 billion, 72 percent of which was donated by individuals, and the rest by foundations, corporations, and bequests. Moreover, "64.5 million adults volunteered 7.9 billion hours of service, worth an estimated value of $ 175 billion." See also www.gallup.com/poll/166250/americans-practice-charitable-giving-volunteerism.aspx.

54 While almost all people use "knowledge" and "information" interchangeably, they are not synonymous. We will return to this point in a later section. Here it suffices it to note that "knowledge entails information, interpretation and judgment" (Daniel Klein, 2012, p. 79).

55 The field of "mechanism design" to a large extent rests on Hayek's theory of market, in particular his 1945 essay. For a survey of this field, see the Nobel lectures of Leonid Hurwicz (2008), Roger Myerson (2007), and Eric Maskin (2007).

56 Steve Horwitz (2010) documents altruistic actions by business corporations such as Walmart, Home Depot, McDonald's, and Marriott towards their employees, customers, and the community in the aftermath of Hurricane Katrina in the United States

in 2005. These businesses knew the needs of people in distress and thus helped them even though substantial financial and non-financial assistance were provided by the government as well as by charitable organizations.

57 Pierre Force (2003) cites a few references in the eighteenth century literary and scientific works to the invisible hand that either have connotations different from Smith's use of the phrase or appeared after the publication of *The Theory of Moral Sentiments* in 1759. See also D. D. Raphael (1997, p. 67) for the use of the invisible hand with theological connotations prior to Adam Smith.

58 On the historical origin of "the invisible hand of Jupiter," see Gloria Vivenza (2008).

59 As we saw above, about half a century before Smith, Mandeville had argued that the "vice" of consuming luxuries is actually a social "virtue." Alexander Pope in 1731 had also expressed the same idea in his poems. On Pope's contribution to the debate on luxury, see McCloskey (2010, pp. 146–147).

60 Istvan Hont (2005, p. 91) believes that Smith's reference to the invisible hand in *The Theory of Moral Sentiments* has a theological connotation and relates to Smith's analysis of Jean Jacques Rousseau's *Discourse on Inequality*. Deidre McCloskey (2010, p. 144) also notes that in the invisible hand passage in *The Theory of Moral Sentiments* "Smith wants to argue against Rousseau's notion that property brings inequality in its train." But the editors of *The Theory of Moral Sentiments* (footnote on page 183) doubt that Rousseau was the target in the passage, although they do not rule out the possibility. If Smith had Rousseau in mind, he chose to be silent about it. Smith's review of Rousseau's *Discourse on Inequality* was a part of a long letter he sent to *Edinburgh Review* in 1755. This letter is included in Smith (1982a), pp. 242–254.

61 Smith famously wrote, "… defence … is of much more importance than opulence" (1776/1981, pp. 464–465).

62 Since Peter Minowitz (2004) has dissected and critiqued Grampp's paper in details, no further elaboration seems necessary.

63 Smith stipulated a rather long list of government functions, scattered throughout his writings and lectures. Steven Medema (2009, p. 24) presents a summary of these functions (which are quite numerous) and quotes Viner's comment that Smith "would have been astounded" had he been presented "with a complete list of modifications to the principle of laissez faire" that "he had granted his approval."

64 See also Ronald Hamowy, 1987, p. 21.

65 The authors of the *Federalist Papers* expressed the same idea by noting that since the "desire of reward is one of the strongest incentives of human conduct" the "best security for the fidelity of mankind is to make interest coincide with duty" (Alexander Hamilton *et al.*, 1788/1818, p. 452).

66 For further elaboration on the role of institutions in Smith's scholarly project, see Nathan Rosenberg (1960).

67 Edmund Burk (1729–1797) also launched an assault on the colonial policies of Great Britain on the ground that these policies involved coercion and thus violated the rights of people in shaping their own lives. He warned against "breaking the laws of commerce, which are the laws of nature, and consequently the laws of God" (quoted in Muller, 2002, p. 118).

68 For further discussion on Smith's views on slavery, see Spencer Pack (1996), Marvin Brown (2010), Thomas Wells (2010), and Bruce Elmslie (2010).

69 This passage suggests that Smith would have endorsed some regulation of the financial sector. Michael Corkery (2007) describes how unscrupulous individuals in the mortgage industry deepened the financial crisis of 2007 in the United States. Gary Gorton (2010) argues for regulation of the financial sector in his book, *Slapped by the Invisible Hand: The Panic of 2007*.

70 In the words of O'Brian (2004, p. 34), "the work of Adam Smith" served as "the great trunk of the Classical Economic tree."

71 For a concise analysis of classical and neoclassical economics and their seminal figures, see Harry Landreth and David Colander (2002).
72 For a survey of the development of general equilibrium theory see Lionel McKenzie (1987) and John Geanakoplos (1987).
73 Pareto optimality obtains when a change in resource allocation cannot make a person better off without making someone else worse off.
74 The elegant First Welfare Theorem, Blaug (2009, p. 233) further argues, represents "an extreme contrast in economics between 100 percent rigor and 0 percent relevance." The debate on Blaug's argument continues in the literature. For recent contributions, see Pierangelo Garegnani (2011) and Heinz D. Kurz and Neri Salvadori (2011).
75 Effiency also requires that products be rivalrous as well as excludable; otherwise, the private sector may refuse to supply them. For a non-technical analysis of market failure, see Kenneth Arrow (1973); for a rigorous description, see Bernard Salanié (2000); for an economic/philosophical discussion, see Wim Dubbink (2003).
76 For the collection of seminal works on increasing returns see Guang-Zhen Sun (2005), James Buchanan and Yong Yoon (1994), and W. Brian Arthur (1994). See also Chipman (1965, pp. 736–749) for a detailed intellectual history of increasing returns. For non-technical books on increasing returns, see M. Mitchell Waldrop (1992) and (especially) David Warsh (2006).
77 Medema (2009, pp. 103–104) tells the story of a meeting between Coase and twenty Chicago economists (including Milton Friedman, George Stigler, and Aaron Director) all of whom at the start of the meeting opposed Coase, but by the end of the meeting they all accepted his idea.
78 See also Medema (2011) for a highly detailed analysis of the Coase Theorem and its relationship with the invisible-hand proposition.
79 See also Bernard Salanié (2000, chapter 6).
80 See for example, Toni Vogel Carey (1998) and David Hull (1997).
81 Fisher's essay appeared in the journal *Science*, where six decades later Hardin would publish his essay.
82 See also the comments by M. Shaid Alam (1983) on Leibenstein's paper and Leibenstein's reply (1983) to Alam.
83 In the vast literature on the differing views on the role of self-interest and the market, see Jerry Muller (2002). He presents the views of many leading thinkers of the market system from Voltaire to Hayek. These thinkers include economists and non-economists some of whom support while the rest oppose the market economic system.
84 It is no wonder that Fisher believed in eugenics and served as a member of the American Eugenic Society.
85 See also Stiglitz (2000) and Arrow (1994), both of whom try to refute Hayek's argument that knowledge is so widely dispersed in the market that it cannot be made available to any individual or entity.
86 Joseph Schumpeter also believed that "there was a source of energy within the economic system which would of itself disrupt any equilibrium that might be attained" (Francisco Louca, 2010, p. 86).
87 Oskar Morgenstern (1902–1977) notes in his diary that the great physicist Niels Bohr believed the "social sciences are so much more complicated" than physics that economists should not try to imitate physicists in their work. Bohr then pointed out (in a lecture at the Institute for Advanced Study) that Max Planck shared this view. The reference to Bohr and Planck is in Robert Leonard (2010, p. 225).
88 See also Steven Horwitz (2001).
89 For an analysis of Nozik's "invisible-hand explanation," see Edna Ullmann-Margalit (1978).
90 For a detailed and extensive analysis of Schelling's segregation model, see N. Emrah Aydinonat (2008).

91 Francisco Louca (2010, p. 910) notes that under the influence of Moore, John Maynard Keynes "increasingly stressed the organic nature of social process itself at all its levels, that is, the deep rationality of social indeterminateness and complexity." This issue warrants further research, for Keynes' understanding of social processes appears to be similar to that of Hayek but the two thinkers held opposing views on the management of the economy. In fact, as noted in the previous section, Keynes argued against the invisible-hand proposition.

92 In response to my inquiry, both Gabaix and Rose in email communications confirmed that the prevalence of Zipf's law remains unexplained. The physicist Per Bak (1994) has shown that a power law governs the magnitude and the frequency of earthquakes, known as the Gutenberg-Richter law. "For each earthquake of magnitude 6" Bak notes, "there are 10 earthquakes of magnitude 5, 100 earthquakes of magnitude 4, and so on" (1994, p. 478). Bak presents a graph depicting the Gutenberg-Richter law that looks very much like Figures 1.1 and 1.2.

93 Since the emergent outcomes in complex systems are undesigned but orderly, the terms "invisible hand" and "spontaneous order" are sometimes invoked in complexity literature. For example, see Stuart Kauffman (1995, pp. 27–28), Auyang (1998, pp. 132, 136), and Steven Strogatz (2003, pp. 232, 250). In addition to Auyang and Kauffman, for a highly readable book on complexity with extensive reference to economics, see Mitchell Waldrop (1992). For the application of complexity to economics, see the series of edited books titled *The Economy as an Evolving Complex System* published under the auspices of the Santa Fe Institute. See also several articles in the June 2005 issue of *The Economic Journal*, on "markets as complex adaptive systems." In particular, see the survey article by Sheri Markose.

94 I have explored the affinity between the invisible hand and the complexity science in Rassekh (2009).

95 Other examples of complex systems include "the central nervous system, ecologies, immune system, the developmental stages of multi-celled organisms, and the processes of evolutionary genetics" (Holland, 1988, p. 118). See also Holland (1992, 1995).

96 I thank Emrah Aydinonat for bringing Klein's paper to my attention.

97 See also Brian Arthur *et al.* (1996), Joshua Epstein and Robert Axtell (1996), and Ramon Marimon *et al.* (1990). These works are summarized in Kochugovindan and Vriend (1998).

98 Young (1998, p. 4) regards "Adam Smith, David Hume, and Edmund Burke" as well as "Menger, von Hayek, and Schumpeter" as the originators and expounders of the evolutionary perspective on economic and social institutions.

99 Darwin (1859/1991) defined natural selection in the beginning of chapter four of his book *On the Origin of Species* as follows: "This preservation of favourable variations and the rejection of injurious variations, I call Natural Selection."

100 Alfred Russell Wallace (1823–1913), who independently and concurrently discovered the mechanism of natural selection, also received his insight from Malthus' population theory. See Wallace's autobiography (1905).

101 Bertrand Russell (1935, p. 72) notes, "Darwin's theory was essentially an extension to the animal and vegetable world of *laisser-faire* economics." For a lengthy discussion on this point see Peter Bowler (1989).

102 For the citations to these books in Darwin's notes, see Schweber (1980 and 1977).

103 See also Schweber (1985).

104 Many other scholars have written on Smith's influence on Darwin including Toni Vogel Carey (1998), Kim Sterelny (1994), Elias Khalil (2000b), and Geoffrey Hodgson (1996).

105 Hull (1997) addresses the issues that Ylikoski raises about the invisible hand of science. Although he agrees that several differences exist between the invisible hand of the market and of science, he insists that scientists contribute to the greater good despite their interest in personal reward.

106 On the invisible hand of science, in addition to those presented in this section, see Ronald Giere (1988) and Philip Kitcher (1993 and 1994). Kitcher (1993) does not invoke the term "the invisible hand" as others do, but his analysis concerning how science advances unmistakably relies on an invisible-hand process. In particular see pp. 310–311 and 351.

107 A number of scholars including Baumol have noted that Smith wrote "led by an invisible hand" not "led *as though* by an invisible hand" (1978, p. 117, italics in original). On this point, see also Peter Minowitz (2004, p. 409). Baumol's contention that Smith regarded the market as a divine instrument is akin to the theistic interpretation of the Darwinian evolution, which maintains that natural selection is a providential law of nature that ultimately led to the emergence of human beings and the fulfillment of divine intention. On the theistic interpretation of evolution, see Francis Collins (2006).

108 A number of other scholars also believe in the deistic interpretation of the invisible hand. See, for example, T. D. Campbell (1971, p. 61) and Heinz Lubasz (1992).

109 Warren Samuels (2011), Emma Rothschild (2001), and D. D. Raphael (1997, p. 67) are among those who reject the invisible hand as a deistic concept. Elias Khalil (2000a) argues that the invisible hand is the "wisdom of nature."

110 Smith traveled to France in 1764 and met a number of influential French thinkers including physiocrats that he admired greatly. The account of Smith's visit to France is well chronicled by Smith's scholars. See, for example, Andrew Skinner, 2007, pp. 99–102.

111 Rothschild (2001) provides a quote by Dugald Stewart, Smith's student, in which the invisible hand is used (apparently) as a metaphor.

112 This view is inspired by the recent writings of a number of scholars on the invisible hand, above all Warren Samuels (2011) and Gavin Kennedy (2009).

Bibliography

Acemoglu, Daron and James Robinson (2012), *Why Nations Fail: The Origin of Power, Prosperity, and Poverty*, New York, NY: Crown Business.

Alam, Shaid M. (1983), "Intrafirm Productivity: Comment," *American Economic Review* 73, September, pp. 817–821.

Aquinas, St. Thomas (1988), *St. Thomas Aquinas on Politics and Ethics*, Ed. by Paul E. Sigmund, New York, NY: W.W. Norton and Co.

Arrow, Kenneth J. (1973), "Social Responsibility and Economic Efficiency," *Public Policy* 21, Summer, pp. 303–317.

Arrow, Kenneth J. (1994), "Methodological Individualism and Social Knowledge," *American Economic Review*, May, pp. 1–9.

Arrow, Kenneth and Frank Hahn (1971), *General Competitive Analysis*, San Francisco, CA: Holden-Day, Inc.

Arthur, W. Brian (1989), "Competing Technologies, Increasing Returns, and Lock-in by Historical Events," *The Economic Journal* 99, March, pp. 116–131.

Arthur, W. Brian (1994), *Increasing Returns and Path Dependence in Economics*, Ann Arbor, MI: University of Michigan Press.

Arthur, W. Brian (1999), "Complexity and the Economy," *Science* 284, April, pp. 107–109.

Arthur, W. B., J. H. Holland, B. LeBaron, R. Palmer, and P. Tayler (1996), "Asset Pricing Under Endogenous Expectations in an Artificial Stock Market," *Working Paper* No. 96-12-093, Santa Fe Institute.

Ashraf, Nava, Colin Camerer, and George Loewenstein (2005), "Adam Smith, Behavioral Economist," *The Journal of Economic Perspectives* 19, Summer, pp. 131–145.

Auyang, Sunny Y. (1998), *Foundations of Complex-System Theories in Economics, Biology, and Statistical Physics*, Cambridge, UK: Cambridge University Press.

Axtell, Robert (2001), "Zipf Distribution of US Firm Sizes," *Science* 293, pp. 1818–1920.

Aydinonat, N. Emrah (2008), *The Invisible Hand in Economics: How Economists Explain Unintended Consequences*, London, UK: Routledge.

Bak, Per (1994), "Self-Organized Criticality: A Holistic View of Nature," in *Complexity, Metaphors, Models, and Reality*, Proceedings Volume XIX, Ed. by George Cowan, David Pines, and David Meltzer, Santa Fe Institute, Studies in the Sciences of Complexity, Reading, MA: Addison-Wesley Publishing Company.

Barro, Robert J. and Xavier Sala-i-Martin (1995), *Economic Growth*, New York, NY: McGraw-Hill.

Barry, Norman (2004), "The Tradition of Spontaneous Order," The Online Library of Liberty. Accessed January 2016 from www.econlib.org/library/Essays/LtrLbrty/bryTSO1.html

Baumol, William (1978), "Smith versus Marx on Business Morality and the Social Interest," in *Adam Smith and the Wealth of the Nations 1776–1976 Bicentennial Essays*, Boulder, CO: Colorado Associated University Press, pp. 111–122.

Becker, Carl L. (1932), *The Heavenly City of the Eighteenth-Century Philosophers*, New Haven, CT: Yale University Press.

Blaug, Mark (1978), *Economic Theory in Retrospect*, Cambridge, UK: Cambridge University Press.

Blaug, Mark (1992), *The Methodology of Economics or How Economists Explain*, Cambridge, UK: Cambridge University Press.

Blaug, Mark (1998), "The Problem with Formalism," Interview with Mark Blaug, *Challenge*, May–June.

Blaug, Mark (2001), "No History of Ideas, Please, We're Economists," *The Journal of Economic Perspectives* 15, 1, Winter, pp. 145–164.

Blaug, Mark (2007), "The Fundamental Theorems of Modern Welfare Economics, Historically Contemplated," *History of Political Economy* 39, 2, pp. 185–207.

Blaug, Mark (2009), "Trade-Off between Rigor and Relevance: Sraffian Economics as a Case in Point," *History of Political Economy* 41, 2, pp. 219–247.

Boland, Lawrence A. (2003), *The Foundation of Economic Method: A Popperian Perspective*, London, UK and New York, NY: Routledge.

Bowler, Peter J. (1989), *Evolution: The History of an Idea*, Berkeley, CA: University of California Press.

Brewer, Anthony (2009), "On the Other (Invisible) Hand," *History of Political Economy* 41, 3, pp. 519–544.

Brown, Marvin (2010), "Free Enterprise and the Economics of Slavery," *Real-World Economics* 52, pp. 28–39.

Buchanan, James and Yong Moon (1994), *The Return to Increasing Returns*, Ann Arbor, MI: University of Michigan Press.

Buchanan, James and Viktor Vanberg (1991), "The Market as a Discovery Process," *Economics and Philosophy*.

Buckle, Henry Thomas (1873), *History of Civilization in England*, Volume 1, 2nd London Edition, New York, NY: D. Appleton and Company.

Butler, Joseph (1726/1965), "Sermons," in *British Moralists*, 2 Volumes, Ed. by L.A. Shelby-Bigge, New York, NY: Dover Publications.

Campbell, T. D. (1971), *Adam Smith's Science of Morals*, London, UK: George Allen & Unwin LTD.

Carey, Toni Vogel (1998), "The Invisible Hand of Natural Selection and Vice Versa," *Biology and Philosophy* 13, pp. 427–442.

Chipman, John S. (1965), "A Survey of the Theory of International Trade: Part 2, the Neoclassical Theory," *Econometrica* 33, 4, October, pp. 685–760.

Clower, Robert (1994), "Economics as an Inductive Science," *Southern Economic Journal* 60, 4, April, pp. 805–814.

Coase, Ronald H. (1960), "The Problem of Social Cost," *Journal of Law and Economics* 3, pp. 1–44.

Colander, David (2000), *Complexity and the History of Economic Thought*, London, UK and New York, NY: Routledge.

Collins, Francis (2006), *The Language of God*, New York, NY: Free Press.

Corkery, Michael (2007), "Fraud Seen as a Driver in Wave of Foreclosure," *The Wall Street Journal*, December 21.

Darwin, Charles (1859/1991), *On the Origin of Species by Means of Natural Selection*, Buffalo, NY: Prometheus.

Darwin, Charles (1887/1958), *The Autobiography of Charles Darwin*, London, UK and New York, NY: W.W. Norton & Company.

Debreu, Gerard (1987), "Existence of Equilibrium," in *The New Palgrave: A New Dictionary of Economics*, Volume 2, Ed. by John Eatwell, Murray Milgate, and Peter Newman, London, UK: MacMillan Press, pp. 216–219.

Diamond, Jared (2012), "*Why Nations Fail: The Origins of Power, Prosperity, and Poverty* by Daron Acemoglu and James A. Robinson," New York Review of Books, June 7, 2012.

Dubbink, Wim (2003), *Assisting the Invisible Hand*, Dordrecht, NED, Boston, MA, and London, UK: Kluwer Academic Publishers.

Easterly, William (2009), "Can We Save Africa," *Journal of Economic Literature* XLVII, 2, pp. 373–447.

Ekeland, Ivar (2006), *The Best of All Possible Worlds: Mathematics and Destiny*, Chicago, IL: University of Chicago Press.

Elmslie, Bruce (2010), "Did Smithian Economics Promote Slavery," *Real-World Economics* 53, pp. 150–155.

Epstein, Joshua and Robert Axtell (1996), *Growing Artificial Societies: Social Science from the Bottom Up*, Cambridge, MA: The MIT Press.

Evensky, Jerry (2005), *Adam Smith's Moral Philosophy: A Historical and Contemporary Perspectives on Markets, Law, Ethics, and Culture*, Cambridge, UK: Cambridge University Press.

Ferguson, Adam (1767/1995), *An Essay on the History of Civil Society*, Ed. by Fania Oz-Salzberger, Cambridge, UK: Cambridge University Press.

Ferguson, Adam (1792), *Principles of Moral and Political Science; Being Chiefly a Retrospect of Lectures Delivered in the College of Edinburgh*, 2 Volumes, Edinburgh, UK: W. Creech.

Finley, Moses (1987), "Aristotle," in *The New Palgrave: A New Dictionary of Economics*, Volume 1, Ed. by John Eatwell, Murray Milgate, and Peter Newman, London, UK: MacMillan Press, pp. 112–113.

Fisher, Irving (1907), "Why Has the Doctrine of Laissez Faire Been Abandoned?" *Science* XXV, 627, pp. 18–27.

Foley, Duncan (2006), *Adam's Fallacy: A Guide to Economic Theology*, Cambridge, UK: The Belknap Press of Harvard University Press.

Force, Pierre (2003), *Self-interest before Adam Smith: A Genealogy of Economic Science*, Cambridge, UK: Cambridge University Press.

Friedman, Milton (1962), *Capitalism and Freedom*, Chicago, IL: University of Chicago.

Friedman, Milton (1970), "The Social Responsibility of Business Is to Increase Its Profits," *New York Times Magazine*, September 13, pp. 32–33, 122–126.

Freidman, David (1987), "Just Price," in *The New Palgrave: A Dictionary of Economics*, Volume 2, Ed. by John Eatwell, Murray Milgate, and Peter Newman, London, UK: MacMillan Press, pp. 1043–1044.

Fukuyama, Francis (1995), *Trust: The Social Virtues and the Creation of Prosperity*, New York, NY: The Free Press.

Gabaix, Xavier (2009), "Power Laws in Economics and Finance," *Annual Review of Economics* 1, pp. 255–294.

Garegnani, Pierangelo (2011), "On Blaug Ten Years Later," *History of Political Economy* 43, 3, pp. 591–605.

Geanakoplos, John (1987), "Arrow-Debreu Model of General Equilibrium," in *The New Palgrave: A New Dictionary of Economics*, Volume 1, Ed. by John Eatwell, Murray Milgate, and Peter Newman, London, UK: MacMillan Press, pp. 116–124.
Giere, Ronald (1988), *Explaining Science: A Cognitive Approach*, Chicago, IL: The University of Chicago Press.
Gomes, Leonard (2003), *The Economics and Ideology of Free Trade: A Historical Review*, Cheltenham, UK and Northampton, MA: Edward Elgar.
Gomory, Ralph E. and William Baumol (2000), *Global Trade and Conflicting National Interests*, Cambridge, MA: The MIT Press.
Gordon, Barry (1975), *Economic Analysis before Adam Smith: Hesiod to Lessius*, New York, NY: Harper and Row Publishers.
Gorton, Gary (2010), *Slapped by the Invisible Hand: The Panic of 2007*, Oxford, UK: Oxford University Press.
Gould, Stephen Jay (1980), *The Panda's Thumb: More Reflections in Natural History*, New York, NY: W.W. Norton.
Gould, Stephen Jay (1993), "Darwin and Paley Meet the Invisible Hand," in *Eight Little Piggies: Reflections in Natural History*, New York, NY: W.W. Norton & Company.
Grampp, William D. (2000), "What Did Smith Mean by the Invisible Hand?" *The Journal of Political Economy* 108, 3, pp. 441–465.
Gray, Alexander (1931), *The Development of Economic Doctrine; An Introductory Survey*, Longmans, Green.
Hahn, Frank (1982), "Reflections on the Invisible Hand," *Lloyds Bank Review* 144, April, pp. 1–21.
Haidt, Jonathan (2012), *The Righteous Mind: Why Good People Are Divided by Politics and Religion*, New York, NY: Pantheon.
Hamilton, Alexander, James Madison, and John Jay (1788/1818), *The Federalist Papers on the New Constitution*, Washington, DC: Jacob Gideon.
Hamowy, Ronald (1987), *The Scottish Enlightenment and the Theory of Spontaneous Order*, Carbondale and Edwardsville, IL: Southern Illinois University Press.
Hardin, Garrett (1968), "The Tragedy of the Commons," *Science* 162, pp. 1243–1248.
Hayek, Friedrich August von (1945), "The Use of Knowledge in Society," *American Economic Review* 35, September, pp. 519–530.
Hayek, Friedrich August von (1946/1980), "The Meaning of Competition," in *Individualism and Economic Order*, Chicago, IL and London, UK: The University of Chicago Press, pp. 92–106.
Hayek, Friedrich August von (1967a), "The Results of Human Action but Not of Human Design," in *Studies in Philosophy, Politics, and Economics*, Ed. by F. A. Hayek, Chicago, IL: The University of Chicago Press.
Hayek, Friedrich August von (1967b), "Dr. Bernard Mandeville," *Proceedings of the British Academy*, Volume LII, in *New Studies in Philosophy, Politics, Economics and the History of Ideas*, Ed. by F. A. Hayek, Chicago, IL: The University of Chicago Press.
Hayek, Friedrich August von (1968/2002), "Competition as a Discovery Procedure," Translated by Marcellus S. Snow, *Quarterly Journal of Austrian Economics* 5, 3, pp. 9–23.
Hayek, Friedrich August von (1973), *Law, Legislation and Liberty*, Volume 1, Chicago, IL: The University of Chicago Press.
Hayek, Friedrich August von (1974/1989), "The Pretense of Knowledge," *The American Economic Review* 79, 6, pp. 3–7.
Hayek, Friedrich August von (1976/1978), "The New Confusion about 'Planning,'" *The Morgan Guaranty Survey*, reprinted in *New Studies in Philosophy, Politics, Economics, and the History of Ideas*, Ed. by F. A. Hayek, Chicago, IL: The University of Chicago Press, pp. 232–248.

Hayek, Friedrich August von (1988), *The Fatal Conceit*, Chicago, IL: The University of Chicago Press.

Hazlitt, Henry (1946/1979), *Economics in One Lesson*, New York, NY: Three River Press.

Herman, Arthur (2001), *How the Scots Invented the Modern World*, New York, NY: Random House.

Hetherington, Norriss S. (1983), "Isaac Newton's Influence on Adam Smith's Natural Laws in Economics," *Journal of the History of Ideas* 44, pp. 497–505.

Hirschman, Albert (1977), *The Passions and the Interests*, Princeton, NJ: The Princeton University Press.

Hobbes, Thomas (1651/1946), "Leviathan or the Matter, Forme, and Power of a Commonwealth Ecclesiastical and Civil," Ed. by Michael Oakeshott, Oxford, UK: Basil Blackwell.

Hodgson, Geoffrey M. (1996), *Economics and Evolution: Bring Life Back to Economics*, Ann Arbor, MI: The University of Michigan Press.

Hodgson, Geoffrey M. and Thorbjørn Knudsen (2010), *Darwin's Conjecture: The Search for General Principles of Social Evolution*, Chicago, IL and London, UK: The University of Chicago Press.

Holcombe, Randall G. (1999), "Equilibrium versus the Invisible Hand," Review of Austrian Economics 12, pp. 227–243.

Holland, John H. (1988), "The Global Economy as an Adaptive Process," in *The Economy as an Evolving Complex System*, Volume V, Ed. by Philip W. Anderson, Kenneth J. Arrow, and David Pines, Santa Fe Institute Studies in the Sciences of Complexity, Redwood City, CA: Addison-Wesley Publishing Company.

Holland, John H. (1992), *Adaptation in Natural and Artificial Systems: An Introductory Analysis with Application to Biology, Control, and Artificial Intelligence*, Cambridge, MA: The MIT Press.

Holland, John H. (1995), *Hidden Order: How Adaptation Builds Complexity*, New York, NY: Basic Books.

Hont, Istvan (2005), *Jealousy of Trade*, Cambridge, MA: The Belknap Press of Harvard University Press.

Horwitz, Steven (2001), "From Smith to Menger to Hayek Liberalism in the Spontaneous-Order Tradition," *The Independent Review* VI, 1, Summer, pp. 81–97.

Horwitz, Steven (2010), "Doing the Right Things: The Private Sector Response to Hurricane Katrina as a Case Study in the Bourgeois Virtues," in *Accepting the Invisible Hand*, Ed. by Mark D. White, New York, NY: Palgrave Macmillan, pp. 169–190.

Hosseini, Hamid S. (2007), "Contributions of Medieval Muslim Scholars to the History of Economics and Their Impact: A Refutation of the Schumpeterian Great Gap," in *A Companion to The History of Economic Thought*, Ed. by Warren J. Samuels, Jeff E. Biddle, and John B. Davis, Malden, MA: Blackwell Publishing, pp. 28–45

Hull, David L. (1988), *Science as a Process*, Chicago, IL: The University of Chicago Press.

Hull, David, L. (1997), "What's Wrong with the Invisible Hand Explanations?" *Philosophy of Science* 64, Proceedings, 4, pp. S117–S126.

Hume, David (1739/1951), *A Treatise of Human Nature*, Volume 1 and 2, London, UK: J. M. Dent & Sons LTD.

Hume, David (1748/2000), *An Enquiry Concerning Human Understanding*, in *The Clarendon Edition of the Works of David Hume*, Ed. by T. L. Beauchamp, Oxford, UK: Oxford University Press.

Hume, David (1758/1955), "Of the Jealousy of Trade," in *David Hume: Writings on Economics*, Ed. by Eugene Rotwein, Madison, WI: University of Wisconsin Press, pp. 78–82.

Hume, David (1777/1987), *Essays Moral Political and Literary*, Indianapolis, IN: Liberty Classics.

Hurwicz, Leonid (2008), "Who Will Guard the Guardians?" May 13. Accessed January 2016 from www.econ.umn.edu/workingpapers/hurwicz_guardians.pdf.

Ingrao, Bruna and Giorgio Israel (1990), *The Invisible Hand: Economic Equilibrium in the History of Science*, Translated by Ian McGilvary, Cambridge, MA: The MIT Press.

Irwin, Douglas (2006), *Against the Tide: An Intellectual History of Free Trade*, Princeton, NJ: Princeton University Press.

Iyengar, Radha (2008), "I'd Rather be Hanged for a Sheep than Lamb: The Unintended Consequences of 'Three-Strikes' Laws," National Bureau of Economic Research, February, *NBER Working Paper* No. W13784.

James, Harvey and Farhad Rassekh (2000), "Smith, Friedman, and Self-Interest in Ethical Society," *Business Ethics Quarterly* 10, 3, pp. 659–674.

Kauffman, Stuart (1995), *At Home in the Universe: The Search for the Laws of Self-Organization and Complexity*, New York, NY: Oxford University Press.

Kennedy, Gavin (2009), "Adam Smith and the Invisible Hand: From Metaphor to Myth," *Econ Journal Watch* 6, 2, pp. 239–263.

Kennedy, Gavin (2010), "Paul Samuelson and the Invention of the Modern Economics of the Invisible Hand," *History of Economic Ideas* 9, pp. 105–119.

Keynes, John Maynard (1924), "The End of *Laissez-Faire*." Accessed January 2016 from www.panarchy.org/keynes/laissezfaire.1926.html.

Keynes, John Maynard (1936/1997), *The General Theory of Employment, Interest, and Money*, Amherst, NY: Prometheus Books.

Khalil, Elias (2000a), "Making Sense of Adam Smith's Invisible Hand: Beyond Pareto Optimality and Unintended Consequences," *Journal of the History of Economic Thought* 22, 1, pp. 49–63.

Khalil, Elias (2000b), "Beyond Natural Selection and Divine Intervention: The Lamarckian Implication of Adam Smith's Invisible Hand," *Journal of Evolutionary Economics* 10, pp. 373–393.

Kitcher, Philip (1993), *The Advancement of Science*, Oxford, UK: Oxford University Press.

Kitcher, Philip (1994), "Contrasting Conception of Social Epistemology," in *Socializing Epistemology: The Social Dimensions of Knowledge*, Ed. by Frederick F. Schmitt London, UK: Rowman & Littlefield.

Klein, Daniel B. (1997), "Convention, Social Order, and the Two Coordinations," *Constitutional Political Economy* 8, pp. 319–335.

Klein, Daniel B. (2009), "In Adam Smith's Invisible Hand: Comments on Gavin Kennedy," *Econ Journal Watch* 6, 2, pp. 264–279.

Klein, Daniel B. (2012), *Knowledge and Coordination: A Liberal Interpretation*, Oxford, UK: Oxford University Press.

Kochugovindan, Sreekala and Nicolaas J. Vriend (1998), "Is the Study of Complex Adaptive Systems Going to Solve the Mystery of Adam Smith's 'Invisible Hand'?" *The Independent Review* III, 1, Summer, pp. 53–66.

Krugman, Paul (1996), *The Self-Organizing Economy*, Cambridge, UK: Blackwell Publishers.

Krugman, Paul (2006), "The Pin Factory Mystery," *New York Times Book Review*, Sunday, May 7, p. 14.

Kuhn, Thomas (1962), *The Structure of Scientific Revolution*, Chicago, IL: The University of Chicago Press.

Kurz, Heinz D. and Neri Salvadori (2011), "In Favor of Rigor and Relevance: A Reply to Blaug," *History of Political Economy* 43, 3, pp. 607–616.

Lal, Deepak (1998), *Unintended Consequences: The Impact of Factor Endowments, Culture, and Politics on Long-Run Economic Performance*, Cambridge, MA: The MIT Press.

Lal, Deepak and Hla Myint (1996), *The Political Economy of Poverty, Equity and Growth*, Oxford, UK: Clarendon Press.

Landes, David (1998), *The Wealth and Poverty of Nations: Why Some Are So Rich and Some So Poor*, London, UK: Little Brown and Company.

Landreth, Harry and David C. Colander (2002), *History of Economic Thought*, Boston, MA: Houghton Mifflin.

Langholm, Odd (2006), *The Legacy of Scholasticism in Economic Thought*, Cambridge, UK: Cambridge University Press.

Leibenstein, Harvey (1982), "The Prisoners' Dilemma in the Invisible Hand: An Analysis of Intrafirm Productivity," *American Economic Review Proceedings* 72, May, pp. 92–97.

Leibenstein, Harvey (1983), "Intrafirm Productivity: Reply," *American Economic Review* 73, September, pp. 822–823.

Leijonhufvud, Alex (2006), "Agent-Based Marco," in *Handbook of Computational Economics*, Ed. by Leigh Tesfatsion and Kenneth Judd, Amsterdam, North Holland, 2, pp. 1626–1637.

Leonard, Robert (2010), *Von Neumann, Morgenstern, and the Creation of Game Theory*, Cambridge, UK: Cambridge University Press.

Leonard, Thomas C. (2002), "Reflection on Rules in Science: An Invisible-Hand Perspective," *Journal of Economic Methodology* 9, 2, pp. 141–168.

Louca, Francisco (2010), "Bounded Heresies. Early Intuitions of Complexity in Economics," *History of Economic Ideas* 18, 2, pp. 77–113.

Lowry, S. Todd (1979), "Recent Literature on Ancient Greek Economic Thought," *Journal of Economic Literature* 17, March, pp. 65–86.

Lowry, S. Todd (2007), "Ancient and Medieval Economics," in *A Companion to The History of Economic Thought*, Ed. by Warren J. Samuels, Jeff E. Biddle, and John B. Davis, Malden, MA: Blackwell Publishing, pp. 11–27.

Lubasz, Heinz (1992), "Adam Smith and the Invisible Hand of the Market?" in *Contesting Markets*, Ed. by Roy Dilley, Edinburgh, UK: Edinburgh University Press, pp. 37–56.

Macfie, Alec (1955/2009), "The Scottish Tradition in Economic Thought," *Economic Journal Watch* 6, 3, pp. 389–410.

Macfie, Alec (1971), "The Invisible Hand of Jupiter," *Journal of History of Ideas* 32, 4, October–December, pp. 595–599.

Magnusson, Lars (1995), "Introduction," in *Mercantilism*, Volume 1, Ed. by Lars Magnusson, pp. 1–48.

Magnusson, Lars (2007), "Mercantilism," in *A Companion to The History of Economic Thought*, Ed. by Warren J. Samuels, Jeff E. Biddle, and John B. Davis, Malden, MA: Blackwell Publishing, pp. 46–60.

Mandeville, Bernard (1714/1924), *The Fable of the Bees: Private Vices, Publick Benefits*, Oxford, UK: The Clarendon Press.

Marimon, Ramon, Ellen McGrattan and Thomas Sargent (1990), "Money as a Medium of Exchange in an Economy with Artificially Intelligent Agents," *Journal of Economic Dynamics and Control* 14, pp. 329–373.

Markose, Sheri M. (2005), "Computability and Evolutionary Complexity: Markets as Complex Adaptive Systems," *The Economic Journal* 115, June, pp. F159–F192.

Mas-Colell, Andreu, Michael D. Winston, and Jerry R. Green (1995), *Microeconomic Theory*, Oxford, UK: Oxford University Press.

Maskin, Eric S. (2007), "Mechanism Design: How to Implement Social Goals," Price Lecture, December 8.

McCloskey, Deidre N. (2010), "Life in the Market Is Good for You," in *Accepting the Invisible Hand*, Ed. by Mark White, New York, NY: Palgrave Macmillan, pp. 139–168.

McCulloch, John Ramsay (1825/1830), *The Principles of Political Economy with a Sketch of the Rise and Progress of the Science*, 2nd Edition, London, UK: Longman's.

McKenzie, Lionel (1987), "General Equilibrium," in *The New Palgrave: A New Dictionary of Economics*, Volume 2, Ed. by John Eatwell, Murray Milgate, and Peter Newman, London, UK: MacMillan Press, pp. 498–513.

McMillan, John (2002), *Reinventing the Bazaar: A Natural History of the Markets*, New York, NY: W. W. Norton.

Medema, Steve (2009), *The Hesitant Hand*, Princeton, NJ: Princeton University Press.
Medema, Steve (2011), "HES Presidential Address: The Coase Theorem," *Journal of the History of Economic Thought* 33, 1, March, pp. 1–18.
Meek, Ronald (1963), *The Economics of Physiocracy: Essays and Translation*, Cambridge, MA: Harvard University Press.
Meikle, Scott (1995), *Aristotle's Economic Thought*, Oxford, UK: Clarendon Press.
Menger, Carl (1871/1976), *Principles of Economics*, Translated by James Dingwall and Bret F. Hoselitz, Auburn, AL: Mises Institute.
Milgate, Murray and Shannon Stimson (2009), *After Adam Smith: A Century of Transformation in Politics and Political Economy*, Princeton, NJ: Princeton University Press.
Minowitz, Peter (2004), "Adam Smith's Invisible Hands," *Econ Journal Watch* 1, 3, December, pp. 381–412.
Mirowski, Peter (1997), "On Playing the Economic Trump Card in the Philosophy of Science: Why It Did Not Work for Michael Polanyi," *Philosophy of Science* 64, Proceedings, pp. S127–S138.
Mirowski, Philip (2013), "2012 HES Presidential Address: Does the Victor Enjoy the Spoils? Paul Samuelson as Historian of Economics," *Journal of the History of Economic Thought* 35, 1, March, pp. 1–18.
Montes, Leonidas (2008), "Newton's Real Influence on Adam Smith and Its Context," *Cambridge Journal of Economics* 32, pp. 555–576.
Moore, George Edward (1902), *Principia Ethica*, Cambridge, UK: Cambridge University Press.
Muller, Jerry Z. (1993), *Adam Smith in His Time and Ours*, Princeton, NJ: Princeton University Press.
Muller, Jerry Z. (2002), *The Mind and the Market: Capitalism in Modern European Thought*, New York, NY: Knopf.
Mun, Thomas (1664/1959), *England's Treasure by Forraign Trade*, Oxford, UK: Blackwell Publishers.
Myers, Milton (1983), *The Soul of Modern Economic Man*, Chicago, IL: Chicago University Press.
Myerson, Roger B. (2007), "Perspectives on Mechanism Design Theory in Economic Theory," Prize Lecture, December 8.
Newton, Isaac (1686/1954), *Mathematical Principles of Natural Philosophy*, Chicago, IL: The University of Chicago Press.
Newton, Isaac (1704/1954), *Optics*, Chicago, IL: The University of Chicago Press.
Nozick, Robert (1974), *Anarchy, State, and Utopia,* New York, NY: Basic Books.
O'Boyle, Edward J. (2006), "Classical Economics and the Great Irish Famine: A Study in Limits," *Forum for Social Economics* 35, 2, pp. 21–53.
O'Brian, D.P. (2004), *The Classical Economics Revisited*, Princeton, NJ: Princeton University Press.
Ostrom, Elinor (1990), *Governing the Commons: The Evolution of Institutions for Collective Actions*, Cambridge, MA: Cambridge University Press.
Pack, Spencer (1993), "Adam Smith on the Limits of Human Reason," in *Perspectives on the History of Economic Thought*, Ed. by Robert F. Hebert, Cheltenham, UK: Edward Elgar, pp. 53–62.
Pack, Spencer (1994), "Adam Smith's Invisible Hand/Chain/Chaos," in *Joseph A. Schumpeter, Historian of Economics*, Ed. by Laurence S. Moss, London, UK and New York, NY: Routledge, pp. 181–195.
Pack, Spencer (1996), "Slavery, Adam Smith's Economic Vision and the Invisible Hand," *History of Economic Ideas* IV, pp. 253–269.
Paganelli, Maria Pia (2009), "Approbation and the Desire to Better One's Condition in Adam Smith," *Journal of History of Economic Thought* 31, March, pp. 79–92.
Perlman, Mark and Charles R. McCann Jr. (2001), *The Pillars of Economic Understanding: Ideas and Traditions*, Ann Arbor, MI: The University of Michigan Press.

Pigou, Arthur C. (1936), "State Action and Laisser-Faire," in *Economics in Practice*, Ed. by A. C. Pigou, London, UK: Macmillan and Co., pp. 107–128.
Pigou, Arthur C. (1952), *The Economics of Welfare*, 4th Edition, London, UK: Macmillan and Co.
Plutarch (1927), "On Whether Water or Fire Is More Useful," in *Plutarch's Moralia*, Volume 12, Loeb Classical Library.
Polanyi, Michael (1962/1969), "The Republic of Science: Its Political and Economic Theory," in *Knowing and Being: Essays by Michael Polanyi*, Ed. by Marjorie Grene, Chicago, IL: The University of Chicago Press, pp. 49–72.
Pomeranz, Kenneth and Steven Topik (1999), *The World that Trade Created*, Armonk, NY: M. E. Sharpe.
Pope, Alexander (1734/1931), "An Essay on Man," in *The Complete Works of Alexander Pope*, Ed. by Henry W. Boynton, Boston, MA: Houghton Mifflin.
Rainer, Helmut and Thomas Siedler (2006), "Does Democracy Foster Trust?" Social Science Research Network, IZA Discussion Paper No. 2154, May.
Raphael, D. D. (1997), "Smith," in *Three Great Economists*, Ed. by Keith Thomas, Oxford, UK: Oxford University Press, pp. 1–104.
Rassekh, Farhad (2009), "In the Shadow of the Invisible Hand," *History of Economic Ideas* XVII, 3, pp. 147–165.
Reid, Thomas (1788/1967), *Essays on the Active Powers of Man*, in *Philosophical Works*, in *Sir William Hamilton*, 8th edition, 2 Volumes, Hildesheim, GER: George Olms Verlagsbuchhandlung.
Ricardo, David (1816/2004), "Proposals for Economical and Secure Currency," in *The Works and Correspondence of David Ricardo*, Volume IV, Ed. by Piero Sraffa, Indianapolis, IN: Liberty Fund, pp. 49–142.
Ricardo, David (1817/1996), *Principles of Political Economy and Taxation*, Great Mind Series, Amherst, NY: Prometheus Books.
Robbins, Lionel (1953), *The Theory of Economic Policy in English Classical Political Economy*, Reprint, New York, NY: St. Martin Press.
Robbins, Lionel (1998), *A History of Economic Thought: The LSE Lectures*, Ed. by Steven Medema and Warren Samuels, Princeton, NJ: Princeton University Press.
Rose, Andrew K. (2006), "Cities and Countries," *Journal Money, Banking and Credit* 8, pp. 2,225–2,246.
Rosenberg, Nathan (1960), "Some Institutional Aspects of the *Wealth of Nations*," *Journal of Political Economy* 68, pp. 557–570.
Ross, Ian (1995), *The Life of Adam Smith*, Oxford, UK: Clarendon Press.
Rothbard, Murray N. (1999), *Economic Thought before Adam Smith: An Austrian Perspective on the History of Economic Thought*, Volume I, Cheltenham, UK: Edward Elgar.
Rothschild, Emma (2001), *Economic Sentiments: Adam Smith, Condorcet, and the Enlightenment*, Cambridge, MA: Harvard University Press.
Russell, Bertrand (1935), *Religion and Science*, New York, NY: Henry Holt and Company.
Sachs, Jeffrey (1997), "The Limits of Convergence: Nature, Nurture and Growth," *The Economist*, June 14, pp. 19–22.
Salanié, Bernard (2000), *Microeconomics of Market Failures*, Cambridge, MA: The MIT Press.
Samuels, Warren (2011), *Erasing the Invisible Hand: Essays on an Elusive and Misused Concept in Economics*, Cambridge, UK: Cambridge University Press.
Schelling, Thomas C. (1978), *Microbehavior and Macrobehavior*, New York, NY: W.W. Norton and Company.
Schumpeter, Joseph A. (1954), *History of Economic Analysis*, New York, NY: Oxford University Press.
Schweber, Silvan S. (1977), "The Origin of the *Origin* Revisited," *Journal of the History of Biology* 10, 2, Fall, pp. 229–316.

Schweber, Silvan S. (1980), "Darwin and the Political Economists: Divergence of Character," *Journal of the History of Biology* 13, 2, Fall, pp. 195–289.
Schweber, Silvan S. (1985), "The Wider British Context in Darwin's Theorizing," Ed. by David Kohn, *The Darwinian Heritage*, Princeton, NJ: Princeton University Press, pp. 35–70.
Sen, Amartya (1987), *On Ethics and Economics*, Oxford, UK: Basil Blackwell.
Sen, Amartya (1999), *Development as Freedom*, New York, NY: Anchor Books.
Seymour-Smith, Martin (1998), *The 100 Most Influential Books Ever Written*, New York, NY: Citadel Press.
Skinner, Andrew S. (2007), "Adam Smith (1723–1790): Theories of Political Economy," in *A Companion to The History of Economic Thought*, Ed. by Warren J. Samuels, Jeff E. Biddle, and John B. Davis, Malden, MA: Blackwell Publishing, pp. 94–111.
Skousen, Mark (2001), *The Making of Modern Economics: The Lives and Ideas of the Great Thinkers*, Armonk, NY: M.E. Sharpe.
Smith, Adam (1759/1984), *The Theory of Moral Sentiments*, Indianapolis, IN: Liberty Fund.
Smith, Adam (1776/1981), *An Inquiry into the Nature and Causes of the Wealth of Nations*, Indianapolis, IN: Liberty Fund.
Smith, Adam (1793/1982), *Essays on Philosophical Subjects*, Ed. by W.P.D. Wightman and J.C. Bryce 1982, Indianapolis, IN: Liberty Fund.
Smith, Adam (1982a), "The History of Astronomy," in *Essays on Philosophical Subjects*, Ed. by W.P.D. Wightman and J.C. Bryce, 1982, Indianapolis, IN: Liberty Fund.
Smith, Adam (1982b), *Lectures on Jurisprudence*, Indianapolis, IN: Liberty Fund.
Smith, Adam (1985), *Lectures on Rhetoric and Belles Letters*, Indianapolis, IN: Liberty Fund.
Smith, Adam (1987), *The Correspondence of Adam Smith*, Indianapolis, IN: Liberty Fund.
Smith, Craig (2006), *Adam Smith's Political Philosophy: The Invisible Hand and Spontaneous Order*, London, UK and New York, NY: Routledge.
Stark, Rodney (2005), *The Victory of Reason*, New York, NY: Random House.
Sterelny, Kim (1994), "Science and Selection," *Biology and Philosophy* 9, pp. 45–62.
Stewart, Dugald (1793/1982), "Account of the Life and Writings of Adam Smith," in *Essays on Philosophical Subjects*, Indianapolis, IN: Liberty Fund, pp. 269–351.
Stiglitz, Joseph (2000), "The Contribution of the Economics of Information to the Twentieth Century Economics," *Quarterly Journal of Economics* 115, 4, pp. 1441–1478.
Stiglitz, Joseph E. (2002), "Information and the Change in the Paradigm in Economics," *The American Economic Review* 92, 3, June, pp. 460–501.
Strogatz, Steven (2003), *Sync: The Emerging Science of Spontaneous Order*, New York, NY: Hyperion Books.
Sun, Guang-Zhen (2005), *Readings in the Economics of the Division of Labor: The Classical Tradition*, New Jersey: World Scientific.
Thornton, Mark (2006), "The Mystery of Adam Smith's Invisible Hand Resolved," Mises Institute.
Tobin, James (1992), "The Invisible Hand in Modern Macroeconomics," in *Adam Smith's Legacy: His Place in the Development of Modern Economics*, Ed. by Michael Fry, London, UK: Routledge.
Trever, Albert Augustus (1916/1978), *History of Greek Economic Thought*, Philadelphia, PA: Porcupine Press.
Ullmann-Margalit, Edna (1978), "Invisible-Hand Explanations," *Syntheses* 39, pp. 263–291.
Verburg, Rudi (2012), "The Rise of Greed in Early Economic Thought: From Deadly Sin to Social Benefit," *Journal of the History of Economic Thought* 34, 4, pp. 491–514.
Viner, Jacob (1927/1991), "Adam Smith and Laissez Faire,'" in *Essays on the Intellectual History of Economics*, Ed. by Douglas A. Irwin, Princeton, NJ: Princeton University Press, pp. 86–113.

Viner, Jacob (1959/1991), "The Intellectual History of Laissez Faire," in *Essays on the Intellectual History of Economics*, Ed. by Douglas A. Irwin, Princeton, NJ: Princeton University Press, pp. 200–225.

Viner, Jacob (1960/1991), "The 'Economic Man,' or the Place of Self-Interest in a 'Good Society,'" in *Essays on the Intellectual History of Economics*, Ed. by Douglas A. Irwin, Princeton, NJ: Princeton University Press, pp. 69–77.

Viner, Jacob (1968/1991), "Adam Smith," in *Essays on the Intellectual History of Economics*, Ed. by Douglas A. Irwin, Princeton, NJ: Princeton University Press, pp. 248–261.

Viner, Jacob (1991), *Essays on the Intellectual History of Economics*, Ed. by Douglas A. Irwin, Princeton, NJ: Princeton University Press.

Vivenza, Gloria (2008), "A Note on Adam Smith's First Invisible Hand," *Adam Smith Review* 4, pp. 26–29.

Vriend, Nicolaas J. (1995), "Self-Organization of Markets: An Example of a Computational Approach," *Computational Economics* 8, pp. 205–231.

Waldrop, M. Mitchell (1992), *Complexity*, New York, NY: Touchstone, Simon and Schuster.

Wallace, Alfred Russell (1905), *My Life: A Record of Events and Opinions*, 2 Volumes, London, UK: Chapman and Hall.

Walras, Leon (1874/1954), *Elements of Pure Economics*, Homewood, IL, Published for the American Economic Association by Richard D. Irwin, Inc.

Warsh, David (2006), *Knowledge and the Wealth of Nations: A Story of Economic Discovery*, New York, NY: W.W. Norton.

Wells, Thomas (2010), "Adam Smith's Views on Slavery: A Reply to Marvin Brown," *Real-World Economics* 53, pp. 156–160.

Witztum, Amos (2010), "Interdependence, the Invisible Hand, and Equilibrium in Adam Smith," *History of Political Economy* 42, 1, Spring, pp. 155–192.

Ylikoski, Petri (1995), "The Invisible Hand and Science," *Science Studies* 8, pp. 32–43.

Young, H. Peyton (1998), *Individual Strategy and Social Structure: An Evolutionary Theory of Institutions*, Princeton, NJ and Oxford, UK: Princeton University Press.

Young, H. Peyton (2001), "The Dynamics of Conformity," in *Social Dynamics*, Ed. by Steven N. Durlauf and H. Peyton Young, Cambridge, MA: The MIT Press, pp. 133–152.

2 The theory of comparative advantage

"Ricardo's theory of comparative advantage … as if by magic … shows that there is indeed a free lunch – the free lunch that comes from not-previously-obvious geographical specialization that increases world potential production of all possible commodities." (Paul Samuelson, 1998, p. 22)

Chapter contents

1. Introduction

At the core of the theory of comparative advantage (also known as comparative costs) lies the proposition that imports can be beneficial even though the importing country can produce them more efficiently than the exporting country. Thus a country may be able to produce everything with fewer resources than (i.e., having an absolute advantage relative to) another country, but she cannot produce everything at lower costs (i.e., she cannot have a comparative advantage in everything). In a later section we will delve into David Ricardo's model of comparative advantage, which he introduced in 1817; here, it suffices to quote his lucid and short explication of the theory:

> a country possessing very considerable advantages in machinery and skill, and which may therefore be enabled to manufacture commodities with much less labor than her neighbors, may, in return for such commodities, import a portion of the corn required for its consumption, even if its land were more fertile and corn could be grown with less labor than in the country from which it was imported. (Ricardo 1817/1996, p. 95)

In Ricardo's exposition, a country may possess superior efficiency over her neighbors in both manufacturing and agriculture, yet she is better off importing corn and paying for it with manufactured goods because her advantage is greater in manufacturing than in agriculture.

The theory demonstrates that every country has a comparative advantage in some good and no country can have a comparative advantage in all goods. This remains true regardless of the educational, technological, and institutional attainments of the economies engaged in international trade. Moreover, the theory remains valid under any income structure in an economy relative to its trading partners. As Roy Ruffin (2002, p. 734) has noted, "Every country has a place at the table of world markets, no matter how high the country's competitively determined wages or how poor its circumstances of production…" Thus, more productive economies cannot outcompete less productive economies in all goods; nor can low-wage economies outcompete high-wage economies in all goods. A corollary of this implication is that if an import-competing industry improves its competitiveness and acquires a comparative advantage, then in the same economy another industry in the export sector at no fault of its own may lose its comparative advantage.[1]

The theory implies that strong equilibrating forces direct every economy towards the production of goods in which it has a comparative advantage and exchange them for goods in which other economies have a comparative advantage. The theory further implies that under free trade all economies gain from trade and no economy gains at the expense of another economy.[2] The source of the mutual gains is the unequal levels of productivity across economies (and across individuals within an economy). Moreover, the operation of comparative advantage will maximize gains from trade which are shared (not necessarily equally) by the trading economies. The logic of comparative advantage applies equally to individuals as well as business firms in the sense that every economic entity has a comparative advantage in the production of some good. Thus the theory of comparative advantage, similar to the invisible-hand proposition, offers an optimistic view of the market economic system. It maintains that if economic agents are free to pursue their own goals, they gravitate (led by an invisible hand, as Adam Smith might put it) towards the production of goods in which they have a comparative advantage.

This chapter explores the intellectual history of comparative advantage, tracing its roots, early insight, discovery, formulation, extensions, and applications. Ricardo (1772–1823) deserves the central place in this intellectual odyssey similar to the role of Adam Smith in the invisible-hand proposition. Ricardo, as we shall explain, laid out the intricacies of comparative advantage and expressed the theory in a simple model that nearly 200 years later continues to be analyzed theoretically as well as empirically and even historically. Our analysis will be confined to the Ricardian comparative advantage while making a few remarks about other models of trade theory. Since comparative advantage constitutes the cornerstone of the theory of international trade, we begin with a (brief) review of the influential ideas on long-distance trade over the two millennia prior to the formulation of comparative advantage.

2. Theories of foreign trade before David Ricardo

Theories of foreign trade have always been an integral part of the general theory of market, which itself, as described in chapter one, remained largely undeveloped until well into the seventeenth century. Moreover, the intensity and composition of foreign trade as well as commercial policies and international relations have played important roles in the development of trade theories. In this section, we consider three periods prior to the formulation of the theory of comparative advantage. The first period covers classical antiquity up to the sixteenth century; the second period focuses on the mercantilist theories of foreign trade in the sixteenth and seventeenth centuries; finally, we focus on relatively advanced theories in the eighteenth century that prepared the path towards the formulation and articulation of comparative advantage in the early nineteenth century.

2.1. From classical antiquity to the sixteenth century

A fairly large repertoire of historical accounts by the Greeks and Romans in antiquity reveals that commercial activities included commodity arbitrage across the known world. Major cities such as Athens, Rome, Alexandria, and Constantinople imported olive, wine, grain, silk, spices, and handcrafted items from numerous places. The commercial network in antiquity was so strong and the movement of "people, goods, and information" was so free and frequent that "the Greek and Roman worlds would have looked very different without wine, or imported fine-ware pottery, or incense" (Morley, 2007, p. 96).[3] Morley (Ibid.) further notes, "If Egypt had suddenly been conquered by the Persians, one might suggest, the effects on the city of Rome would have been catastrophic." Just as in the twenty-first century China produces goods for North American markets, in the first century "Attic potters and pot-painters" in distant places "produced shapes and designs especially for the Etruscan market…" (Ibid.).

While long-distance trade remained a fact of life in antiquity, certain influential Greek philosophers including Plato and Aristotle generally advocated self-sufficiency, but allowed for imports only when it was necessary.[4] However, there were other contemporary thinkers who had sympathetic views towards foreign trade. For instance, Greek historian Xenophon (430–354) called attention to the advantage of transporting goods in pursuit of profits. Merchants, he noted, buy grains where it is abundant and ship it to where it is scarce (Morley, 2007, pp. 30–31). Xenophon's observation of commodity arbitrage still propels international trade. Cicero (106–46 B.C.E.) made the same observation, but he focused primarily on the proper conduct of trade rather than its economic consequences. Thus he approved of imports "from all parts of the world and distributing to many" as long as it is done "without misrepresentation" (Irwin, 1996, p. 13). Cicero discerned the following moral dilemma:

> Suppose that there is a time of dearth and famine at Rhodes, with provisions being sold at fabulous prices; and suppose that an honest man has imported a large cargo of grain from Alexandria and that to his certain knowledge several other importers have set sail from Alexandria, and that in the course of the voyage he has sighted their vessels laden with grain and headed for Rhodes; is he bound to report this fact to the people of Rhodes, or is he to keep his own counsel and sell his goods at the highest market prices? (Quoted in Morley, 2007, p. 17)

Cicero's question indicates that long-distance trade in the first century had reached a sufficiently high level to warrant such scrutiny. Apparently, foreign trade has always been a contentious issue on both economic and moral grounds. A few generations after Cicero, the Greek historian Plutarch (46–120 C.E.) observed that foreign trade facilitates consumption of goods that are superior to local goods or not produced at home.

Any insight into the operation of foreign trade in antiquity including Plutarch's, however, was eclipsed by a doctrine that influenced economic thinking for centuries to come. Jacob Viner (1937/1975, p. 100) notes:

> In the ancient Greek and Roman classics is to be found the doctrine that differences in natural conditions in different countries made trade between these countries mutually profitable. The early Christian philosophers took over this doctrine and gave it a theological flavor. God had endowed different regions with limited but varied products to give mankind an incentive to

> trade, so that through a world economy they would become united in a world society. This was apparently common doctrine among the English theological writers of the sixteenth century and later.

In his first lecture at Wabash College in 1959, Viner called this idea "Universal Economy" and referred to it as "the oldest and longest-lived economic doctrine" (1959/1991, p. 42). Viner quotes the historian Florus, a contemporary of Roman Emperor Augustus (63 B.C.E.–14 C.E.), who said, "Suppress commerce and you tear apart the bonds of human race" (Ibid., p. 41). Similarly, Plutarch noted that commerce through "[The sea] has rendered sociable and tolerable our existence" and that "the exchange of goods" has brought "community and friendship" (Ibid., p. 41). However, since foreign commerce took place largely over the sea and sailors faced the risk of piracy, conflict, and storms, some observers objected to the doctrine of universal economy. Nonetheless, this doctrine carried the day because commerce proved to be beneficial. More importantly, the doctrine entered theological discourse and received the endorsement of influential religious thinkers. John Chrysostom, a fourth-century preacher, summed up this doctrine as follows: "God filled the earth with goods but gave each region its own particular products, so that, moved by need, we would communicate and share among ourselves, giving others that of which we have abundance and receiving that which we lack" (quoted in Morley, 2007, p. 20).

Stripped of its theological garb, however, two aspects of this doctrine have survived. The first one, which attributes trade to resource endowments, is embodied in the influential theory of Eli Heckscher (1919/1991) and Bertil Ohlin (1933). In this theory resource endowments are the primary source of comparative advantage in international trade. The second aspect of the doctrine of universal economy – the idea that commerce promotes amity and unity among nations – became quite popular in the eighteenth and nineteenth centuries. Albert Hirschman (1982) calls this idea the "*doux-commerce*" thesis. The historian Jacques Barzun (1981, p. 703) notes that the eighteenth-century thinkers regarded international commerce as a means of establishing world peace. For example, Montesquieu (1689–1755) argued that "the spirit of commerce unites nations" and Benjamin Rush, a signer of the U.S. Declaration of Independence, viewed commerce as "the means of uniting the different nations of the world" (both quotations are in Ralph Lerner, 1979, p. 15). John Stuart Mill (1848/2006, pp. 581–582) articulated the idea as follows:

> Commerce is now what war once was, the principal source of this contact.... It is commerce which is rapidly rendering war obsolete, by strengthening and multiplying the personal interests which are in natural opposition to it. And it may be said without exaggeration that the great extent and rapid increase of international trade, in being the principal guarantee of the peace of the world, is the great permanent security for the uninterrupted progress of the ideas, the institutions, and the character of the human race.

Although World War One shattered the optimism in Mill's statement, the formation of the European Union after World War Two was predicated on the Millian premise that economic integration can cause and maintain peace among countries that had historically been hostile to each other.

2.2. The era of mercantilism

Lars Magnusson (2007, p. 49) has defined mercantilism

> as a literature of pamphlets and books, mainly of English origin, which primarily dealt with practical political and economic policy issues, roughly between 1620 and 1750. However, an overall objective in much of this literature was the question how England should be able to achieve national wealth and power.

As noted in chapter one, mercantilism emerged as a logical and rational response to "commercial rivalry – 'jealousy of trade' as it was called" that ruled the continent of Europe in the sixteenth and seventeenth centuries (Gomes, 2003, p. 6). This commercial rivalry resulted from the exploration of the rest of the world that began in a systematic way in the fifteenth century and contributed to the expansion and acceleration of international trade in subsequent centuries. As an example of this expansion, consider that exports of pepper from Southeast Asia increased from 950 tons in the year 1500 to 5,300 tons in 1700, of which the share of Europe and Middle East soared from a meager 50 tons in 1500 to a staggering 2,600 tons in 1700.[5] This colossal increase becomes even more impressive when we consider that over the 200-year period the European population increased by only 45 percent and the per capita GDP by 32 percent.[6]

In the opening paragraph on mercantilism in the *Wealth of Nations* Adam Smith (1776/1981, p. 429) writes, "That wealth consists in money, or in gold and silver, is a popular notion which naturally arises from the double function of money, as the instrument of commerce, and the measure of value." He further notes that this confusion of wealth with money has led to trade policies intended "for enriching the country." In particular he (Ibid., p. 450) mentions "restraints upon importation, and encouragements to exportation". Such a view is generally supported by quoting Thomas Mun (1571–1641), a director of the British East Indies Trading Company, who recommended that England "prevent the importation of Hemp, Flax, Cordage, Tobacco and diverse other things which we now fetch from strangers to our great impoverishing" (1664/1959, p. 7).[7]

Although Mun is generally regarded as the most influential expositor of mercantilism, mercantilist tracts appeared long before Mun wrote his book. For example, in 1549 Sir Thomas Smith had argued that foreign trade deficit impoverishes the national economy and benefits the trading partners.[8] Indeed, mercantilist policies ostensibly aimed at generating a trade surplus in order to cause an inflow of precious metals. According to Viner (1937/1975, p. 3) many mercantilists went as far as declaring foreign trade as "the only source of wealth". The mercantilist literature justified and fueled the desire of newly established European nations for international domination and contributed to the colonial aspirations and policies that lasted through the twentieth century. As William Allen (1987, p. 446) notes, "The precepts and proposals of mercantilism were the economic component of state-building, providing much of the rationale and suggesting some of the procedures of national unification, seen especially in England, France and Spain."[9]

However, as noted in chapter one, Magnusson in several publications has challenged this orthodox view of mercantilism. For example, he (2007, p. 55) notes that if mercantilists recommended policies to increase the stock of gold and silver, they did so, not because they confused money with wealth, rather because they aimed at increasing the supply of money, which they deemed necessary "to finance a greater volume of trade." Although mercantilists aimed to enhance national wealth and power, they lacked a unified and coherent system of theory that would guide them to achieve this goal. More importantly, mercantilism evolved over time as the later thinkers (e.g., Charles Davenant) embraced free trade even though they still had the same goal of enhancing national wealth and power.

The intellectual origin of mercantilism can be traced to the Greek poet and merchant Solon who lived in the early sixth century B.C.E. Barry Gordon in *Economic Analysis before Adam Smith, Hesiod to Lessius* (1975, pp. 7–8) notes that Solon considered

> foreign trade ... as the leading edge of an expansionary movement. In a list of six worthy occupations, sea commerce is given first place ahead of agriculture, manufactures, teaching, prophecy and medicine. This emphasis on trade, monetization of the economy, and the alliance of political with economic power suggest that it is appropriate to apply the term 'mercantilist' to Solon's programne. The future of Athens was being shaped in accordance with policies akin to those adopted by nation-states of Europe in the late sixteenth and early seventeenth centuries A.D.

Gordon (1975, p. 17) cites a surviving treatise, titled *Ways and Means to Increase the Revenues of Athens*, "written about the middle of the fourth century B.C. by a contemporary of Plato ... [which] remained the only essay to be devoted exclusively to this particular topic [mercantilism] for well over 1500 years." The treatise argues that the prosperity of a city depends on the amount of silver it can acquire. Gordon further notes that the Greek sophist-philosophers, who "were a potent force in the intellectual life of Athens between about 450 and 350 B.C.," advanced economic views that "had a strong mercantilist bias" (Ibid., p. 17). Socrates, Plato, and Aristotle argued against the sophist philosophy, but made no attempt to refute their mercantilist views. The refutation had to wait until the eighteenth century when, as we shall see, David Hume and Adam Smith, two leading figures of classical economics, appeared on the scene.

What explains the nearly two millennia hiatus between the appearance of the essay *Ways and Means* and the emergence of the mercantilist literature of the later period? A possible explanation is that the period from 400 B.C.E. to 1500 C.E. roughly corresponds to the time when empires ruled vast areas. These empires, including Greek, Persian, Roman, Carolingian, Sung, Islam, and Mongol, were more interested in expanding and/or preserving their territories than self-enrichment through foreign trade. By and large, they adopted a relatively free market system, which simply did not lend itself to mercantilist ideologies and policies. Hence no substantive literature on mercantilism appeared for nearly 2000 years.

The mercantilist conviction that an economy benefits from trade surplus but suffers from trade deficit rests on a fallacy called "the balance-of-labor doctrine," according to which employment is *the end* to be achieved by *the means* of trade surplus.[10] The next section will show why the argument is fallacious.

2.3. The eighteenth century – laying the foundation

While mercantilist ideology has always been appealing to politicians and merchants, keen observers have noticed that trade policies that are opposite to those of mercantilism have often coincided with economic prosperity. For example, in the year 1670 Roger Coke noted that "The Dutch we see import all, yet thrive upon trade, and the Irish export eight times more than they import, yet grow poorer" (quoted in Irwin, 1996, p. 48). Three hundred years later in our time, economists have resorted to the same logic to debunk the mercantilist myth that trade surplus signifies economic strength. For example, George Hatsopoulos *et al.* (1988, p. 299) have noted, "from 1980 through 1986 Bolivia consistently ran a trade surplus. Exports exceeded imports by more than 60% in most years … yet from 1980 to 1986 the per capita output in the already desperately poor Bolivian economy fell by 26%." More recently, Peter Lindert and Jeffrey Williamson (2003) have pointed out that there is not even one country

> that chose to be less open to trade and factor flows in the 1990s than in the 1960s and rose in the global living-standard ranks at the same time. As far as we can tell, there are no anti-global victories to report for the postwar Third World. We infer that this is because freer trade stimulates growth in Third World economies…

Although empirical observations that contradict the predictions of a proposition sufficiently reject the general validity of the proposition, theoretical analysis is necessary to expose the fallacy of an entrenched idea such as mercantilism. An intellectual development in the latter part of the seventeenth century significantly contributed to debunking mercantilism and making the case for free trade. It centered on the observation concerning the harmony between private interests and public interests, which several thinkers extended to international trade, arguing that free trade enhances public interest. The most prominent figures in this group of thinkers include Dudley North (1641–1691), Charles Davenant (1656–1714), and Henry Martyn (d. 1712) whose views were briefly covered in chapter one of the present work.

Here we present the writings of Henry Martyn, David Hume, and Adam Smith, who advanced the most influential and sophisticated analysis of trade theory in the eighteenth century and prepared the path for the discovery of comparative advantage. In fact these authors realized that some forces similar to comparative advantage propel international markets. As Istvan Hont (2005, p. 68) has noted, "Hume and Smith (and, in a way, Davenant and Martyn) had already grasped the basics of the principle without as yet using the confusing term 'comparative advantage' even if its detailed exegesis came only with Ricardo in the early nineteenth century."[11] The evidence that Davenant and Hume had grasped the basics of comparative advantage rests, not on specific statements, but on their entire writings, which advocate trade among *all* countries. But, as we shall see shortly, Martyn advanced an analytical framework that served as the foundation of the Ricardian comparative advantage. Section 2.6 below and Appendix I describe Smith's expression of the operation of comparative advantage.

2.4. Henry Martyn

In the seventeenth century, England experienced a rapid expansion of international trade. Joel Mokyr (2009, p. 18) notes that in England "between 1622 and 1700 both imports and exports just about doubled, and a new commercial activity, re-exports, had emerged." According to Maddison (2007, p. 112), the number of ships sailing from England to Asia increased from 811 in the seventeenth century to 1,865 in the eighteenth century. These figures correspond to the exports of gold and silver from England to Asia which increased from 1,300 metric tons in the seventeenth century to over 3,900 in the eighteenth century. Because of such substantial increase in the volume of foreign trade and the lingering effects of mercantilist theories, the closing decades of the seventeenth century witnessed strong protectionist sentiments in England. The East-India company, a major player in England's foreign trade, came under increasing pressure to reduce its imports, but the company was able to resist the pressure until the onset of the Glorious Revolution of 1688. Daron Acemoglu and James Robinson (2012, p. 212) describe the evolution of protectionism at the time of the Revolution, and note, "The tide changed after 1688" to the point that between the years 1696 and 1698 domestic manufacturers of woolen and silk products coalesced to bring about legislation restricting imports. In 1701, the English Parliament passed the following law: "All wrought silks, bengals and stuffs, mixed with silk of herba, of the manufacture of Persia, China, or East-India, all Calicoes painted, dyed, printed, or stained there, which are or shall be imported into this kingdom, shall not be worn" (Ibid., p. 200).

On the eve of the passage of this law Martyn published a fairly sophisticated tract, titled *Considerations upon the East-India Trade* (1701).[12] Martyn made his objective very clear in the early part of his tract. He (1701, p. III) noted, "by means of this Trade, no Imployment of the People is lost that is worth our keeping; no Manufacture is destroy'd which is profitable to the Kingdom." He advanced a case for the expansion of foreign trade on the grounds that international exchange, similar to technical progress, saves domestic labor, which can be deployed to more productive employment than to the production of the importables. He argued, "If the same Work is done by one, which was done before by three; if the other two are forc'd to sit still, the Kingdom got nothing before by the Labour of the two, and therefore loses nothing by their sitting still" (Ibid., p. 34). This logic led Martyn to an argument against protectionism:

> a Law to restrain us to use only English Manufactures, is to oblige us to make them first, is to oblige us to provide for our Consumption by the labour of many, what might as well be done by that of few, is to oblige us to consume the labour of many when that of few might be sufficient. Certainly we lose by being refrain'd to the Consumption of our own, we cannot be so much impoverish'd by the free and indifferent use of Manufactures. (Ibid., p. 48)

Accordingly, protectionism wastes resources and breeds inefficiency.

Martyn was well aware of the principle of opportunity cost. He wrote, "To imploy to make Manufacturers here, more Hands than are necessary to procure the like things from the *East-Indies*, is not only to imploy so many to no profit, it is also the labour of so many Hands which might be imploy'd to the profit of the kingdom" (Ibid., p. 54). His deep insight into the advantages of foreign trade shines through in the following argument:

> If nine cannot produce above three Bushels of Wheat in *England*, if by equal Labour they might procure nine Bushels from another Country, to imploy these in agriculture at home, is to imploy nine to do no more work than might be done as well by three; is to imploy six to do no more work than might be done as well without them; is to imploy six to no profit, which might be imploy'd to procure as many Bushels of Wheat to England; is the loss of six Bushels of Wheat; is therefore the loss of so much value. (Ibid., p. 55)

Jacob Viner (1937/1975, p. 440) dubbed Martyn's insight "the eighteenth century rule," and defined it as follows: "it pays to import commodities from abroad whenever they can be obtained in exchange for exports at a smaller real cost than their production at home would entail."[13] Viner (Ibid.) goes on to say that "Such gain from trade is always possible when, and is only possible if, there are comparative differences in costs between the countries concerned." Viner (Ibid.) further comments that the "doctrine of comparative costs is, indeed, but a statement of some of the implications of this rule, and adds nothing as a guide for policy." He (Ibid., p. 441) even notes the "statement that imports could be profitable even though the commodity imported could be produced at less cost at home than abroad was, it seems to me, the sole addition of consequence which the doctrine of comparative costs made to the eighteenth century rule."[14]

In a detailed analysis of Matryn's tract, Maneschi (2002) quotes P. J. Thomas and William Barber, who gave much credit to Martyn for his insight into comparative advantage. Thomas in a 1926 publication noted that Martyn "foreshadowed the modern theory of comparative costs" (quoted in Maneschi, 2002, p. 245); and in 1975 Barber wrote, "in all essential particulars, the analysis the nineteenth century was to know as the theory of comparative advantage can be found" in Martyn's book (quoted in Maneschi, 2002, p. 245). Section three will show how Ricardo built his comparative advantage model on Martyn's eighteenth-century rule.[15]

2.5. David Hume

The rapid increase in international trade that had begun in the seventeenth century accelerated in the eighteen century. Joel Mokyr (2009, p. 167) notes that total exports rose from £3.8 million in 1700 to £28.4 million in 1801, representing more than a 100 percent increase in exports as a share of the GDP from 5.8 percent to 12.3 percent. This increase took place despite the fact that during this period the British economy "was heavily taxed and regulated, with strong protection for many imports and 'bounties' (subsidies) for some exports" (Ibid., p. 396). Mercantilism was alive and well in the eighteenth-century Britain.

In a series of essays, David Hume (1711–1776) consistently and persuasively argued for the expansion of foreign trade and stressed the benefits of not just exports but imports as well.[16] In an essay titled "Of Commerce" Hume (1752a/1955, p. 13) noted, "a kingdom, that has a large import and export, must abound more with industry, and that employed upon delicacies and luxuries, than a kingdom which rests contended with its native commodities." The inclusion of "large import" in the statement and the expression of its benefits marked a radical departure from mercantilism, which had stressed import restrictions. In particular, Hume exposed the fallacy of mercantilism with two arguments. The first one centers on the specie-flow mechanism, which he presented in an essay titled, "Of the Balance of Trade."[17] In this essay Hume argued that a change in the quantity of money causes a proportional change in the price level with no long-run impact on the economy's output.[18] Whether "four-fifths of all the money in GREAT BRITAIN to be annihilated in one night" or "all the money of GREAT BRITAIN were multiplied fivefold in a night … the price of all labour and commodities" change "in proportion" to the change in the money supply (Hume 1752b/1955, pp. 60–61). The mercantilist policy of increasing exports, which causes an inflow of gold and silver, is unsustainable and self-defeating because prices

> rise to such an exorbitant height, that no neighbouring nations could afford to buy from us; while their commodities, on the other hand, became comparatively so cheap, that, in spite of all the laws which could be formed, they

> would be run in upon us, and our money flow out; till we fall to a level with foreigners, and lose that great superiority of riches … (Ibid., p. 63)

Hume exhibits a deep understanding of a self-regulating system of international payments through the endogenous changes in the exchange rate. He writes, "When we import more goods than we export, the exchange turns against us, and this becomes a new encouragement to export …" (Ibid., p. 64). A trade deficit lowers the value of domestic currency, which increases exports while reducing imports, and a trade surplus strengthens the currency leading to the opposite outcomes. Thus Hume effectively exposed the fallacy of mercantilism by showing that imports and exports are inextricably linked and that a trade surplus is not sustainable. Endogenous forces tend to shrink both a trade a surplus and a trade deficit.

Hume's second argument against mercantilism centers on a dominant view in the seventeenth and eighteenth centuries, called "jealousy of trade." Istvan Hont (2005, p. 2) notes that "jealousy of trade" had mutated from "Jealousy of State," extracted from Thomas Hobbes' *Leviathan* (1650) in which he had written of "Jealousy of Kings and Persons of Sovereign Authority." Hont (Ibid., pp. 3–6) points out that in the seventeenth and eighteenth centuries the term jealousy connoted "a competitive stance motivated by ambition, envy, and resentment" and it "was a disparaging phrase, referring to a pathological conjunction between politics and the economy that turned the globe into a theater of perpetual commercial war." Hume and Smith argued that jealousy of trade is driven by prejudice (towards other countries) and ignorance (concerning the benefits of international commerce). The sentiments that jealousy of trade evokes have survived to the present time.

In "Of the Balance of Trade" Hume (1752b/1955, pp. 66–67) notes "Our jealousy and our hatred of France are without bounds; and … have occasioned innumerable barriers and obstructions upon commerce.… But what have we gained by the bargain? We lost the FRENCH market for our woollen manufactures, and transferred the commerce of wine to SPAIN and PORTUGAL, where we buy worse liquor at a higher price."[19] Hume's most comprehensive refutation of mercantilism appears in an essay titled, "Of the Jealousy of Trade" in which he argues all nations gain from trade (a basic implication of comparative advantage) and that the prosperity spills over to one's trading partners. In the opening paragraph of the essay he (1758/1955, p. 78) writes:

> Nothing is more usual, among states which have made some advances in commerce, than to look on the progress of their neighbours with a suspicious eye, to consider all trading states as their rivals, and to suppose that it is impossible for any of them to flourish, but at their expense. In opposition to this narrow and malignant opinion, I will venture to assert, that the encrease of riches and commerce in any one nation, instead of hurting, commonly promotes the riches and commerce of all its neighbours; and that a state can

> scarcely carry its trade and industry very far, where all the surrounding states are buried in ignorance, sloth, and barbarism.

Here Hume invokes a sort of divine economy doctrine to argue that "a diversity of geniuses, climates, and soils" among different nations secures "mutual intercourse and commerce" (Ibid., p. 79). His advocacy of trade among all nations suggests that Hont (2005, p. 68) is right in asserting that "Hume … had already grasped the basics of the" theory of comparative advantage. Hume (1758/1955, p. 82) concludes the essay with these words:

> I shall therefore venture to acknowledge, that, not only as a man, but as a BRITISH subject, I pray for the flourishing commerce of GERMANY, SPAIN, ITALY, and even FRANCE itself. I am at least certain, that GREAT BRITAIN, and all those nations, would flourish more, did their sovereigns and ministers adopt such enlarged and benevolent sentiments towards each other.[20]

2.6. Adam Smith

One year after the appearance of "Of the Jealousy of Trade," Adam Smith published his first book *The Theory of Moral Sentiments* (1759/1984). In a section of the book on "Character of Virtues" Smith writes, "The love of our own nation often disposes us to view, with the most malignant jealousy and envy, the prosperity and aggrandizement of any other neighbouring nation" (1759/1984, p. 228). He then uses the example of France and England to argue against jealousy of trade:

> France and England may each of them have some reason to dread the increase of the naval and military power of the other; but for either of them to envy the internal happiness and prosperity of the other, the cultivation of its lands, the advancement of its manufactures, the increase of its commerce, the security and number of its ports and harbours, its proficiency in all the liberal arts and sciences, is surely beneath the dignity of two such great nations. These are all real improvements of the world we live in. Mankind are benefited, human nature is ennobled by them. In such improvements each nation ought, not only to endeavour itself to excel, but from the love of mankind, to promote, instead of obstructing the excellence of its neighbours. These are all proper objects of national emulation, not of national prejudice or envy. (Ibid., p. 229)

By invoking the nobility of human nature and the love of mankind, Smith's argument against jealousy of trade assumes a moral dimension, which in addition to the economic one resonates well with Hume's view on international commerce.

Smith's case against mercantilism rests primarily on his conviction that in any society and economy "every man" should have the opportunity "to pursue his own interest in his own way, upon the liberal plan of equality, liberty, and justice" (1776/1981, p. 664). This philosophy put Smith at odds with mercantilists who advocated government actions and interventions, particularly in foreign trade, to enhance national wealth and power. For Smith, such actions and interventions would fail to accomplish the intended goal, since "no human wisdom or knowledge could ever be sufficient" for "superintending the industry of private people, and of directing it towards the employments most suitable to the interest of the society" (Ibid., p. 687). Indeed, to advance the interests of the society, the "great body of the people" should have the freedom "to buy whatever they want of those who sell it cheapest" (Ibid., pp. 493–494). This freedom extends to purchasing imported goods: "If a foreign country can supply us with a commodity cheaper than we ourselves can make it, better buy it of them with some part of the produce of our own industry employed in a way in which we have some advantage" (Ibid., p. 457). Moreover,

> No regulation of commerce can increase the quantity of industry in any society beyond what its capital can maintain. It can only divert a part of it into a direction into which it might not otherwise have gone; and it is by no means certain that this artificial direction is likely to be more advantageous to the society than that into which it would have gone of its own accord. (Ibid., p. 453)

To Smith, mercantilism seeks to enhance and protect the interests of "merchants and manufacturers" at the expense of the interests of the consumers:

> It cannot be very difficult to determine who have been the contrivers of this whole mercantile system; not the consumers, we may believe, whose interest has been entirely neglected; but the producers, whose interest has been so carefully attended to; and among this latter class our merchants and manufacturers have been by far the principal architects. In the mercantile regulations, which have been taken notice of in this chapter, the interest of our manufacturers has been most peculiarly attended to; and the interest, not so much of the consumers, as that of some other sets of producers, has been sacrificed to it. (Ibid., pp. 661–662)

Smith argues that the expansion of international trade widens the extent of the market, deepens division of labor, fosters productivity, enhances economic efficiency, increases living standards, and reduces poverty. He notes that the "discovery of America" opened "a new and inexhaustible market to all the commodities of Europe," and "gave occasion to new divisions of labour and improvements of art" (Ibid., p. 448). In a lecture in 1763 he observed that the living standards of a "day-labourer in England or Holland" exceed those of an "Indian prince" or an "African king" (1982, pp. 339–340).[21] He attributes the higher living standards to deeper division of labor that results from the extension of commercial activities to foreign markets.

Smith, however, puts forth, "two cases in which it will generally be advantageous to lay some burden upon foreign, for the encouragement of domestick industry. The first is when some particular sort of industry is necessary for the defence of the country" (1776/1981, p. 463). Thus Smith endorsed the Navigation Acts which were enforced in his time and provided Britain with a strong naval power for national defense.[22] "The second case, in which it will generally be advantageous to lay some burden upon foreign for the encouragement of domestick industry, is, when some tax is imposed at home upon the produce of the latter. In this case, it seems reasonable that an equal tax should be imposed upon the like produce of the former" (Ibid., p. 465). Further, Smith (Ibid., p. 468) endorses retaliatory measures "when there is a probability that they will procure the repeal of the high duties or prohibitions" but when "there is no probability that any such repeal can be procured, it seems a bad method of compensating the injury done to certain classes of our people, to do another injury ourselves, not only to those classes, but to almost all the other classes of them."

Despite the few exceptions noted above, Smith remains the patron saint of free trade in the annals of economic history. His writings have never ceased to influence economic thought and policies. In 1793, three years after Smith's death, his student Dugald Stewart (1752–1828) gave an "Account of the Life and Writings of Adam Smith" before the Royal Society. In the "Account" Stewart (1793/1982, p. 270) referred to Smith as "a genius, which was destined not only to extend the boundaries of science, but to enlighten and reform the commercial policy of Europe."

Before we end the section on Smith, let us explore the question of whether he was aware of the operation of comparative advantage in international trade. Smith is generally known for having relied on absolute advantage, and has been criticized for failing to discover the theory of comparative advantage. Arthur Bloomfield (1975/1994, p. 138), while praising Smith for his "over-all performance in the analysis of international trade," chides him on the grounds that he "did not come up with comparative costs, reciprocal demand or others of the concepts and tools that were to be developed by later classical writers." Following Bloomfield, virtually all subsequent commentators on Smith's contribution to trade theory mention Smith's alleged failure to discover comparative advantage.[23] Leaving aside the absurdity of such criticism (for it is akin to chiding Isaac Newton for not having discovered the theory of relativity), the charge against Smith is an extravagant exaggeration if not a myth. We already quoted Hont who said that Smith had "grasped the basics of the principle without as yet using the confusing term 'comparative advantage'" (Hont, 2005, p. 68). Magnusson (2004, pp. 30–31) goes farther and refers to Smith as "a founding father of the comparative cost theory." Even Bloomfield (1975/1994, p. 111) writes, "Almost at the beginning of his book he does make a statement that could have been developed into a theory of comparative costs, but fails to follow through."

While Smith's analysis of foreign trade lacks an explicit exposition of comparative advantage, Bruce Elmslie (1994), by delving into Smith's writings (including the passage that Bloomfield mentions) and connecting the dots, demonstrates that not only was Smith well aware of the operation of comparative advantage in international trade, he actually "did make use of some form of comparative advantage" (Elmslie, 1994, p. 254).[24] In a nutshell, Smith observed that two main sectors of the economy (manufacturing and agriculture) operate in rich countries as well in poor countries. He further observed that even though a poor country has an absolute productivity disadvantage relative to a rich country, she produces the agricultural good (but not the other one) at a lower cost. This is evident from the fact that the poor country exports the agricultural good to the rich country. Exporting a good despite having an absolute disadvantage is the central implication of the theory of comparative advantage. Uncharacteristically of Smith, however, his analysis that leads to the comparative advantage outcome is quite abstruse, and he mentions it (almost in passing) in the context of division of labor, not foreign trade. In fact Smith seems to have serendipitously stumbled upon comparative advantage while analyzing the consequences of division of labor.[25]

3. Formulation and articulation of comparative advantage

As we argued above, Henry Martyn laid the foundation of the theory of comparative advantage; and, as Appendix I shows, a model of comparative advantage can be built based on the writings of Adam Smith. Nonetheless, the formulation and articulation of comparative advantage in a systematic and methodical way had to wait for the optimal intellectual climate and an economist with an uncanny ability for abstract analysis.

The first few decades of the nineteenth century witnessed an unprecedented increase in the volume of international trade, which, as documented before, had begun to rise rapidly in the eighteenth century. According to Findlay and O'Rourke (2007, p. 327) "Britain's total imports rose over sevenfold from £20.3 million in 1784–86 to £151.18 million in 1854–56..." But the increase in international trade was not limited to Britain; it was a global phenomenon.[26] O'Rourke and Williamson (2002, p. 456) have characterized the dramatic changes in the world economy that began around the year 1820 as "a very big global bang."[27] The growth of global trade in this period was significantly propelled by inventions and innovations in the transportation industry which included steamship, train, and mechanical refrigeration.[28]

The unprecedented rise in international trade required deeper theoretical analysis than the theories of Martyn, Hume, and Smith to explain the forces that were shaping international trade and the global economy. The need for such analysis led to the publication of a number of influential economic treatises and books that analyzed, among other subjects, the workings of international trade.[29] As a result, the intellectual climate for the cultivation and fruition of the theory of comparative advantage emerged in the early decades of the nineteenth century.

It was in this climate that David Ricardo introduced the theory of comparative advantage.

3.1. David Ricardo's model of comparative advantage

Robert Torrens, in an essay published in 1815, presented a clear statement of comparative advantage. He (1815/1827, p. 263) wrote,

> If England should have acquired such a degree of skill in manufacturing, that with any given portion of her capital, she could prepare a quantity of cloth, for which the Polish cultivator would give a greater quantity of corn, than she [England] could, with the same portion of capital, raise from her own soil, then, tracts of her territory, though they should equal, nay, even though they should be superior, to the lands in Poland, will be neglected; and a part of her supply of corn will be imported from that country.

Torrens deserves credit for his intuition and insight, but not for having developed the theory of comparative advantage, because his statement is devoid of proof and the intricacies a scientific theory requires. David Ricardo, in all likelihood having read Torrens' essay and being familiar with the insight, was well prepared to formulate the theory of comparative advantage within a conceptual structure including the requisite assumptions. He did that in 1816 when he finished the first seven chapters of his book (including the chapter on foreign trade) and sent them to James Mill. We will return to the correspondence between Ricardo and Mill in the next section.[30]

Ricardo presents his comparative advantage model in chapter VII ("On Foreign Trade") of his *Principles of Political Economy and Taxation* (1817/1996). A few paragraphs before introducing the model, he (1817/1996, p. 93) observes, "The same rule which regulates the relative value of commodities in one country does not regulate the relative value of commodities between two or more countries." The reason, Ricardo argues, is that labor and capital are immobile between countries and, as a result, the labor theory of value does not apply to international trade. To elaborate, he uses the example of England exchanging cloth for Portuguese wine. It turns out that this example was neither arbitrary nor hypothetical. Findlay and O'Rourke (2007, p. 252) note that England in 1703 had signed the Methuen Treaty with Portugal "by which England had preferential access for cloth exports to Portugal in exchange for reciprocal preferences for Portuguese wine exports to England, the trade immortalized by David Ricardo's use of it to illustrate his theory of comparative advantage." Moreover, Mary Morgan (2012, p. 45) notes that in the eighteenth century Portugal had given up "making textiles" and specialized "in wine to trade with English cloth." Ricardo's example of the two countries and the two goods must have been familiar to his audience.

Since the labor theory of value does not apply to foreign trade, Ricardo (1817/1996, p. 94) argues, "The quantity of wine which she [Portugal] shall give in exchange for the cloth of England is not determined by the respective quantities of labor devoted to the production of each, as it would be if both commodities were manufactured in England, or both in Portugal." He then uses a numerical example to support his argument. He writes, "England may be so circumstanced that to produce the cloth may require the labor of 100 men for one year and if she attempted to make the wine, it might require the labor of 120 men for the same time. England would therefore find it [sic] her interest to import wine, and to purchase it by the exportation of cloth" (Ibid., p. 94). Ricardo here argues that England gains from trade because instead of allocating the labor of 120 men to make, say, Y quantity of wine, she allocates 100 men to make, say, X quantity of cloth, which can be exchanged for Y quantity of wine. The specialization and the consequent exchange would therefore save England the labor of 20 men who can boost the production of cloth by 20 percent.[31]

John Chipman (1965, p. 479) has argued that Ricardo's conclusion about England "is a *non-sequitur*, since nothing has been said about Portugal." Chipman's point is that to determine the comparative advantage of a country one must know the production functions in both countries. Ruffin (2002, p. 741) has argued that Chipman overlooked "the fact that Ricardo was in effect starting with the terms of trade" implying that in Ricardo's analysis trade had already taken place. That is the reason Ricardo chose England and Portugal – they had been exchanging cloth and wine for over a century. Maneschi (2004, p. 435) has supported Ruffin's argument by noting that Ricardo in the above quote uses "the terms 'the cloth' and 'the wine'" in reference to the goods *actually* traded. Hence the labor inputs that Ricardo assigns to England, Maneschi notes, establish "her comparative advantage in cloth without requiring any knowledge of Portugal's labor inputs" (Ibid., p. 436).[32] An alternative (and perhaps a more persuasive) response to Chipman's criticism is that up to this point Ricardo is trying to demonstrate the non-applicability of the labor theory of value in foreign trade rather than introducing the theory of comparative advantage. This response is supported by the fact that, as we shall soon see, Ricardo makes his comparative advantage statement *after* he added Portugal to the model.

Ricardo expanded his model by writing, "To produce the wine in Portugal might require only the labor of 80 men for one year, and to produce the cloth in the same country might require the labor of 90 men for the same time. It would therefore be advantageous for her to export wine in exchange for cloth" (1817/1996, p. 94). Thus Portugal saves the labor of 10 men who can boost Portugal's wine output by 12.5 percent (10/80). The additional 20 percent cloth and the 12.5 percent more wine can be shared by both countries through trade. Ricardo's model is presented in Table 2.1.

Ricardo's comparative advantage model is a brilliant application of the eighteenth-century rule: a country gains from importing a good when it costs less (in terms of inputs) to purchase the good with exports than producing it at home. From this "rule" Ricardo deduced the theory of comparative advantage. He (Ibid., p. 94) wrote, "this exchange" between England and Portugal "might even take place notwithstanding that the commodity imported by Portugal could

Table 2.1 Ricardo's Model

	Workers Needed to Produce	
	X Quantity of Cloth	*Y Quantity of Wine*
England	100	120
Portugal	90	80

be produced there with less labor than in England." This statement established the theory of comparative advantage.

Ricardo applied his insight in a correspondence with Malthus who had argued, "The rapid increase of the United States of America, taken as a whole, has undoubtedly been aided very greatly by foreign commerce, and particularly by the power of selling raw produce, obtained with little labour, for European commodities which have cost much labour" (Ricardo, 2004, Vol. II, p. 427). In his critique of Malthus' statement, Ricardo pointed out, "It can be of no consequence to America, whether the commodities she obtains in return for her own, cost European much, or little labor; all she is interested in, is that they shall cost her less labor by purchasing them than by manufacturing them herself" (Ibid.). Thus the United Sates gained from importing European commodities even though their production might have required less labor at home.

In the following statement Ricardo explains why the importation of cloth is beneficial to Portugal even though she can make the good at home with less labor:

> Though she could make the cloth with the labor of 90 men, she would import it from a country where it required the labor of 100 men to produce it, because it would be advantageous to her rather to employ her capital in the production of wine, for which she would obtain more cloth form England, than she could produce by diverting a portion of her capital from cultivation of vines to the manufacture of cloth. (Ricardo, 1817/1996, p. 94)

As we have seen in this section, Ricardo's approach hinges entirely on the eighteenth-century rule, but this approach has become completely obsolete; instead, the theory is ubiquitously explained in terms of opportunity costs.[33] For example, Gottfried Haberler (1930/1985, p. 5) reformulated Ricardo's model as follows:

> Portugal has an absolute advantage in both branches of production. But the advantage is larger in wine; it has a comparative advantage because the cost differential in that product is lager: $80/120 < 90/100$. In this case it is advantageous for both countries to specialize: Portugal will produce only wine – where it has a comparative advantage – and England only cloth, i.e., the good in which its disadvantage is relatively small. That both countries profit from this division of labor is clear from following reasoning: The exchange

> ratio between cloth and wine, before the opening of international trade, was 1W:1.2C in England and 1W:0.89C in Portugal. It is therefore of advantage to England to offer less than 1.2C for a unit of wine, and for Portugal to obtain more than 0.89C for a unit of wine. Any price of wine in terms of cloth between 1.2 and 0.89 brings advantage to both countries.[34]

Quite significantly, the validity of the Ricardian model is independent of variables such as wages and the exchange rates between the two countries. If the values of these variables are such that initially the price of each good is lower in one country (say, Portugal) than in England, then England will buy both goods and sell nothing – clearly an unsustainable trade relation. English currency and wages will decline while the opposite happens in Portugal. Consequently, the price of both goods will fall in England and rise in Portugal. This process will continue until the price of only one of the goods – the one in which Portugal has a comparative advantage – will remain lower there than in England. As Eaton and Kortum (2012) demonstrate, the ratio of English wage to Portuguese wage (w^E/w^P) must be between (90/100) and (80/120); for, if initially (w^E/w^P) > (90/100) > (80/120), then "both cloth and wine will be produced more cheaply in Portugal, leaving English labor out of work" (Eaton and Kortum, 2012, p. 68).[35] Similarly, if the wage ratio "is smaller than 80/120, then both cloth and wine will be cheaper in England." Hence for trade to take place, the wage ratio will adjust so that its value will "be somewhere between 2/3 and 9/10" (Ibid., p. 68).[36]

Following the presentation of his model, Ricardo returns to his main argument that labor theory of value does not apply to international trade. He (Ibid., pp. 94–95) writes,

> the produce of the 100 men for the produce of the labor of 80 … could not take place between the individuals of the same country. The labor of 100 Englishmen cannot be given for that of 80 Englishmen, but … may be given for the produce of the labor of 80 Portuguese, 60 Russians, or 120 East Indians. The difference in this respect between a single country and many, is easily accounted for, by considering the difficulty with which capital moves from one country to another, to seek a more profitable employment, and the activity with which it invariably passes from one province to another in the same country.

Having successfully demonstrated that domestic trade and foreign trade obey different rules, Ricardo returns to comparative advantage but in a footnote, which consists of two sentences. The first one, quoted at the beginning of the chapter, is noted below for further analysis:

> a country possessing very considerable advantages in machinery and skill, and which may therefore be enabled to manufacture commodities with much less labor than her neighbors, may, in return for such commodities, import a portion of the corn required for its consumption, even if its land were more

> fertile and corn could be grown with less labor than in the country from which it was imported. (Ricardo, 1817/1996, p. 95)

Here, Ricardo identifies two sources of superior productivity: first, "considerable advantages in machinery and skill" in manufactured commodities; second, "more fertile" land in the production of corn. In his book, before introducing the comparative advantage model, Ricardo refers to "the better distribution of labor, by each country producing those commodities for which by its situation, its climate, and its other natural or artificial advantages" and "exchanging them for the commodities of other countries" (Ibid., p. 92). Clearly for Ricardo technology is only one of the sources of comparative advantage, but international trade literature invariably focuses on technology as the only source. As Edward Leamer (1984, p. 37) has pointed out, "The source of comparative advantage was not Ricardo's concern, but it has been interpreted by many modern writers as 'technological differences.'"[37]

The second sentence of the footnote (Ricardo, 1817/1996, p. 95) is as follows:

> Two men can both make shoes and hats, and one is superior to the other in both employments; but in making hats he can exceed his competitor by one-fifth or 20 percent, and in making shoes he can excel him by one-third or 33 percent; – will it not be for the interest of both that the superior man should employ himself exclusively in making shoes, and the inferior man in making hats?

The hats–shoes model is a clear deduction from the cloth–wine model; in fact they are convertible to each other. However, here Ricardo applies a different method of determining comparative advantage, which may be expressed as follows: an economy (or an individual) that enjoys superior productivity in all goods relative to another economy (or individual) has a comparative advantage in goods where its productivity is most superior; and the other economy (or individual) has a comparative advantage in goods where its productivity is least inferior.[38] To carry out this analysis further, suppose the "two men" in Ricardo's example are Edward and Pedro. If Edward in one month can make 100 hats or 100 pairs of shoes, then Pedro's monthly output will be 120 hats or 133 pairs of shoes. Pedro has an absolute advantage over Edward. Table 2.2 presents the model.

Table 2.2 Ricardo's Model of Two Men

	Monthly Output	
	Hat (H)	*Shoes (S)*
Edward	100	100
Pedro	120	133

According to the model, for Edward one hat costs one pair of shoes while for Pedro the cost is 1.10 (i.e., 133/120) pairs of shoes. Thus Edward has a comparative advantage in making hats because his cost is lower. Similarly, while for Edward one pair of shoes costs one hat, for Pedro the cost is 0.90 hats. Thus Pedro has a comparative advantage in making shoes just as Ricardo implied in his rhetorical question. This analysis means that with complete specialization based on comparative advantage the same amount of output can be produced at lower costs as compared with partial or no specialization. The flip side is that if resources are employed where they have a comparative advantage, more output can be produced without additional resources.[39] The validity of the results is independent of where Edward and Pedro reside. They both could be living in London or Lisbon or one in London and the other in Lisbon. Moreover, the cost ratios place a limit on the wages that Pedro and Edward can earn. This is demonstrated in Appendix II.

Clearly, Ricardo's comparative advantage model is ingenious, methodical, and thoughtful.[40] However, the complete reliance on the eighteenth-century rule led Ricardo to conclude that technical advancement might bring trade to a halt. Consider the following statement (Ibid., p. 96), which appears almost immediately following Ricardo's discussion of comparative advantage:

> Now suppose England to discover a process of making wine, so that it should become her interest to grow rather than import; she would naturally divert a portion of her capital from the foreign trade to the home trade; she would cease to manufacture cloth for exportation, and would grow wine for herself.... Cloth would continue for some time to be exported from this country, because its price would continue to be higher in Portugal than here; but money instead of wine would be given in exchange for it, till the accumulation of money here, and its diminution aboard, should so operate that it would cease to be profitable for the two countries to exchange employments ...

Suppose the discovery of "a process of making wine" reduces England's requirement of labor from 120 to 95, as shown in Table 2.3.

Since in both counties fewer workers are needed to make wine than to make cloth, the eighteenth-century rule would imply that they both want "to export wine

Table 2.3 Modified Ricardo's Model

	Workers Needed to Produce	
	X Quantity of Cloth	*Y Quantity of Wine*
England	100	95
Portugal	90	80

in exchange for cloth." Thus as Ricardo concluded in the above quote, trade would cease to exist. In fact he (Ibid., p. 98) also wrote,

> Let there be more difficulty in England in producing cloth, or in Portugal in producing wine, or let there be more felicity in England in producing wine, or in Portugal in producing cloth, and the trade must immediately cease.
>
> No change whatever takes place in the circumstances of Portugal; but England finds that she can employ her labor more productively in the manufacture of wine and instantly the trade of barter between the two countries changes. Not only is the exportation of wine from Portugal stopped, but a new distribution of the precious metals takes place, and her importation of cloth is also prevented.

If we analyze Table 2.3 in light of modern approach to comparative advantage (as opposed to the eighteenth century rule), trade will continue between the two countries. The reason is that to produce X quantity of cloth Portugal needs 90 percent of labor that England needs while to make Y quantity of wine she needs 84 percent (80/90). This means Portugal retains a comparative advantage in wine and (the reciprocal of the ratios show) England keeps her comparative advantage in cloth. To solidify the point, consider that the opportunity cost of X units of cloth in England is 100Y/95 = 1.052Y while in Portugal it is 90Y/80 = 1.125Y. Further, the opportunity cost of Y units of wine in England is 95X/100 = 0.95X while in Portugal it is 80X/90 = 0.88Y. Thus trade would continue because both countries can import a good made at lower cost abroad. As Edward Leamer and James Levinsohn, in reference to the Ricardian model, have noted (1995, p. 1344) "*Except when labor requirements are identical across countries, there exist gains from trade*" (italics in original). As shown in the next section, James Mill's contribution to comparative advantage revolves around this very point stressed by Leamer and Levinsohn.

3.2. James Mill

As noted above, when Ricardo completed the first seven chapters of his book, he sent them to James Mill. He did that on 14 October 1816. Mill communicated his comments to Ricardo on 16 November 1816. He wrote,

> The inquiry concerning foreign trade … is like the rest, original, and sound, and excellently demonstrated. That foreign trade augments not the value of a nations [sic] property: that it may be good for a country to import commodities from a country where the production of those same commodities costs more, than it would cost at home: that a change in manufacturing skill in one country, produces a new distribution of the precious metals, are new propositions of the highest importance, and which you fully prove. (Ricardo, 2004, Vol. VII, p. 99)

Table 2.4 James Mill's Model

	Days of Labor Needed to Produce	
	X Quantity of Cloth	*Y Quantity of Corn*
England	150	200
Poland	100	100

In his book, *Elements of Political Economy* (published in 1821), Mill advanced Ricardo's analysis of comparative advantage to a higher level. He introduced a model in which a certain quantity of cloth and corn each requires "100 days' labour in Poland" but "150 days' labour in England" (Mill, 1821/1844, p. 120). Hence Poland has an absolute advantage but neither country can have a comparative advantage. Mill then says, suppose "the quantity of cloth, which, in Poland, is produced with 100 days' labour, can be produced in England with 150 days' labour"; but "the corn, which is produced in Poland with 100 days' labour," now "requires 200 days' labour in England" (Mill, 1821/1844, p. 120). Mill's model is presented in Table 2.4.

The application of the eighteenth-century rule would lead to the wrong conclusion that only England has an interest in trade and Poland does not. But Mill (1821/1844, p. 120) realized that "it will be in the interest of Poland to import her cloth from England" and it is advantageous to England to import corn from Poland. The reason is that if Poland imports X quantity of English cloth in exchange for Y quantity of her corn, England will reallocate 200 days of labor from corn to the cloth industry. Since X quantity of cloth in England requires 150 days of labor, the additional 50 days of labor will boost production of cloth by one-third (50/150), which the two countries can share through trade while leaving each country with the same amount of corn as before. Perhaps Mill chose the particular labor requirements for Poland to make the point that the theory of comparative advantage is richer and more consequential than appears from Ricardo's Portugal–England example.[41] Mill's contribution influenced other economists of the time, notably his son John Stuart Mill.

3.3. John Stuart Mill

In an 1829 essay John Stuart Mill (1806–1873) provided a precise description of the theory of comparative advantage:

> It is not a difference in the *absolute* cost of production, which determines the interchange, but a difference in the *comparative* cost. It may be to our advantage to procure iron from Sweden in exchange for cottons, even though the mines of England as well as her manufactories should be more productive than those of Sweden; for if we have an advantage of one-half in cottons, and only an advantage of a quarter in iron, and could sell our cottons to Sweden at the price which Sweden must pay for them if she produced them

herself, we should obtain our iron with an advantage of one-half, as well as our cottons. (Mill, 1829/2006, p. 233)

Mill quotes this passage in his *Principles of Political Economy* (1848/2006, p. 598). He (Ibid., p. 596) also reintroduces (with minor modifications) from his father's book a comparative advantage example. But Mill's crucial contribution lies in making an early foray into the theory's generalization by analyzing the Ricardian model in a multi-country and multi-good setting. He (1848/2006, p. 600) notes, "Trade among any number of countries, and in any number of commodities, must take place on the same essential principles as trade between two countries and in two commodities." Mill (1848/2006, p. 602) further argues that adding more commodities and countries does not change the fact that ultimately the demand must equal supply through an adjustment in the value of the goods. As a result, Mill maintains, the outcome of the two-country and two-good model remains intact in higher dimensions.[42] As we shall see in section five, in the twentieth century theoretical works demonstrated that the operation of comparative advantage in multilateral models is more complex and the results are less certain than Mill presented in his statement. Nonetheless, Mill is fundamentally right that the principle of comparative advantage governs trade in multilateral cases.

Mill's most enduring and consequential contribution to trade theory is the theory of reciprocal demand, which focuses on the distribution of the gains from trade between the trading countries. Citing his own 1829 essay as the origin of the theory, Mill (1848/2006, p. 595) argues, "The value of a thing in any place, depends on the cost of its acquisition in that place; which in the case of an imported article, means the cost of production of the thing which is exported to pay for it." Mill begins his analysis with a clear explication of the law of demand and supply and the emergence of equilibrium, which he extends to international markets. Mill notes that the terms of trade between two countries results from the interaction between the demand functions of the trading countries. The demand function in this context represents the various units of imports a country is willing to exchange with her exports.[43] The farther the terms of trade is from a country's production cost of imports (measured in terms of forgone exports), the larger the gains from trade. This analysis implies that under free trade, a small (poor) country (that is, a price-taker in world markets) benefits more than a large (rich) trade partner because the terms of trade would be closer to the cost (price) ratio of the large country and thus (relatively) farther from that of the small country.[44] This result would be reversed if the large country imposed a tariff on its imports from the small country, against which the small country cannot retaliate because she imports too little.[45] This theory sowed the seeds of the optimum tariff argument.[46]

4. Comparative advantage and free trade

The economic case for free trade rests on two deductively derived propositions: first, free trade leads countries to the production of the goods in which they have a comparative advantage; second, production based on comparative advantage results in efficient resource allocation. Hence free trade maximizes efficiency and the gains from trade. Indeed, the theory of comparative advantage provides a powerful case for free trade.[47] Historically, however, support for free trade did not always rest on comparative advantage. In fact, the classical economists from Ricardo to J. S. Mill usually invoked the theory of comparative advantage not to justify free trade but to explain *why* trade takes place among all countries. Moreover, when they did advance a case for free trade they often resorted to the type of arguments we encounter in the *Wealth of Nations*. Even Ricardo, in making a case for free trade, advanced an argument reminiscent of Smith's invisible-hand passage in the *Wealth of Nations*. Consider the following passage:

> Under a system of perfectly free commerce, each country naturally devotes its capital and labour to such employments as are most beneficial to each. *This pursuit of individual advantage is admirably connected with the universal good of the whole.* By stimulating industry, by rewarding ingenuity, and by using most efficaciously the peculiar powers bestowed by nature, it distributes labour most effectively and most economically: while, by increasing the general mass of productions, it diffuses general benefit, and binds together by one common tie of interest and intercourse, the universal society of nations throughout the civilized world. It is this principle which determines that wine shall be made in France and Portugal, that corn shall be grown in America and Poland, and that hardware and other goods shall be manufactured in England. (Ricardo, 1817/1996, p. 93, emphasis added)

Ricardo says all this – making a case for free trade – without a hint to comparative advantage, and in fact immediately *before* he introduces his comparative advantage model. Similarly, J. S. Mill in two essays, one titled, "The Corn Laws" (1825/2006) and the other, "Petition on Free Trade" (1841/2006) argues that protective tariffs benefit one group at the expense of another one, which is a restatement of Adam Smith's argument that protectionism benefits "merchants and manufacturers" at the expense of the "great body of people."

Most notably, consider the arguments regarding repeal of the Corn Laws in England that was debated between the years 1815 and 1846. The leading economists of the time including Ricardo, Nassau Senior, James Mill, and J. S. Mill all favored the repeal, but none of them invoked comparative advantage to support their position. Cheryl Schonhardt-Bailey (2006, p. 28) in her detailed book on the repeal of Corn Laws notes:

> that interests drove repeal to the doors of Parliament, ideas inspired constituents and legislators alike to endorse free trade .... and institutions shaped *and* shaped by the interests and ideas that drove repeal. In short, repeal must be understood as the product of interests, ideas, *and* institutions. (Italics in original)

Schonhardt-Bailey (Ibid.) further argues that "economic interests led Britain to repeal, but ideas and institutions delivered the final outcome." Curiously, the most important idea in international trade theory (i.e., comparative advantage) never entered into the debate. The term comparative advantage is not even mentioned in Schonhardt-Bailey's 426 page long book. As Gomes (1990, pp. 4–5) points out, although the

> economists were on the side of free trade ... arguments based on comparative-cost reasoning featured only marginally, if at all, in their attacks on agricultural protection. Ricardo, for instance, never made use of the comparative-cost idea in his criticism of the Corn Laws, but relied instead on absolute cost differences between Great Britain (in manufactures) and the rest of the world (in agriculture).

The classical view of comparative advantage as a positive and descriptive theory eventually morphed into a normative and prescriptive one, particularly in the twentieth century. As an example, Haberler (1930/1985, p. 4), while defending the theory of comparative advantage against some charges, wrote, "The proof that free trade is advantageous" for all countries including those poorly "endowed and which work in less favorable conditions of production than others ... is ... furnished by the theory of comparative costs which is indeed but an exact formulation of the theorem of the international division of labor."

The opponents of free trade must try (and have tried) to refute the validity of the theory of comparative advantage.[48] In his influential book titled *Unequal Exchange* (1969/1972), Arghiri Emmanuel devotes the lengthy introduction of his book almost entirely to an analysis of the theory of comparative advantage. He notes that this theory enjoys a unique position in economics because all major economic thinkers support it. In reference to the theory, he (1969/1972, p. ii) notes, "To get Ricardo and Walras, John Stuart Mill and Pareto, Cairness and Jevons, Marshall and Viner, all to agree in this way is an achievement that is quite out of the ordinary." He then argues that this theory should be evaluated based on its assumptions, in particular that of factor immobility, which he contends does not hold. Emmanuel's argument is flawed both economically and epistemologically.

It is true that Ricardo built his comparative advantage model on his observation that capital and labor are immobile between countries; otherwise, he argued, both inputs would move to the country that has absolute advantage, which in his model is Portugal. He (1817/1996, p. 95) wrote,

> It would undoubtedly be advantageous to the capitalists of England, and to the consumers in both countries, that under such circumstances [factor mobility] the wine and the cloth should be made in Portugal, and therefore that the capital freely flowed toward those countries where it could be most profitably employed; there could be no difference in the rate of profit, and no other difference in the real or labor required to convey them to the various market where they were to be sold.

Emmanuel's argument was revived in 2004 when Chuck Schumer and Paul Craig Roberts raised the issue that the Ricardian model of comparative advantage is no longer a valid guide to international trade because in recent years significant offshore outsourcing has violated the assumption of factor immobility across countries.[49] The economic flaw in the Emmanuel–Schumer/Roberts argument is that for factor mobility to vitiate the theory of comparative advantage, the mobility must be, not haphazard and partial, but complete. In fact partial factor mobility across countries has always existed. As we saw in chapter one, the context of Adam Smith's invisible-hand passage (1776/1981, p. 456) involves an individual who is deciding whether to invest at home or abroad. Surely Ricardo was aware of the fact that both labor and capital were mobile in the early decades of the nineteenth century, but he also knew that the mobility was not perfect. In a critique of the Schumer/Roberts argument, Donald Boudreaux (2004, p. 376) points out that "If even a single person remains in a country … then this person will almost certainly enjoy a comparative advantage at producing some quantity of some good or service over the people" in other countries.[50] And if the entire population of a country moves to another country then the whole issue, Boudreaux (Ibid.) notes, "makes no more sense than lamenting the absence of comparative advantage and trade between Earth and Jupiter." Finally, Alan Deardorff's analysis of comparative advantage theory under numerous conditions and assumptions shows (2005, p. 1013) that the theory remains valid for trade in "services" as well as in "intermediate goods" just as it does for "final goods." Outsourcing of services is the reason behind the objection of people like Schumer and Roberts. We will return to Deardorff's contributions in the next section.

Epistemologically, Leamer (1994, p. 66) notes, "A model is a powerful device for organizing our thoughts; it is not literally true; indeed it derives its power from the very fact that it is not literally true." Leamer's description fits the Ricardian model perfectly, for the model is not literally true, but it helps us think clearly about trade relations among all countries, and demonstrates why free trade provides an opportunity for all countries to participate beneficially in the global economy.[51] The real question, as Milton Friedman (1953) persuasively argued, is not whether a scientific model rests on realistic assumptions, but, whether it has significant explanatory and predictive power. We will present the empirical works on comparative advantage in section six.

In a paper titled, "Deconstructing the Mythology of Free Trade: Critical Reflections on Comparative Advantage," Carmen Gonzalez (2006) opposes free trade. In the early part of the paper the author rightfully chastises the high-income countries for protecting their own agricultural sector while preaching to the low-income countries (which are also pressured by the World Bank and the IMF) to eliminate or reduce their protective measures. However, Gonzalez (2006, p. 69) errs when she argues that the theory of comparative advantage does not apply to low-income countries, and that these "countries must be permitted to utilize tariffs, subsidies and other forms of state intervention in order to promote those industries most likely to contribute to long-term national welfare." Such a policy recommendation, she notes (Ibid., pp. 78–79), rests on the influential and well-known writings of Raul Prebisch and Hans Singer, who shortly after the Second World War argued for protective measures in low-income countries.

But Gonzalez does not mention the fact that many countries in South and Central America, Africa, and Asia did follow the Prebisch–Singer recommendation and implemented inward-looking/import-substitution policies. These policies turned out to be generally unsuccessful because the industries that they spawned were shielded from global competition, and produced goods in which they had a comparative *dis*advantage. Besides, they had little incentive to improve efficiency and quality. The failure of these policies became apparent in the 1970s and 1980s. But consider countries such as Singapore, South Korea, Hong Kong, and Taiwan that adopted outward-looking/export-oriented policies which subjected domestic producers and manufacturers to the test of global markets. Such policies led to vibrant economies producing and exporting goods in which they have a comparative advantage.[52] These countries, which were considered poor or at best middle income in the 1960s or 1970s, now rank as high income.[53] Empirical works show that the economies that are more globally integrated tend to grow faster, reduce poverty further, and improve health and education more effectively.[54]

5. Extension and evolution of the Ricardian comparative advantage

The Ricardian model of comparative advantage – built with two countries, two goods, and one factor of production (labor) – is the simplest possible trade model. This raises a question: can this simple model offer insights into the working of international trade in the real world of multi-country, multi-commodity, and multi-factor? As noted above, J. S. Mill's intuition led him to an affirmative answer. But many trade theorists have delved into this question more deeply and their efforts have proven highly fruitful in shedding light on the intricacies of international trade. In fact, the path-dependency of economics in this context is quite palpable as Ricardo's comparative advantage model has spawned numerous theoretical and empirical works. Much of the theoretical research revolves around the generalization of comparative advantage (i.e., whether the Ricardian model survives under different circumstances) while the empirical investigations generally attempt to determine whether comparative advantage can explain the pattern of international trade.

As early as 1835, Mountifort Longfield extended the Ricardian comparative advantage to more than two goods.[55] He (1835/1971, p. 70) noted,

> Let us suppose the productiveness of English labor to be ten times as great as that of any other nation, in the production of tin, calico, coals, cutlery, and pottery. The wages of her laborers will, in consequence, be much greater than those in any other nation; suppose them eight times as great, and suppose that English labor is only twice as productive as foreign labor, in the manufacture of other commodities. These latter, therefore, will be fabricated in the rest of the world, at the fourth part of the price which it will cost to make them in England.

The theory of comparative advantage implies that, in Longfield's analysis, in industries where labor productivity is more than eight times, England has a comparative advantage and where it is less than eight times (but still more than the labor productivity abroad) England has a comparative disadvantage.[56], As we shall see in the next section, several studies have empirically analyzed this implication of the theory.

Another important contribution to the multi-commodity version of the Ricardian model was made in 1863 by the German economist Hans Karl Mangoldt, and introduced to the English-speaking economists in 1894 by Francis Edgeworth. In Mangoldt's model, the production costs of tradable goods in a representative country are arrayed in descending order. There is an intermediate good whose production cost is the same in the trading countries, and hence it does not get traded. In a typical trading country all goods whose production costs lie to the left of the intermediate good get imported and the rest exported. Mangoldt further argues that reciprocal demands play a crucial role in determining exports and imports. Indeed, a change in the reciprocal demand of either country might cause exports and imports switch places.[57]

Edgeworth (1894b, p. 633) elaborates on Mangoldt's work and argues that in a multi-commodity model

> it is not in general possible to determine *a priori*, from a mere observation of the costs of production in the respective countries before the opening of the trade, which commodities will be imported and which produced at home. 'Comparative cost' cannot be ascertained by simply comparing the costs of different articles in the two countries.

Indeed the *autarkic* cost of producing a good may be lower in country A than in country B but trade might reveal that A has a comparative *dis*advantage in the production of the good. Edgeworth (Ibid., p. 633) further notes that whether a good is imported or produced at home "depends not only on the costs of production in each country, but also on the law of demand in each country for the different commodities."

Edgeworth's contemporary influential economists, including Alfred Marshall (1842–1924), Vilfredo Pareto (1848–1923), Frank Tausig (1859–1940), and Eli Heckscher (1879–1952), made important contributions to trade theory in general.[58] Of the next generation, Jacob Viner (1892–1970), Frank Graham (1890–1949), and Gottfried Haberler (1900–1995) wrote extensively on the Ricardian model of comparative advantage. Viner elucidated the model in the context of its intellectual history, culminating in chapter eight of his book (1937), part of which we covered above. Similarly, we already presented Haberler's main contributions to the Ricardian comparative advantage. Here, we add that Haberler demonstrated how the theory of comparative advantage remains valid in the case of many commodities.[59] As for Graham (1948), he launched an attack on comparative advantage on the grounds that the implications of Ricardo–Mill trade models will not necessarily hold in higher dimensions. Graham's work led to important theoretical contributions in two papers by Lionel McKenzie (1954 and 1956) in which he showed that free trade remains optimal in Graham's multidimensional model. McKenzie's work in turn motivated a paper by Jones (1961) in which among other things, he investigated comparative advantage in a multi-country and multi-commodity model. In particular, Jones extended "McKenzie's contributions and developed the necessary and sufficient conditions for efficient multilateral specialization." He demonstrated that the minimization of unit labor input in the production process constitutes "efficient multilateral specialization." McKenzie and Jones solidified the validity of the Ricardian model in higher dimensions.[60]

Further theoretical works, however, have shown that in multi-dimensional models the straightforward comparative advantage results do not necessarily hold. For example, while the Ricardian model with two goods and one factor of production predicts the pattern of trade based on comparative advantage, James Melvin (1968) demonstrated that in a model with three goods and two factors of production the pattern of trade will be indeterminate. Similarly, mathematical analysis of Avinash Dixit and Victor Norman (1980, p. 95) led them to *reject* the hypothesis that "a country will export each good in which it has a comparative advantage." But Dixit and Norman's deeper and further analytical work rescued comparative advantage by showing that there exits "a *correlation* between comparative advantage and the pattern of trade" (1980, p. 95, emphasis in original). By "*correlation*" the authors mean "a country tends to import goods that are relatively more expensive there than in the rest of the world in autarky, and export goods that are relatively cheap at home in a no-trade equilibrium" (Ibid., p. 95). Since the results hold only on average, and not for every single good, Dixit and Norman describe this finding as "a very weak version of the comparative advantage hypothesis" (Ibid., p. 95).

Independently and simultaneously, Alan Deardorff (1980) reached the same conclusion as Dixit and Norman. In particular, he (1980, p. 942) found "a negative correlation between any country's relative autarky prices and its pattern of net exports" and that "on average, high autarky prices are associated with imports and low autarky prices are associated with exports." To Deardorff, his findings represent, "the validity of a weak form of the Law of Comparative Advantage" (Ibid., p. 941). The correlation concept, however, has bestowed substantial utility for analyzing the theory's robustness in various conditions. The rest of this section draws largely on Deardorff (2005) in which he presents a summary of his research on the validity of comparative advantage conducted over a quarter a century.[61]

Among many questions that Deardorff investigated is whether the theory of comparative advantage applies only to final goods. He (2005, p. 1012) finds that "the correlation result is proved for a formulation of technology that imposes no meaningful restriction in the use of goods as inputs to other goods. Thus all goods may be final goods, intermediate goods, or both." Moreover, as noted above, "the correlation result continues to hold" for "services" (Ibid., p. 1013). He also addresses the possibility that the productive factors may not be mobile within a country, and shows that "the comparative advantage correlations still go through." Further, comparative advantage remains valid "for all possible shapes of preferences" as well as for "dated" goods (regardless of when they are produced) and "differentiated" goods (Ibid., p. 1013).

Trade economists have argued that impediments such as tariffs and transportation costs can reduce or even eliminate trade. But such barriers do not invalidate the theory of comparative advantage just as preventing an object from falling does not vitiate the law of gravity. Similarly, a large enough subsidy, granted to an import-competing industry, could cause the industry to export its product despite its comparative disadvantage. But again the validity of the theory of comparative advantage remains intact just as throwing an object into the air leaves the law of gravity intact.[62]

So far, the theory of comparative advantage has survived under a number of circumstances. Two conditions, however, present difficulty for the theory, namely, "domestic distortions" and "increasing returns." A distortion "such as a negative externality from production, for example, if it occurs in an export sector," Deardorff (2005, p. 1014) points out, "may reverse the gains from trade." Since an externality such as pollution imposes a cost that is not reflected in the price, the export sector may produce units of output whose costs to society exceed their benefits. This means some resources in this sector would have created more value elsewhere in the economy. Globally, however, there may not be a net loss; for, "if the same distortion occurs in an import-competing sector," Deardorff (Ibid., p. 1014) points out, "it will increase the gains from trade. And since a given sector must exist as both export and import-competing in different countries, there may be no presumption that the existence of this distortion reduces the gains from trade worldwide."

Nevertheless, a distortion in the export sector poses a problem for the operation of comparative advantage. A solution to this problem was proposed by Bhagwati and Ramaswami (1963), who argued that if a distortion (such as pollution) is targeted directly and corrected with appropriate policy measures (e.g., a pollution tax), then free trade and comparative advantage will again maximize the value of the output and the gains from trade. But in the absence of an effective policy, Deardorff (2005, p. 1014) argues, "we must accept that domestic distortions interfere with the case for comparative advantage working its magic."

As noted above, one of the assumptions underlying the Ricardian model is constant returns to scale. This assumption implies that the unit cost of output remains constant as the output level changes whereas under increasing returns (economies of scale) the unit cost is inversely correlated with the level of output.[63] In the presence of *internal* increasing returns, a firm can gain market power and produce a socially suboptimal level of output. In this case, as Deardorff (2005, pp. 1013–1014) puts it, " … economies will fail to maximize the value of their output, perhaps with and without trade, and the arguments for comparative advantage do not go through … increasing returns are hard to reconcile with comparative advantage."[64]

Another issue concerns import-competing goods that are subject to increasing returns. In this case, the exporter must be further down on the average cost curve, enjoying a lower unit cost and higher labor productivity than the domestic producer of the good in the importing country. But the domestic producer has to match the lower price of the imported good to stay in the market. This in turn requires paying lower wages, which would make the importing country worse off. Thus the basic implication of comparative advantage that trade is mutually beneficial regardless of the trading countries' circumstances does not hold in this case.[65] Nevertheless, globally the net effect may be positive because the gains to the exporting economy might exceed the loss to the importing economy.[66] Regardless of this possibility, some scholars including J. S. Mill and Frank Graham have argued for temporary protection for industries that are subject to increasing returns.[67]

Despite the two cases of distortion and increasing returns, Deardorff (Ibid., p. 1014) notes, "the theory gives good reason to believe that comparative advantage works, on average, to provide the potential for gain from trade and to explain what the nature of beneficial trade is likely to be." Finally, Deardorff's voluminous writing on the theory of comparative advantage has led him to the following conclusion:

> Perhaps there is structure that we have not explored that will bias the net effects of all these complications in one direction or the other, either for or against trade. I don't know. My point here is just that the mere presence of frequent instances of distortion and increasing returns suggests only that we are ignorant, not necessarily that we are wrong. (Deardorff, 2005, p. 1014)

6. Empirical studies of the Ricardian comparative advantage

In a general and broad sense history has validated the theory of comparative advantage because international trade has never excluded a country from world markets. Such an historical approach, however, would not satisfy the scientific curiosity of most economists who depend on econometric methods for empirical analysis.

Of considerable relevance to this section is an argument put forth by Leamer and Levinsohn who (1995, p. 1342) note, "The proper function of empirical work is not to test the validity of the theory but to determine if the theory is working adequately in its limited domain." Hence we should discard a theory that fails to have sufficient explanatory power "in its limited domain." The empirical works on the Ricardian comparative advantage model seem to have followed the Leamer–Levinsohn dictum by aiming to find out if the theory adequately explains the reality of international trade. For example, in a pioneering study on comparative advantage, using 1937 data, G.D.A. MacDougall (1951, p. 697) remarks,

> According to that theory [of comparative costs], when based on a labour theory of value and assuming two countries, each will export those goods for which the ratio of its output per worker to that of the other exceeds the ratio of its money wag-rate to that of the other. Before the war, American weekly wages in manufacturing were roughly double the British, and we find that, where American output per worker was more than twice the British,

> the United States had in general the bulk of the export market, while for products where it was less than twice as high the bulk of the market was held by Britain.... Out of twenty-five products taken, twenty (covering 97% of the sample by value) obey the general rule, and two of the remaining five would cease to be exceptional if a different measure of output per worker were chosen.

The theory of comparative advantage implies a *positive* correlation between the ratio of U.S. to U.K. exports and the ratio of their labor productivities. MacDougall's finding supports the implication. Robert Stern (1962) and Bela Balassa (1963), respectively, using data in the years 1950 and 1951 confirmed the validity of the same implication. Stephen Golub and Chang-Tai Hsieh (2000) used a different method and like their predecessors, they, too, found substantial support for the theory of comparative advantage.

More recent noteworthy empirical works on the Ricardian model include Arnaud Costinot, Dave Donaldson, and Ivana Komunjer (2012) as well as Jonathan Eaton and Samuel Kortum (2012). In a sample of 21 countries and 13 manufacturing sectors using 1997 data, Costinot *et al.* (2012, p. 600) confirm the validity of an implication of the comparative advantage theory by finding that "relative exports levels across countries and industries ... are positively correlated with relative productivity levels across countries and industries." Eaton and Kortum (2012) use the Ricardian framework to estimate the gains from trade for 25 countries in 2006 and the percentage change in the gains since 1996. They (2012, p. 82) limit their work to manufacturing, and write,

> Clearly, gains from trade are substantial, particularly for small countries: for example over 25 percent of income for Denmark, Estonia, and Hungary. For the largest countries, Japan and the United States, gains from trade amounted to 2–3 percent of GDP 20 years ago. But those gains are now over 50 percent higher.

The works reviewed above may be labeled an "indirect approach" of the theory. In fact a "direct approach" of the Ricardian model (with complete specialization) seems impossible because it requires data on labor inputs in autarky. But such data do not exist since all countries engage in trade.[68] However, Daniel Bernhofen and John Brown (2004) found a case that allowed them to conduct a "direct test" of comparative advantage. In 1659 Japan adopted an isolationist policy, which lasted until 1858 when under American pressure the country opened up to the rest of the world. Peter Lindert and Jeffery Williamson (2003, p. 236) refer to Japan's transformation as:

> Probably the greatest nineteenth century "globalization shock".... Japan switched from virtual autarky to free trade in 1858. It is hard to imagine a more dramatic switch from closed to more open trade policy. In the

> fifteen years following 1858, Japan's foreign trade rose 70 times, from virtually nil to 7 percent of national income.

Daniel Bernhofen and John Brown (2004, p. 65) call this case of Japan a "natural historical experiment." They apply the correlation concept of comparative advantage as developed by Deardorff (1980) as well as by Dixit and Norman (1980). Bernhofen and Brown's findings correspond to the predictions of the comparative advantage theory. They (Ibid., p. 65) note, "The historical narrative demonstrates that the Japanese economy during the time period of our investigation was compatible with the assumptions of the underlying theory."

Finally, Costinot and Donaldson (2012) investigate Ricardo's prediction that relative factor productivity (denoted by *A*) determines comparative advantage, but they do so without comparing the relative productivity in a given country with that in other countries. Specifically, they (2012, p. 2) note:

> If two factors f_1 and f_2 located in country *c* are such that $A^{g2}{}_{cf2}/A^{g1}{}_{cf2} > A^{g2}{}_{cf1}/A^{g1}{}_{cf1}$ for two goods g_1 and g_2, then field f_2 has a comparative advantage in g_2. (Italics in original)

Note that Costinot and Donaldson determine comparative advantage of country *c* without knowing the corresponding productivity in the trading country. Their approach raises the same question we encountered when we presented Ricardo's model. What if the inequality (in the above quote) holds also in the trading country? If so, we seemingly arrive at the untenable conclusion that both countries have a comparative advantage in g_2! But in Costinot and Donaldson's formulation the inequality *cannot* hold in both countries because they use the actual trade data. As just noted, their approach is reminiscent of Ricardo's approach in that he determined the pattern of trade between England and Portugal from England's labor input alone (see section 3.1 above). Similarly, Costinot and Donaldson (2012) determine the comparative advantage of country *c* without comparing her productivity with that of a trading country.[69] Their sample includes "17 agricultural crops and 55 major agriculture-producing countries in 1989." The analysis of the sample produces "significant explanatory power in the data" in support of Ricardo's prediction (Ibid., p. 6).[70]

7. A final note

Let's ponder a counter-factual question: how would the world economy have looked if the theory of comparative advantage were not true? The answer is that the volume of global trade would have been substantially less than the current level because trade would have been based on absolute advantage, not comparative advantage, and consequently, the structure of world economy and even international relations would have been quite different from the present one. If the theory of comparative advantage were not true, poor and small countries would not have been able to participate in the world economy in any meaningful way since they generally have an absolute disadvantage in almost all goods. But thanks to the operation of comparative advantage, even the tiniest, poorest, and least well-endowed countries can beneficially and fully participate in global trade. The world economy is indeed shaped by the forces of comparative advantage.

Appendix I: a model of comparative advantage based on the writings of Adam Smith

In the opening chapter of the *Wealth of Nations*, Smith observes that the manufacturing sector enjoys a faster productivity growth than the agricultural sector because it is subject to deeper and finer division of labor. He (1776/1981, p. 16) writes, "The labour … which is necessary to produce any one complete manufacture, is almost always divided among a great number of hands.… The nature of agriculture, indeed, does not admit of so many subdivisions of labour, nor of so complete separation of one business from another, as manufactures." Smith further observes that rich countries enjoy superior productivity relative to poor countries in both manufacturing and agriculture. He writes that tracts of land in rich countries

> are in general better cultivated, and having more labour and expence bestowed upon them, produce more in proportion to the extent and natural fertility of the ground. But this superiority of produce is seldom much more than in proportion to the superiority of labour and expence. In agriculture, the labour of the rich country is not always much more productive than that of the poor; or, at least, it is never so much more productive, as it commonly is in manufactures. (1776/1981, p. 16)

Smith's argument implies that if the rich country's productivity exceeds the poor country's productivity in manufacturing by the factor α and in agriculture by the factor β, then, $\alpha > \beta$.[71] This implication helps us demonstrate how Smith's observation and analysis led to his insight into comparative advantage. By drawing on Smith's writings, the following model presents a rational reconstruction of Smith's thought process on comparative advantage. The notations are common in international trader literature.

Rich country = Home country
Poor country = Foreign country, denoted by an "*"
a_i = Required labor to produce a unit of good i where i denotes manufactures (M) or agriculture (A)
$1/a_i$ = Units of good i that one unit of labor can produce; i.e., labor productivity

The relationship between the two countries' productivities can be expressed as follows:

$$1/a_M = \alpha(1/a_M^*) \text{ or } a_M^* = \alpha\, a_M \quad (1)$$

$$1/a_A = \beta(1/a_A^*) \text{ or } a_A^* = \beta\, a_A. \quad (2)$$

Smith observes that division of labor increases productivity and improves the living standards of all groups of people. He (Ibid., p. 22) argues, "It is the great multiplication of the productions of all the different arts, in consequence of the division of labour, which occasions, in a well-governed society, that universal opulence which extends itself to the lowest ranks of the society." Moreover, "In consequence of better machinery, greater dexterity, and of a more proper division and distribution of work … a smaller quantity of labour becomes requisite for executing any particular piece of work; and … the real price of labour should rise considerably" (Ibid., p. 260).[72] These passages imply that in the rich country where labor productivity is higher than in the poor country, the wage rate (w) is also higher; that is, $w > w^*$. Labor mobility within each country ensures that in the rich country both industries pay workers the same wage w, and in the poor country w^*. Suppose w exceeds w* by the factor γ such that

$$w = \gamma\, w^*. \quad (3)$$

How is the value of γ determined? The positive correlation between wages and labor productivity implies that if both countries produced only manufactured goods (or only agricultural goods), γ would be equal to α (or β), as defined above. But since both countries produce both types of goods, the value of γ must lie somewhere between α and β depending on the relative shares of manufacturing and agricultural output in the economy.[73] Thus

$$\alpha > \gamma > \beta. \quad (4)$$

Equations (1)–(4) help us discern the emergence of comparative advantage from Smith's further analysis. He (Ibid., p. 16) observes, "though the poor country, notwithstanding the inferiority of its cultivation, can, in some measure, rival the rich in the cheapness and goodness of its corn, it can pretend to no such competition in its manufactures; at least if those manufactures suit the soil, climate, and situation of the rich country." Thus the rich country, which has an absolute advantage over the poor country, cannot produce both manufactures and corn at lower costs than the poor country. To demonstrate the validity of Smith's argument, using the above model, let c_M denote the unit production costs in manufacturing and c_A denote the unit production costs in agriculture. The unit costs are:[74]

$$c_M = wa_M\,;\; c_A = wa_A \quad (5)$$

and

$$c_M^* = w^*a_M^*;\; c_A^* = w^*a_A^*. \quad (6)$$

If we incorporate equation (3) into equation (5), we obtain

$$c_M = \gamma w^* a_M \, ; \, c_A = \gamma w^* a_A. \tag{7}$$

If we incorporate equations (1) and (2) into equation (6), we obtain

$$c_M^* = \alpha w^* a_M \, ; \, c_A^* = \beta w^* a_A. \tag{8}$$

Since $\beta < \gamma < \alpha$, it follows that $c_M < c_M^*$ and $c_A^* < c_A$; that is, the manufactured good is produced more cheaply in the rich country and the agricultural good in the poor country even though the rich country is more efficient in agriculture. Given that Smith presents this analysis in the early part of the *Wealth of Nations*, wherever in the rest of book he says the price of a good is lower in a foreign country, the lower price might well have resulted from the operation of, not absolute, but comparative advantage. Consider the statement we quoted above: "If a foreign country can supply us with a commodity cheaper than we ourselves can make it, better buy it of them with some part of the produce of our own industry employed in a way in which we have some advantage" (Ibid., p. 457). In light of the analysis and the model presented above, the "foreign country" in Smith's statement, just like the poor country in the model, might well have an absolute disadvantage in the production of the "commodity" but she can produce it at a lower cost because of her comparative advantage. The rest of the statement advances a case for free trade, which can be read in light of comparative advantage:

> The general industry of the country, being always in proportion to the capital which employs it, will not thereby be diminished, no more than that of the above-mentioned artificers; but only left to find out the way in which it can be employed with the greatest advantage. It is certainly not employed to the greatest advantage when it is thus directed towards an object which it can buy cheaper than it can make. The value of its annual produce is certainly more or less diminished when it is thus turned away from producing commodities evidently of more value than the commodity which it is directed to produce. According to the supposition, that commodity could be purchased from foreign countries cheaper than it can be made at home. It could, therefore, have been purchased with a part only of the commodities, or, what is the same thing, with a part only of the price of the commodities, which the industry employed by an equal capital would have produced at home, had it been left to follow its natural course. (Ibid., p. 457)

Smith's insight imparts a central message of the theory of comparative advantage: more productive countries cannot outcompete less productive countries in all commodities and thus do not drive them out of world markets; nor can low-wage countries outcompete high-wage countries in all goods in the global economy. This message, however, became fundamental in trade theory only after Ricardo presented his comparative advantage model.[75]

Appendix II: how comparative costs ratios set limits on wages

Haberler (1930/1985) develops a numerical model, which I will adapt to Ricardo's example of "two men" in his footnote introduced above. Recall that Ricardo (1817/1996, p. 95) writes, "Two men can both make shoes and hats, and one is superior to the other in both employments; but in making hats he can exceed his competitor by one-fifth or 20 percent, and in making shoes he can excel him by one-third or 33 percent." Suppose the "two men" are Pedro and Edward. Pedro has an absolute advantage, and his monthly wage rate is, say, $1000 and Edwards's $800. Labor wages are the only production costs. This example can be summarized in the following table, which also includes the productivity values from Table 2.2 in section 3.1 above:

Monthly Output and Wages

	Hat (H)	*Shoes (S)*	*Wages*	*Unit Cost/H*	*Unit Cost/S*
Edward	100	100	$800.00	$8.00	$8.00
Pedro	120	133	$1000.00	$8.33	$7.52

Since Pedro's superiority is greater in making shoes than in making hats he has a comparative advantage in shoes. And since Edward's inferiority is less in making hats than in making shoes, he has a comparative advantage in making hats. For Edward and Pedro to specialize, if the monthly wage of Pedro is $1000.00, then Edward's wage must exceed $750 but not $830, because if it is less than $750 (or more than $830), then he will produce both goods at lower (higher) costs than Pedro. Similarly, if Edward's wage is $800, then Pedro's wage must remain between $960 and $1060.40. If the wages are not in the range noted above, they will adjust so that each person will produce only the good in which he has a comparative advantage. The exact value of wages depends on the reciprocal demands of the two countries for each other goods.

Appendix III: Mountifort Longfield's generalization of the Ricardian model

Suppose the home country (England) and foreign country (the rest of the world, denoted by an asterisk) can potentially produce n tradable goods. Consider the following standard notations in international trade literature:

a_i = the amount of labor needed to produce a unit of good i in the home country

a_i^* = the amount of labor needed to produce a unit of good i in the foreign country

w and w* = the wage rate in the home and foreign country

wa_i = the unit cost of good i in the home country
$w^*a_i^*$ = the unit cost of good i in the foreign country.

Since a_i and a_i^* are the inverse of labor productivity, if $a_i < a_i^*$ the home country is more efficient than the foreign country in the production of good i. Longfield assumes that the home country has an absolute advantage; that is she has superior labor productivity in all goods. He further assumes that the home country *on average* is eight times (for the sake of generality, let's say, γ times) as productive as the foreign country. This means the wage rate in the home country is γ times the wage rate in the foreign country. Thus,

$$w = \gamma w^*. \tag{1}$$

There are three possibilities regarding the representative good i. The first one is that the home country is exactly γ times more efficient in the production of good i than the foreign country. That is,

$$\gamma a_i = a_i^*. \tag{2}$$

Multiplying equation (2) by equation (1) results in

$$a_i w = a_i^* w^*. \tag{3}$$

According to equation (3), since the home country's productivity advantage is offset by her wage rate being γ times higher, the unit production cost of good i is the same in both countries. Hence, good i will not be traded.

The second possibility is that the home country's productivity advantage for good i is larger than γ times; that is,

$$\gamma a_i < a_i^*. \tag{4}$$

Multiplying equation (4) by equation (1) results in

$$a_i w < a_i^* w^*. \tag{5}$$

This means the production cost of good i is lower at home and hence the home country will export good i. Finally, if $\gamma a_i > a_i^*$, then $a_i w > a_i^* w^*$ and the home country will import good i.

Longfield's analysis embodies what later was termed "the chain of comparative advantage," which can be explained as follows. Suppose in the home country we array all goods from the highest labor productivity to the lowest, and for one good (good i) in this chain the first possibility holds; that is, $a_i w = a_i^* w^*$. Hence good i is not traded, but all goods to the left of i are exported (because the home country can produce them at a lower cost) and all to the right of i are imported.

Appendix IV: Haberler's multi-goods case of comparative advantage

Harberler (1930/1985, p. 11, italics in original) makes the following general statement: "*Country I possesses a comparative advantage as against country II in all export goods compared with all import goods* (the same holds, of course, *vice versa* for country II)." He then proceeds to demonstrate a chain of comparative advantage as follows. Suppose the two countries (I and II) produce goods A, B, C, ... Further, suppose:

a_j = work days necessary to produce a unit of A in country j
where j = I, II (1)
p_{aj} = price of good A in country j (2)
w_j = money wages in country j. (3)

Thus,

$$p_{aj} = a_j w_j \quad (4)$$

r = the number of currency units of country II that a unit of the currency of country I can purchase.

Haberler then notes that the necessary condition for country I to export A is that $p_{a1} < p_{a2}$, meaning the autarky price of A in country I must be lower than in country II. Equation (4) shows this condition is the same as $a_1 w_1 r < a_2 w_2$, or

$$a_1/a_2 < w_2/w_1 r. \quad (5)$$

For country I to import B, the inequality $p_{b2} < p_{b1}$ must hold, that is $b_2 w_2 < b_1 w_1 r$ or

$$b_1/b_2 > w_2/w_1 r. \quad (6)$$

The two inequalities (5) and (6) imply

$$a_1/a_2 < b_1/b_2. \quad (7)$$

The inequality (7) means country I has a comparative advantage in A and II has a comparative advantage in B. The inequality can be extended to all traded goods:

$$a_1/a_2 < b_1/b_2 < c_1/c_2 < d_1/d_2 < e_1/e_2 < f_1/f_2 < g_1/g_2 < h_1/h_2 < i_1/i_2 \ldots \quad (8)$$

In this chain, the location of the wage ratio $w_2/w_1 r$ will determine exports and imports. Haberler (1930/1985, p. 11) notes if the wage ratio "is located between E and F," then "goods A to E are exported and the rest imported." Haberler's analysis implies that any disequilibrium in the balance of payments would trigger movements in the wage rates and in the exchange rates. Such movements would relocate the wage ratio in the chain, alter the pattern of trade, and eventually restore equilibrium.

Notes

1 An industry or a business can acquire a comparative advantage by raising productivity, lowering wages, or receiving a government subsidy.
2 There are a few exceptions to this general implication in that free trade may not maximize the value of output and a trading country may lose from trade. We shall discuss these few cases later.
3 Ancient empires such as the Persian, Greek, and Roman as well as relatively more recent empires of Islam and Mongol generally instituted a market economy which allowed for free movement of people, goods, and ideas within their territories. For example, Ronald Findlay and Kevin O'Rourke (2007, p. 61) note that within the Islamic territories during the few centuries following the advent of the religion in the seventh century, there existed "apparently no restrictions at all on the free flow of people, ideas, techniques, fashions, goods, and capital … in spite of the frequent political conflicts and warfare between individual Muslim states."
4 For the views of these philosophers on foreign trade, see Douglas Irwin (1996, chapter one).
5 These figures are from Ronald Findlay and Kevin O'Rourke (2007, pp. 203 and 282).
6 Angus Maddison (2001, pp. 231 and 164).
7 Mun wrote *England's Treasure by Forraign Trade* in 1630 but it was published posthumously by his son in 1664.
8 See Irwin (1996, p. 27).
9 For a concise summary of Mercantilist thought, see Laura Lahaye (2008).
10 See Viner (1937/1975, p. 55).
11 For detailed analysis of the views of all four thinkers that Hont mentions (to which one may add Dudley North and Josiah Tucker), see Irwin (1996), Andrea Maneschi (1998), Leonard Gomes (2003), and Istvan Hont (2005).
12 The tract was published anonymously. But C. MacLeod (1983) has shown Martyn was the author. It is unclear whether the last name of the tract's author is spelled "Martyn" or "Martin." Here, I use the more common "Martyn."
13 Jorge Morales Meoqui (2011, p. 745) has argued that this rule should be renamed "the classical rule for specialization" because it guided the thinking of all classical economists on foreign trade and comparative advantage.
14 The language here might be confusing. By "less cost" Viner means the imported commodity could be produced with fewer resources at home. He employs the same vocabulary that Ricardo and his contemporary economists used to explain comparative advantage. They measured cost, not by the monetary expenses on resources used in the production process, but by the amount of resources which went into the production of the good; they called this "real cost." Thus a country that has an absolute advantage produces everything at lower *real* cost. However, in world markets her goods in which she has a comparative disadvantage will be priced higher than those of the same goods offered by other countries.
15 Despite his brilliant mind, Martyn was not immune from national prejudice. He vehemently opposed free trade with France (see Gomes, 2003, p. 23).
16 Eugene Rotwein (1955) has collected all of Hume's writings on economics in one volume, which the present chapter uses as the source for exploring Hume's views on mercantilism.
17 This essay was published in 1752. But Hume had already laid out the operation of the specie-flow mechanism in a letter to Montesquieu in 1749. For details concerning Hume's correspondence with Montesquieu, see chapter four of the present book.

18 This argument is the essence of the quantity theory of money. For detailed analysis, see chapter four of the present book.

19 Mokyr (2009, p. 20) notes, "The British tariff on French wine finalized in 1713 made wine so expensive that Britain became a nation of ale and whisky drinkers, with French wines (known as clarets) confined largely to the privileged few."

20 Although in a series of essays Hume extolled the virtues of foreign trade, in "Of the Balance of Trade" he wrote, "All taxes, however, upon foreign commodities, are not to be regarded as prejudicial or useless.... A tax on German linen encourages home manufactures, and thereby multiplies our people and industry. A tax on brandy increases the sale of rum, and supports our southern colonies" (1752b/1955, p. 76). However, Eugene Rotwein (1955), the editor of Hume's *Writings on Economics*, rightly points out that "this appears to be his [Hume's] only major concession to the case of tariff-protection. It is pointedly repudiated in" Hume's 1758 essay "Of the Jealousy of Trade."

21 This argument did not originate with Smith. Henry Martyn in *Considerations upon the East India Trade* (1701, p. 73) had made an almost identical observation. Martyn wrote, "a king of India is not so well lodg'd and cloathed as Day Labourer of England."

22 The first Navigation Act of 1651 "stipulated that all goods imported into England or her territories had to be carried in English ships, unless they were carried directly from a European country of origin on ships owned and crewed by citizens of that country of origin, and that no foreign vessels could engage in the coastal trade among English port. Furthermore, no type of slated fish or fishing by-product of the type usually caught and processed by English people could be imported unless it was caught and processed by an English ship" (Laura Lahaye, 2008, p. 568).

23 Examples include Hla Myint (1977), E.G. West (1978), Kurz (1992), and Robert Blecker (1997). Bruce Elmslie (1994) supplies references to several authors who prior to Bloomfield leveled the same criticism against Smith.

24 See also Elmslie and James (1993).

25 For further analysis, see Rassekh (2015) and Appendix I.

26 See Maddison (2007, p. 81).

27 Maddison (1995) also identifies 1820 as the beginning of modern globalization era. On the history of globalization, see also Gary Gereffi (2005).

28 See O'Rourke and Williamson (1999, p. 33).

29 They include, but are not limited to, James Mill (1808/1997 and 1821/1965), Robert Torrens (1808/2000 and 1815/1827), David Ricardo (1817/1996), and Mountiford Longfield (1835/1971).

30 The dispute over priority on the discovery of comparative advantage has been covered in numerous publications for over a century. For the most recent analysis, see Ruffin (2002, 2005) and Morales Meoqui (2012b). Ruffin is quite convincing that Ricardo is the true discoverer of the theory of comparative advantage. Morales Meoqui (2012b), while quoting Francis Darwin, who observed, "In science the credit goes to the man who convinces the world, not to the man to whom the idea first occurs," argues that Ricardo was the first economist who convinced the world of the validity of comparative advantage. Here there is a parallel between Ricardo's theory of comparative advantage and Charles Darwin's theory of evolution: both ideas had already (and simultaneously) occurred to more than one thinker in their respective fields but credit goes to Ricardo and Darwin for the discoveries because only after they published their work did the ideas influence the thinking of their fellow scholars.

31 This assumes Ricardo's model operates on constant returns to scale, which is a common assumption in the literature. For example, Edward Leamer (1994, p. 69) says Ricardo's model "includes two countries (England and Portugal), two goods (cloth and wine), a single input (labour) and constant ratios of output to input."

32 See also Piero Sraffa (1930). Ruffin (2002, pp. 742–743) points out that "John Stuart Mill was responsible for the rational reconstruction of Ricardo in which the labor cost coefficients were interpreted as the amounts used in a unit of each good produced

rather than Ricardo's labor cost of producing the amounts contained in a typical trading bundle."

33 Maneschi (2008) shows how Ricardo, if he were alive, would have taught the theory of comparative advantage.

34 The 1930 paper was published in German and translated into English in 1985. However, Haberler presented virtually all the arguments in the paper in his other writings, especially in his book (1936).

35 The reason is that if $(w^E/w^P) > (90/100)$, then the cost of English cloth $(100 \times w^E)$ will exceed the cost of Portuguese cloth $(90 \times w^P)$. Moreover, if $(w^E/w^P) > (80/120)$, the cost of English wine $(120 \times w^E)$ will exceed the cost of Portuguese wine $(80 \times w^P)$.

36 Section 4 below, based on Haberler (1930/1985), shows how the same argument applies when there are more than two goods.

37 In contrast to Ricardo, the Heckscher–Ohin (H-O) model of international trade is primarily concerned with the source of comparative advantage, attributed to resource endowments. In the H-O model, the trading countries employ the same technology in the production of goods. In the hands of many trade theorists (above all Paul Samuelson) this model has become one of the most celebrated achievements in all of economics. For a summary of the H-O model and its theorems, see Ron Jones (2008).

38 The following draws on Rassekh (2015). I am grateful to the editors of *History of Economic Ideas* for their permission to use my paper in this chapter.

39 Wilfredo Pareto (1906/1971), however, argued that complete specialization does not necessarily increase the total output as compared with partial or no specialization. Since Pareto's arguments have been thoroughly covered and dealt with in the literature, here I only refer the interested readers to Gottfried Haberler (1930/1985), John Chipman (1965), Leonard Gomes (1990), and Andrea Maneschi (1998). Pareto contributed to the theory of comparative advantage by reformulating it in terms of utility, marginal utility, and opportunity cost.

40 Joseph Schumpeter (1954/1994, pp. 472–473) has criticized Ricardo's method which involves making simplified assumptions that inevitably lead to the desired conclusion. He derisively called it "The Ricardian Vice." Notwithstanding Schumpeter's criticism, the Ricardian model and method impart a profound insight.

41 Mill (1821/1844, p. 122) presented a second numerical example that further clarifies why it is comparative rather than absolute advantage that matters in trade. A pamphlet by an anonymous author was published in 1818, which includes a model similar to Mill's second example although it appears that the author was not familiar with the work of Ricardo, Mill, Torrens, and others. Alan Plant (1933) reprinted the pamphlet and argued that it contains a statement on comparative advantage. But Viner (1937/1975, p. 482) dismissed the statement as a "fallacy." The statement comes close to articulating the theory of comparative advantage but falls short.

42 Mill's argument that comparative advantage holds in higher dimensions was likely influenced by Ricardo's England–Portugal model. As Ruffin (2002, p. 742) points out, Ricardo's analysis can be extended to any "number of goods and countries.… For example, if cloth, corn, and wine trade on the world market at the ratios X:Y:Z, then any single country, among possibly many countries, will devote its resources to the good requiring the least amount of labor to produce X cloth, Y corn, or Z wine."

43 Alfred Marshall (1842–1924) presents this analysis by a geometrical device, known as the offer curves. For an early explication of the offer curves, see Francis Edgeworth (1894a).

44 See Gomes (1990, p. 30).

45 Robert Torrens had realized the possibility that a tariff could be beneficial to an importing country at the expense of the exporting country, but (just as for the theory of comparative advantage) he failed to articulate the intricacies of how it might happen. On this point, see Irwin (1996, pp. 101–115).

46 The optimum tariff theory maintains that a large country by imposing a certain tariff rate can improve her terms of trade and maximize her gains at the expense of the small

country. Mathematically, the optimum tariff rate is the inverse of the elasticity of the foreign export supply curve. On this point, see Ethier (1995, p. 222).

47 There are of course other reasons to support free trade. Consider the free-trade arguments of Adam Smith and David Hume, presented above. Alfred Marshall supported free trade "mainly on the account of political corruption involved in tariff lobbying in a democratic society and consideration of the interests of the agricultural classes" (Gomes, 2003, p. 105).

48 Irwin (1996, part 2) and Maneschi (1998, chapter 5) present the influential theories that oppose free trade. For recent papers challenging the validity of comparative advantage, see John Duffield (2010), Ian Fletcher (2010), and Reinhard Schumacher (2013). An earlier online version of Schumacher's paper garnered several responses. As an example, see Morales Meoqui (2012a). John Pullen (2006) denies altogether that Ricardo proposed a theory of comparative advantage.

49 Offshore-outsourcing from the U.S. is documented in Alan Blinder (2006) and Greg Mankiw and Philip Swagel (2006).

50 Mankiw and Swagel (2006) have argued that economically there is no meaningful distinction between trade via ships or planes and trade via phone lines or the Internet. Both are driven by comparative advantage. See also Bhagwati *et al.* (2004) as well as Bhagwati and Blinder (2009).

51 George Box's and Norman Draper's (1987, p. 424) dictum that "all models are wrong, but some are useful" places Ricardo's model in the category of useful models.

52 This issue has been extensively explored in the literature. As an example, see Jagdish Bhagwati (2004) who explains clearly the difference between the two types of policies and their consequences.

53 The GDP per capita of these countries in 2008 based on purchasing power parity were: South Korea, $28,120; Singapore, $47,940; Taiwan, $35,800; and Hong Kong, $43,960. In comparison, the GDP per capita of the U.S.A. in 2008 was $46,970. The data are from World Bank's *World Development Report 2010*.

54 See Rassekh (2014) and Rassekh and John Speir (2009) for detailed analysis and evidence.

55 The case of multi-commodity trade is more important and more complicated than the case of multi-country trade because in a multi-country setting we can always focus on (say) the home country and regard the rest of the world as the trading partner.

56 I have demonstrated Longfield's analysis algebraically in Appendix III.

57 On Mangoldt, I have drawn on Gomes (1990, pp. 22–25). Viner (1937/1975, pp. 458–562) and Maneschi (1998, pp. 134–135) have also covered Mangoldt.

58 See Leonard Gomes (1990) for the coverage of the contributions of these and other neoclassical scholars to international economics.

59 Appendix IV presents Haberler's demonstration of comparative advantage in the multi-good case.

60 Frank Graham (1948) argued that in a multi-commodity case demand is not as important as supply in the determination of the terms of trade. Maneschi (1998, p. 133) has commented on Graham's argument, "While it is true that in a multicommodity model a given commodity may be produced by both trading countries, and that a shift in demand may cause a quantity adjustment rather than a change in prices, it is demand factors which initially determine the borderline commodity."

61 All of Deardorff's papers on comparative advantage (along with his papers in other areas) are compiled in Stern (2011).

62 Deardorff (1980) has shown that tariffs and transport costs cannot reverse the trade flow while a subsidy can.

63 Economics literature distinguishes between external increasing returns and internal increasing returns. External increasing returns refer to falling average costs in each firm within an industry when the industry expands its output, a possibility that is compatible with competitive markets. Internal increasing returns refer to falling average costs when

a firm within an industry expands its output, a possibility that is not compatible with competitive markets and poses a problem for the operation of comparative advantage. For a detailed discussion on internal and external returns to scale as well as when the returns are national versus when they are international, see Ethier (1995, chapter 2).

64 As most textbooks in international trade explain, increasing returns could well serve as a basis for trade. John Stuart Mill (1848/2006, pp. 918–919) put it this way: "The superiority of one country over another in a branch of production, often arises only from having begun it sooner. There may be no inherent advantage on one part, or disadvantage on the other, but only a present superiority of acquired skill and experience. A country which has this skill and experience yet to acquire, may in other respects be better adapted to the production than those which were earlier in the field..." Here, unlike the Ricardian model, the pattern of trade is indeterminate.

65 See Ethier (1995, p. 56).

66 See Maneschi (1998, p. 206).

67 See Irwin (1996, chapter nine). The literature on increasing returns in international trade is quite vast. The interested reader may consult Krugman (2009).

68 On this point, see Deardorff (1984, p. 470).

69 In an email communication on March 26, 2013, Donaldson in response to a question of mine explained why their approach is legitimate: "The reason is that the inequality is written taken prices as given. In a deeper analysis (like in traditional Ricardian 2x2 theory) the world price would be endogenous and then (if there were two countries and 2 crops ... and one country = one field) then it would be impossible to have both countries have a CA in the same good."

70 Since this chapter focuses on the Ricardian comparative advantage, we do not review the Heckscher–Ohlin model. For a survey of empirical studies on the H-O model, see Deardorff (1984) and Levisohn and Leamer (1995).

71 As an example, if $\alpha = 3$ and $\beta = 2$, the productivity of workers in the rich country's manufacturing is three times the productivity of workers in the poor country's manufacturing while in agriculture it is twice as much.

72 Although these passages indicate that wages depend on productivity, Smith did not think that wages rise by the same percentage increase in productivity. In the *Early Draft* of the *Wealth of Nations*, he calculated that an artisan who makes 2000 pins a day is paid 15 pence, and if he doubles his output to 4000 pins, his wages rise by only one-third to 20 pence (Smith, 1982, p. 566).

73 The exact values of the shares are immaterial as they may assume different values in the two countries, and the values certainly change after trade. What matters is that before trade both countries produce both goods.

74 In this model the unit cost is equal to the marginal cost.

75 Another thinker who understood the operation of comparative advantage in international trade is Josiah Tucker (1713–1779), who famously engaged David Ricardo on the "rich country–poor country" debate. For an analysis of this debate, see Bruce Elmslie (1995) and Istvan Hont (2005, chapter three). Maneschi (1998) provides certain passages from Tucker's writings related to the debate, which demonstrates he "had more than an inkling of the sources of comparative advantage, its shift over time, and the close relationship between trade and economic development" (p. 31).

Bibliography

Acemoglu, Daron and James Robinson (2012), *Why Nations Fail*, New York, NY: Crown Business.

Aldridge, John (2004), "The Discovery of Comparative Advantage," *Journal of History of Economic Thought* 26, 3, pp. 379–399.

Allen, William R. (1987), "Mercantilism," in *The New Palgrave Dictionary of Economics*, Volume 3, Ed. by John Eatwell, Murray Milgate, and Peter Newman, London: The Macmillan Press Limited, pp. 445–449.

Balassa, Bela (1963), "An Empirical Demonstration of Classical Cost Theory," *Review of Economics and Statistics* 4, pp. 231–238.

Barzun, Jacques (1981), "Politics and Society," in *The Columbia History of the World*, Ed. by John A. Garraty and Peter Gay, New York, NY: Harper and Row, Dorest Press, pp. 692–707.

Bernhofen, Daniel and John Brown (2004), "A Direct Test of the Theory of Comparative Advantage: The Case of Japan," *Journal of Political Economy* 112, 1, pp. 48–67.

Bhagwati, Jagdish (2004), *In Defense of Globalization*, Oxford, UK: Oxford University Press.

Bhagwati, Jagdish and Alan S. Blinder (2009), *Offshoring of American Jobs: What Response from U.S. Economic Policy?* Cambridge, MA: The MIT Press.

Bhagwati, Jagdish, Arvind Panagariya, and T.N. Srinivasan (2004), "The Muddles over Outsourcing," *Journal of Economic Perspectives* 18, 4, pp. 93–114.

Bhagwati, Jagdish and V. K. Ramaswami (1963), Domestic Distortions, Tariffs, and the Theory of Optimum Subsidy," *Journal of Political Economy* 71, 1, February, pp. 44–50.

Blecker, Robert (1997), "The 'Unnatural and Retrograde Order': Adam Smith's Theories of Trade and Development Reconsidered," *Economica* 64, pp. 527–537.

Blinder, Alan S. (2006), "Offshoring: The Next Industrial Revolution?" *Foreign Affairs* 85, 2, pp. 113–128.

Bloomfield, Arthur I. (1975/1994), "Adam Smith and the Theory of International Trade," in *Essays in the History of International Trade Theory*, Ed. by Arthur Bloomfield, Cheltenham, UK and Northampton, MA: Edward Elgar, pp. 109–144.

Boudreaux, Donald (2004), "Does Increased International Mobility of Factors of Production Weaken the Case for Free Trade?" *Cato Journal* 23, 3, pp. 373–379.

Box, George E.P. and Norman R. Draper (1987), *Empirical Model Building and Response Surfaces*, New York, NY: Wiley.

Chipman, John (1965), "A Survey of International Trade: Part I, The Classical Theory," *Econometrica* 33, 3, pp. 477–519.

Costinot, Arnaud and Dave Donaldson (2012), "Ricardo's Theory of Comparative Advantage: Old Idea, New Evidence," *The American Economic Review, Papers and Proceedings* 102, 2, pp. 1–6.

Costinot, Arnaud, Dave Donaldson, and Ivana Komunjer (2012), "What Goods Do Countries Trade? A Quantitative Exploration of Ricardo's Ideas," *Review of Economic Studies* 79, pp. 581–608.

Deardorff, Alan V. (1980), "The General Validity of the Law of Comparative Advantage," *Journal of Political Economy* 88, 51, pp. 941–957, Reprinted in Stern (2011), pp. 74–90.

Deardorff, Alan V. (1984), "Testing Trade Theories and Predicting Trade Flows," in *Handbook of International Economics*, Ed. by Ronald Jones and Peter Kenen, Amsterdam, NED: Elsevier Science Publishers, pp. 467–517.

Deardorff, Alan V. (2005), "How Robust Is Comparative Advantage?" *Review of International Economics* 13, 5, pp. 1004–1016, Reprinted in Stern (2011), pp. 183–196.

Dixit, Avinash and Victor Norman (1980), *Theory of International Trade*, Cambridge, UK: Cambridge University Press.

Duffield, John (2010), "Ricardian 'Comparative Advantage' is Illusory," *Real-World Economics Review* 54, pp. 62–78.

Eaton, Jonathan and Samuel Kortum (2012), "Putting Ricardo to Work," *Journal of Economic Perspectives* 26, 2, pp. 65–90.

Edgeworth, Francis (1894a), "Theory of International Values," *The Economic Journal* 4, 15, September, pp. 424–443.

Edgeworth, Francis (1894b), "Theory of International Values," *The Economic Journal* 4, 16, December, pp. 606–638.

Elmslie, Bruce (1994), "Positive Feedback Mechanism in Adam Smith's Theories of International Trade," *The European Journal of the History of Economic Thought* 1, 2, Spring, pp. 253–271.

Elmslie, Bruce Truitt (1995), "Retrospective: The Convergence Debate between David Hume and Josiah Tucker," *Journal of Economic Perspectives* 9, 4, pp. 207–216.

Elmslie, Bruce and Antoinette James (1993), "The Renaissance of Adam Smith in Modern Theories of International Trade," in *Perspectives on the History of Economic Thought*, Volume IX, Ed. by Robert F. Hebert, Published for the History of Economic Society by Edward Elgar.

Emmanuel, Arghiri (1969/1972), *Unequal Exchange*, Translated from French by Brian Pearce, New York, NY and London, UK: Monthly Review Press.

Ethier, Wilfred (1995), *Modern International Economics*, 3rd edition, New York, NY: W.W. Norton and Company.

Findlay, Ronald and Kevin O'Rourke (2007), *Power and Plenty: Trade, War, and the World Economy in the Second Millennium*, Princeton, NJ and Oxford, UK: Princeton University Press.

Fletcher, Ian (2010), "Dubious Assumptions of the Theory of Comparative Advantage," *Real-world Economics Review* 54, pp. 94–105.

Friedman, Milton (1953), "Methodology of Positive Economics," in *Essay in Positive Economics*, Chicago, IL: University of Chicago Press, pp. 3–43.

Gereffi, Gary (2005), "The Global Economy: Organization, Governance, and Development," in *The Handbook of Sociology*, 2nd edition, Ed. by Neil J. Smeler and Richard Swenberg, Princeton, NJ: Princeton University Press, pp. 160–182.

Golub, Stephen and Chang-Tai Hsieh (2000), "Classical Theory of Comparative Advantage Revisited," *Review of International Economics* 8, pp. 221–234.

Gomes, Leonard (1990), *Neoclassical International Economics: An Historical Survey*, New York, NY: St. Martin Press.

Gomes, Leonard (2003), *The Economics and Ideology of Free Trade: A Historical Review*, Cheltenham, UK and Northampton, MA: Edward Elgar.

Gonzalez, Carmen (2006), "Deconstructing the Mythology of Free Trade: Critical Reflections on Comparative Advantage," *Berkeley La Raza Law Journal* 65, pp. 65–93.

Gordon, Barry (1975), *Economic Analysis before Adam Smith: Hesiod to Lessius*, New York, NY: Barnes and Noble Books.

Graham, Frank (1948), *The Theory of International Values*, Princeton, NJ: Princeton University Press.

Haberler, Gottfried (1930/1985), "The Theory of Comparative Costs and Its Use in the Defense of Free Trade," in *Selected Essays of Gottfried Haberler*, Ed. by Anthony Koo, Cambridge, MA: The MIT Press, pp. 3–19.

Haberler, Gottfried (1936), *The Theory of International Trade*, Edinburgh, UK: William Hodge.

Hatsopoulos, George, Paul Krugman, and Lawrence Summers (1988), "U.S. Competitiveness: Beyond the Trade Deficit," *Science* 241, July 15, pp. 299–307.

Heckscher, Eli (1919/1991), "The Effects of Foreign Trade on the Distribution of Income," in *Heckscher-Ohlin Trade Theory*, Ed. by Harry Flam and M. June Flander, Cambridge, MA: The MIT Press.

Hirschman, Albert (1982), "Rival Interpretations of Market Society: Civilizing, Destructive, or Feeble?" *Journal of Economic Literature* 20, December, pp. 1,463–1,484.

Hont, Istavan (2005), *Jealousy of Trade: International Competition and the Nation-State in Historical Perspective*, Cambridge, MA: The Belknap Press of Harvard University Press.

Hume, David (1752a/1955), "Of Commerce," in *David Hume: Writings on Economics*, Ed. by Eugene Rotwein, Madison, WI: University of Wisconsin Press, pp. 3–18.

Hume, David (1752b/1955), "Of the Balance of Trade," in *David Hume: Writings on Economics*, Ed. by Eugene Rotwein, Madison, WI: University of Wisconsin Press, pp. 60–77.

Hume, David (1758/1955), "Of the Jealousy of Trade," in *David Hume: Writings on Economics*, Ed. by Eugene Rotwein, Madison, WI: University of Wisconsin Press, pp. 78–82.

Irwin, Douglas A. (1996), *Against the Tided: An Intellectual History of Free Trade*, Princeton, NJ: Princeton University Press.

Jones, Ronald (1961), "Comparative Advantage and the Theory of Tariffs: A Multi-country, Multi-commodity Model," *Review of Economic Studies* 28, 3, pp. 161–175.

Jones, Ronald (2008), "Heckscher-Ohlin Trade Theory," *The New Palgrave Dictionary of Economics*, 2nd Edition, Ed. by Steven Durlauf and Lawrence Blume, New York, NY: Palgrave MacMillan.

Krugman, Paul (2009), "Increasing Returns in a Comparative Advantage World," in *Comparative Advantage, Growth, and the Gains from Trade and Globalization*, A Festschrift in Honor of Alan Deardorff, Ed. by Robert Stern, New Jersey: World Scientific, pp. 43–51.

Kurz, Heinz (1992), "Adam Smith on Foreign Trade: A Note on the 'Vent-for-Surplus' Argument," *Economica* 59, pp. 475–481.

Lahaye, Laura (2008), "Mercantilism," in *The New Palgrave: Dictionary of Economics*, 2nd Edition, Ed. by Steven Durlauf and Lawrence Blume, pp. 568–569.

Leamer, Edward (1984), *Sources of International Comparative Advantage: Theory and Evidence*, Cambridge, MA: The MIT Press.

Leamer, Edward (1994), "Testing Trade Theory," in *Survey in International Trade*, Ed. by David Greenaway and L. Alan Winters, Oxford, UK: Basil Blackwell, pp. 66–106.

Leamer, Edward and James Levinsohn (1995), "International Trade Theory: The Evidence," in *Handbook of International Economics*, Volume III, Ed. by Gene M. Grossman and Kenneth Rogoff, Amsterdam, NED: Elsevier, pp. 1339–1394.

Lerner, Ralph (1979), "Commerce and Character: The Anglo-American as New-Model Man," *The William and Mary Quarterly* 35, January, pp. 3–26.

Lindert, Peter and Jeffrey Williamson (2003), "Does Globalization Make the World More Unequal?" in *Globalization in Historical Perspective*, Ed. by M. Bordo, Allan M. Taylor and Jeffrey G. Williamson, Chicago, IL: The University of Chicago Press, pp. 227–271.

Longfield, Mountifort (1835/1971), *Three Lectures on Commerce, and on Absenteeism*, New York, NY: Augustus M. Kelley Publishers.

MacDougall, G.D.A. (1951), "British and American Exports: A Study Suggested by the Theory of Comparative Costs," *The Economic Journal* 61, 244, pp. 679–724.

MacLeod, Christine (1983), "Henry Martin and the Authorship of 'Considerations upon the East India Trade,'" *Bulletin of the Institute of Historical Research* 56, 134, pp. 222–229.

Maddison, Angus (1995), *Monitoring the World Economy*, Paris, FRA: OECD Development Center.

Maddison, Angus (2001), *The World Economy: A Millennial Perspective*, Paris, FRA: OECD Development Center.

Maddison, Angus (2007), *Contours of the World Economy, 1–2030 AD: Essays in Macro-economic History*, New York, NY: Oxford University Press.

Magnusson, Lars (2004), *The Tradition of Free Trade*, Abingdon, UK: Rutledge.

Magnusson, Lars (2007), "Mercantilism," in *A Companion to The History of Economic Thought*, Ed. by Warren J. Samuels, Jeff E. Biddle, and John B. Davis, Malden, MA: Blackwell Publishing, pp. 46–60.

Maneschi, Andrea (1998), *Comparative Advantage in International Trade: A Historical Perspective*, Cheltenham, UK and Northampton, MA: Edward Elgar.

Maneschi, Andrea (2002), "The Tercentenary of Henry Martyn's Considerations upon the East-India Trade," *Journal of the History of Economic Thought* 24, 2, pp. 233–249.

Maneschi, Andrea (2004), "The True Meaning of David Ricardo's Four Magic Numbers," *Journal of International Economics* 62, pp. 433–443.

Maneschi, Andrea (2008), "How Would David Ricardo Have Taught the Principle of Comparative Advantage?" *Southern Economics Journal* 74, 4, pp. 1,167–1,176.

Mankiw, N. Gregory and Philip Swagel (2006), "The Politics and Economics of Offshore Outsourcing," *Journal of Monetary Economics* 53, 5, July, pp. 1,027–1,056.

Martyn, Henry (1701), *Considerations upon the East-India Trade*, Eighteenth Century Collections Online Print Edition (available from Amazon.com).

Mason, Edward (1926), "The Doctrine of Comparative Cost," *Quarterly Journal of Economics* 41, 1, pp. 63–93.

McKenzie, Lionel (1954), "Specialization and Efficiency in World Production," *The Review of Economic Studies* 21, 3, pp. 165–180.

McKenzie, Lionel (1956), "Specialization in Production and the Production Possibility Locus," *The Review of Economic Studies* 23, 1, pp. 56–64.

Melvin, James (1968), "Production and Trade with Two Factors and Three Goods," *American Economic Review* 58, pp. 195–205.

Mill, James (1808/1997), "Commerce Defended," in *Free Trade: 1793–1886, Early Sources in Economics*, Volume I, Ed. by Lars Magnusson, London, UK and New York, NY: Routledge, pp. 21–98.

Mill, James (1821/1965), *Elements of Political Economy*, 3rd edition, New York, NY: Augustus M. Kelley, Booksellers.

Mill, John Stuart (1825/2006), "The Corn Laws," in *Essays on Economics and Society, 1824–1845, Collected Works of John Stuart Mill*, Volume IV, Indianapolis, IN: Liberty Fund, pp. 45–70.

Mill, John Stuart (1841/2006), "Petition on Free Trade," in *Essays on Economics and Society, 1824–1845, Collected Works of John Stuart Mill*, Volume V, Indianapolis, IN: Liberty Fund, pp. 761–763.

Mill, John Stuart (1829/2006), "Of the Laws of Interchange Between Nations," in *Essays on Economics and Society, 1824–1845, Collected Works of John Stuart Mill*, Volume IV, Indianapolis, IN: Liberty Fund, pp. 232–261.

Mill, John Stuart (1848/2006), *Principles of Political Economy*, Collected Works of John Stuart Mill, Indianapolis, IN: Liberty Fund.

Mokyr, Joel (2009), *The Enlightened Economy*, New Haven, CT and London, UK: Yale University Press.

Morales Meoqui, Jorge (2011), "Comparative Advantage and the Labor Theory of Value," *History of Political Economy* 43, 4, pp. 743–763.

Morales Meoqui, Jorge (2012a), "Comments on 'Deconstructing the Theory of Comparative Advantage,'" *World Economic Review*, November 14th.

Morales Meoqui, Jorge (2012b), "On the Distribution of Authorship-merits for the Comparative Advantage Proposition," Munich Personal RePEc Archive.

Morgan, Mary (2012), *The World in the Models: How Economists Work and Think*, New York, NY: Cambridge University Press.

Morley, Neville (2007), *Trade in Classical Antiquity*, Cambridge, UK: Cambridge University Press.

Mun, Thomas (1664/1959), *England's Treasure by Forraign Trade*, London, UK: T. Clark.

Myint, Hla. (1977), "Adam Smith Theory of International Trade in the Perspective of Economic Development," *Economica* 44, pp. 231–248.

Ohlin, Bertil (1933), *Interregional and International Trade*, Cambridge, MA: Harvard University Press.

O'Rourke, Kevin H. and Jeffrey G. Williamson (1999), *Globalization and History: The Evolution of a Nineteenth-Century Atlantic Economy*, Cambridge, MA: The MIT Press.

O'Rourke, Kevin H. and Jeffrey G. Williamson (2002), "The Heckscher-Ohlin Model between 1400 and 2000: When It Explained Factor Price Convergence, and When It Did Not, and Why," in *Bertil Ohlin: A Centennial Celebration, 1899–1999*, Ed. by Ronald Findlay, Lars Jonung, and Mats Lundahl, Cambridge, MA: The MIT Press, pp. 431–453.

Pareto, Wilfredo (1906/1971), *Manual of Political Economy*, New York, NY: Augustus M. Kelley Publishers.

Plant, Alan (1933), "A Letter on the True Principles of Advantageous Exportation, 1818," *Economica* 13, pp. 40–50.

Pullen, John (2006), "Did Ricardo Really Have a Law of Comparative Advantage? A Comparison of Ricardo's Version and the Modern Version," *History of Economic Review* 44, Summer, pp. 59–75.

Rassekh, Farhad (2014), "Economic Globalization: An Empirical Presentation and a Moral Judgment," in *Business Ethics*, 2nd Edition, Ed. by Michael Boylan, Wiley-Blackwell, pp. 390–409.

Rassekh, Farhad (2015), "Comparative Advantage in Smith's Wealth of Nations and Ricardo's Principles: A Brief History of Its Early Development," *History of Economic Ideas* 23, 1, pp. 59–76.

Rassekh, Farhad and John Speir (2009), "Can Economic Globalization Lead to a More Just Society?" *Journal of Global Ethics* 6, 1, pp. 27–43.

Ricardo, David (1817/1996), *Principles of Political Economy and Taxation*, Great Mind Series, Amherst, NY: Prometheus Books.

Ricardo, David (2004), *The Works and Correspondence of David Ricardo*, Volumes I through XI, Ed. by Pier Sraffa, Cambridge, UK: Cambridge University Press.

Rotwein, Eugene (1955), *David Hume: Writings on Economics*, Madison, WI: University of Wisconsin Press.

Ruffin, Roy (2002), "David Ricardo's Discovery of Comparative Advantage," *History of Political Economy* 34, 4, pp. 727–748.

Ruffin, Roy (2005), "Debunking a Myth: Torrens on Comparative Advantage," *History of Political Economy* 37, 4, pp. 711–722.

Samuelson, Paul (1998), "The Past and Future of International Trade Theory," in *New Directions in Trade Theory*, Ed. by Jim Levinsohn, Alan Deardorff, and Robert Stern, Ann Arbor, MI: The University of Michigan Press.

Schonhardt-Bailey, Cheryl (2006), *From Corn Laws to Free Trade: Interests, Ideas, and Institutions in Historical Perspective*, Cambridge, MA: The MIT Press.

Schumacher, Reinhard (2013), "Deconstructing the Theory of Comparative Advantage," *World Economic Review* 2, pp. 83–105.

Schumer, Chuck and Paul Craig Roberts (2004), "Second Thought on Free Trade," *New York Times*, 6 January, A 23.

Schumpeter, Joseph A. (1954/1994), *History of Economic Analysis*, New York, NY: Oxford University Press.

Smith, Adam (1759/1984), *The Theory of Moral Sentiments*, Indianapolis, IN: Liberty Fund.

Smith, Adam (1776/1981), *An Inquiry into the Nature and Causes of the Wealth of Nations*, Indianapolis, IN: Liberty Fund.

Smith, Adam (1982), *Lectures on Jurisprudence*, Indianapolis, IN: Liberty Fund.

Sraffa, Piero (1930), "An Alleged Correction of Ricardo," *Quarterly Journal of Economics* 44, 3, pp. 539–544.

Stern, Robert M. (1962), "British and American Productivity and Comparative Costs in International Trade," *Oxford Economic Papers* 14, pp. 275–303.

Stern, Robert M. (2011), *Comparative Advantage, Growth, and the Gains from Trade and Globalization: A Festschrift in Honor of Alan V. Deardorff*, New Jersey: World Scientific.

Stewart, Dugald (1793/1982), "Account of the Life and Writings of Adam Smith," in *Essays on Philosophical Subjects*, Indianapolis, IN: Liberty Fund, pp. 269–351.

Torrens, Robert (1808/2000), "The Economists Refuted," in *Collected Works of Robert Torrens*, Ed. by G.D. Vivo, Bristol, UK: Thoemmes Press.

Torrens, Robert (1815/1827), *An Essay on the External Corn Trade*, 4th edition, London, UK: Longman, Rees, Orme, Brown and Green.

Viner, Jacob (1937/1975), *Studies in the Theory of International Trade*, New York, NY: Augustus M. Kelley Publishers.

Viner, Jacob (1959/1991), "Early Attitudes towards Trade and the Merchant," in *Essays on the Intellectual History of Economics*, Ed. by Douglas A. Irwin, Princeton, NJ: Princeton University Press, pp. 39–44.

West, E.G. (1978), "Scotland's Resurgent Economist: A Survey of the New Literature on Adam Smith," *Southern Economic Journal* 45, 2, pp. 343–369.

World Bank (2010), *World Development Report 2010*, Washington, DC: The International Bank for Reconstruction and Development.

3 The law of markets

"[Jean-Baptiste] Say showed successfully that, however large the phenomenon of overproduction may loom in the historical picture of individual crises, no causal explanation can be derived from it: there is no sense in saying that there is a crisis *because* 'too much' has been produced all round. Though negative, this contribution was very important. It may be said to stand at the fountainhead of the scientific analysis of cycles ..." (Joseph Schumpeter 1954/1994, p. 739, italics in original)

Chapter contents

1. Introduction

The law of markets (also known as Say's law) is a multifaceted theory. In the words of William Baumol (1999, p. 197), the law of markets "is really a complex of ideas." Thomas Sowell (2006, p. 26) has similarly characterized it as "a cluster of related propositions contributed and refined by a number of individuals." Nonetheless, many scholars have presented Say's law in a single sentence or phrase. For example, Paul Lambert (1956, p. 10) defines "the essence of the Law of Markets" as "production itself provides the necessary and sufficient outlet for products." According to William Hutt (1974, p. 3), Say's law "enunciates the principle that 'demands in general' are 'supplies in general' – different aspects of one phenomenon." Mark Blaug (1997, p. 232) notes, "what the classical economists really meant by Say's Law of Markets" is "that a free enterprise capitalist economy has an inherent tendency to return to full employment." Steven Kates (1998, p. 216), who has presented eight propositions as the components of the law of markets, nonetheless, writes, "those who had originally constructed and then defined ... the law of markets ... In accepting the law ... what they had done was to deny flatly that failure of effective demand was a cause of recessions and unemployment." Finally, the most famous and widely accepted definition is John Maynard Keynes' "supply creates its own demand" to which we will return below. These definitions reflect the fact that the law of markets has multiple dimensions and angles.

Two developments – one intellectual and the other historical – led to the formulation and enunciation of the law of markets. The intellectual development rests on certain principles and arguments advanced in the eighteenth century by Adam Smith, the Physiocracts, and a few other thinkers. Their ideas were later incorporated into the law of markets. We shall elaborate on this intellectual development in section 3. The historical development that led to the formulation of the law of markets relates to the unprecedented rise in the productive capability of Western European economies in the latter part of the eighteenth century and the early nineteenth century. This surge in productivity was unleashed by the Industrial Revolution and enhanced by the market economic system whose intellectual foundation Smith had helped establish.[1] Joe Mokyr (2009, p. 30) has argued that the Enlightenment project of free inquiry and free expression made it possible for inventors and innovators to present their ideas without the fear of reprisal. Such a condition played the key role in launching and sustaining the economic momentum in Great Britain where the Enlightenment was in full bloom in the eighteenth century, and also where the Industrial Revolution originated. Indeed while Smith was writing the *Wealth of Nations*, a leading text in the Enlightenment era, James Watt was working on his steam engine, a key invention in the Industrial Revolution. And as it happened, the year 1776 witnessed the publication of Smith's book as well as the first installation of Watt's engine.[2]

Prior to the Industrial Revolution, almost all economies grew at imperceptibly low rates, if at all, and any growth would be interrupted – possibly even reversed – by wars, draught, earthquake, and epidemics. There had been exceptions to this rule throughout history as various empires or countries experienced higher living standards due to conquest or innovation in agriculture or even in basic manufacturing. But no region ever experienced sustained economic growth until the dawn of the eighteenth century. Angus Maddison (2001/2002, p. 28) has estimated the economic growth of the world economy over the past two millennia. He divides the world into seven regions and reports that none experienced economic growth in the first millennium, but from the year 1000 to 1820, Western Europe and her Offshoots grew at 0.14 percent per annum. Since this was the average, some countries failed to experience even this meager growth rate while some grew considerably faster. Peter Temin and David Vines (2014, p. 1) have noted, "in the eighteenth century Britain increased its level of economic activity to a level that had been seen only in first-century Rome and seventeenth-century Holland. But although the residents of these times and places may have been as well off, neither of those precursors was on its way to the Industrial Revolution."

Britain's relatively high economic growth in the eighteenth century had begun in the seventeenth century and accelerated in the nineteenth century. As the Industrial Revolution spread to the market economies of Europe and North America, they all experienced relatively high economic growth rates.[3] But this expansion of economic capacity was accompanied by periods of economic downturns. Roger Fouquet and Stephen Broadberry (2015) have documented the economic performance of six European countries over the last several centuries and found that, to varying degrees, they experienced both positive and negative economic growth.[4] Joseph Schumpeter (1954/1994, p. 738) has pointed out that economic breakdowns had occurred regularly in the eighteenth century just as they did in the nineteenth century. In 1829 John Stuart Mill noted that "the possibility of general over-production … was almost a received doctrine as lately as thirty years ago" (1829/2006, p. 278). At that time the terms "general overproduction" and "general gluts" were used in reference to economic recessions.

The law of markets was developed in the early years of the nineteenth century, in part, to address the issue of overproduction or gluts.[5] Jean-Baptiste Say (1821a/1967, p. 2) in a letter to Malthus noted that his scholarly project aimed to find out, first, "the cause of the general gluts of all the markets in the world"; and second, "the means" by which "this chronic disease" can be "remedied." Such a lofty intellectual venture opened a new vista of inquiry in economics and went beyond the accomplishments of Adam Smith. The architects of Say's law located the source of gluts, not in too much production or too little demand, but rather in disharmonies between the structure of production and the structure of demand. That is, they believed recessions result from misallocation of resources. But they conceded that recessions may have other causes such as monetary contraction. We will return to this point.

Any analysis of the law of markets (particularly a historical one) necessarily and extensively involves John Maynard Keynes' influential 1936 book *The General Theory of Employment, Interest, and Money*. Keynes ingeniously summarized Say's law as "supply creates its own demand" and considered it to be the bedrock of classical economics, which he set out to replace with his own theory. Steven Kates (2003, p. 8), a scholar of the law of markets, maintains, "The Keynesian Revolution was about Say's Law and nothing else." And Paul Sweezy (1947/1960, p. 147) argues, "the Keynesian attacks, though they appear to be directed against a variety of specific theories, all fall to the ground if the validity of Say's Law is assumed." Under Keynes' enormous influence, the phrase "supply creates its own demand" has become the ubiquitous definition of the law of markets and the term "Say's law" its standard name even though he did not coin it.[6]

The present chapter traces the conception, evolution, and policy implications of the law of markets since its enunciation in 1803 by Jean-Baptiste Say (1767–1832) and in 1808 by James Mill (1773–1836). David Ricardo (1772–1823) and J. S. Mill (1806–1873) served as the most effective defenders and expositors of the law of markets.[7] The influence of Ricardo was so pervasive that Keynes on several (but not all) occasions associated the law of markets largely with Ricardo rather than with Say or James Mill even though they both have priority over Ricardo. This chapter will also describe the unusual intellectual history of the law of markets in that most economists in the nineteenth century accepted its tenets (a notable exception being Robert Malthus). In the twentieth century, however, the Great Depression of the 1930s and the publication of the *General Theory* dealt a severe blow to the confidence of many economists and policymakers in the validity and utility of the central theories of classical economics including the law of markets.

Despite its marginalization in economic discourse, largely because of the Keynesian Revolution, Say's law has never ceased to attract attention, although not always for the right reason. Consider the fact that a host of writers have blamed Say's law as either a cause of the 2008–2009 recession or as a reason for the lackluster recovery.[8] The law of markets may have been marginalized, but it cannot be dismissed because many scholars still consider it to be a core proposition in economics. Hutt (1974, p. 3) refers to it as "the most fundamental 'economic law' in all economic theory." While this assertion appears to be hyperbolic, there is no exaggeration in Schumpeter's statement that the law of markets "may be said to stand at the fountainhead of the scientific analysis of cycles …" (1954/1994, p. 739). In the course of the enunciation and explication of Say's law, its defenders delved deeply into the operation of the economy, and bequeathed a rich analysis of market operation that may be regarded as their most consequential and lasting legacy (rather than the law itself). Say, James Mill, Ricardo, and J. S. Mill did not always agree with one another on all aspects of the law of markets, but their writings along with those of other scholars such as Robert Malthus, who opposed the law of markets, made an indelible and indispensable contribution to our understanding of the market economic system.

2. Components of the law of markets

Thomas Sowell (1972, 2006), Andrew Skinner (1967), William Baumol (1977 and 1999), and Steven Kates (1998), among others, have presented the law of markets as a collection of several propositions. Below, we present Sowell's (2006, pp. 26–27) six propositions, which provide a panoramic view of Say's law and help the reader with the rest of this chapter.[9]

1 The total factor payments received for producing a given volume (or value) of output are necessarily sufficient to purchase that volume (or value) of output.
2 There is no loss of purchasing power anywhere in the economy, for people save only to the extent of their desire to invest and do not hold money beyond their transactions needs during the current period.
3 Investment is only an internal transfer, not a net reduction, of aggregate demand. The same amount that could have been spent by the thrifty

consumer will be spent by the capitalists and/or the workers in the investment goods sector.

4 In real terms, supply equals demand *ex ante*, since each individual produces only because of, and to the extent of, his demand for other goods. (Sometimes this doctrine was supported by demonstrating that supply equals demand *ex post*.)
5 A higher rate of savings will cause a higher rate of subsequent growth in aggregate output.
6 Disequilibrium in the economy can exist only because the internal proportions of output differ from consumers' preferred mix – *not* because output is excessive in the aggregate. In short, this implied that there was no such thing as an equilibrium level of national income. (italics in original)

As we shall see in this chapter, the central figures of the law of markets disagreed with one another on some of these propositions.

3. Before Jean-Baptiste Say

The seeds of Say's law were sown in the eighteenth century in the writings of Adam Smith and to some extent those of the Physiocrats as well as a few other thinkers who attempted to refute certain economic views and dogmas of their times. Chief among them was the mercantilist view that consumption benefits while saving harms the economy.[10] In the *General Theory*, Keynes (1936/1997, pp. 358–359) approvingly presents passages from the writings of several mercantilists (in the sixteenth and seventeenth centuries) who praised consumption and denounced saving. In addition, Keynes quotes from Eli Heckscher's classic work on mercantilism. Heckscher notes that the mercantilists held "the deep-rooted belief in the utility of luxury and the evil of thrift. Thrift, in fact, was regarded as the cause of unemployment, and for two reasons: in the first place, because real income was believed to diminish by the amount of money which did not enter into exchange, and secondly, because saving was believed to withdraw money from circulation" (Ibid., p. 358).[11]

In the *Wealth of Nations* Adam Smith argues against the mercantilist position on saving, and points out that saving is necessary for capital formation and economic growth. He (1776/1981, p. 337) writes, "Whatever a person saves from his revenue he adds to his capital, and either employs it himself in maintaining an additional number of productive hands, or enables some other person to do so, by lending it to him for an interest, that is, for a share of the profits." Further, "capitals are increased by parsimony, and diminished by prodigality and misconduct." More importantly,

> What is annually saved is as regularly consumed as what is annually spent, and nearly in the same time too, but is consumed by a different set of people.

> That portion of his revenue which a rich man annually spends is in most cases consumed by idle guests and menial servants, who leave nothing behind them in return for their consumption. That portion which he annually saves, as for the sake of the profit it is immediately employed as a capital, is consumed in the same manner, and nearly in the same time too, but by a different set of people, by labourers, manufacturers, and artificers, who reproduce with a profit the value of their annual consumption. His revenue, we shall suppose, is paid him in money. Had he spent the whole, the food, clothing, and lodging, which the whole could have purchased, would have been distributed among the former set of people. By saving a part of it, as that part is for the sake of the profit immediately employed as a capital either by himself or by some other person, the food, clothing, and lodging, which may be purchased with it, are necessarily reserved for the latter. The consumption is the same, but the consumers are different. (Ibid., pp. 337–338)

Smith's view on saving was later incorporated into the law of markets. Another aspect of Say's law that originated in the *Wealth of Nations* is the possibility of a partial but not general glut. Smith (Ibid., p. 439) notes, "though a particular merchant, with abundance of goods in his warehouse, may sometimes be ruined by not being able to sell them in time, a nation or country is not liable to the same accident." This statement must have influenced the founders of Say's law.

According to the law of markets all transactions are essentially exchanges of goods for goods, and money only facilitates the transactions. J.-B. Say (1821b/1880/1964, p. 230) enunciated this principle in the context of international trade as follows: "No one country can buy of another, except with its own domestic products."[12] Say's pronouncement in essence is the same as the following well-known statement in the *Wealth of Nations* (Smith, 1776/1981, p. 457): "If a foreign country can supply us with a commodity cheaper than we ourselves can make it, better buy it of them with some part of the produce of our own industry employed in a way in which we have some advantage." But Smith is not the only scholar who, prior to Say, understood this point. Paul Lambert (1956, p. 8) notes that "Boisguillbert, Forbonais, Quesnay, Le Mercier de La Riviere, Adam Smith, and Le Tronse" all expressed the idea that market transactions are simply exchanges of goods for goods. In particular, in 1777 Le Tronse wrote, "… products being paid for only with products" (quoted in Lambert, 1956, p. 8). However, Lambert points out that neither Le Tronse nor the Physiocrats went beyond a few premises used in the formulation of Say's law.

Lambert also names three eighteenth-century thinkers who, he argues, understood the law of markets. The first one is Josiah Tucker, who contributed substantially to the discourse on the political economy of his time.[13] The second one is a scholar by the name of Mengotti and the third is the author of an anonymous treatise titled *Sketch of the Advance and Decline of Nations*. Tucker made a statement about the temporary nature of partial gluts. He wrote, "if a particular trade is at any Time over-stocked, will not the Disease cure itself? That is, will not some Persons take to other Trade, and fewer young People be bred up to that which is least profitable?" (quoted in Lambert, 1956, p. 14). Because of this statement, Lambert (Ibid.) calls Tucker "The Founder of the Law of Markets." Tucker certainly deserves credit for understanding the self-adjusting feature of the market, but his rhetorical question hardly qualifies him for the title Lambert bestows upon him.

Lambert (1956, p. 15) notes that the anonymous author of the *Sketch of the Advance and Decline of Nations* put forward a statement of Say's law in which Lambert believes, "Every point has been covered." The statement is this: "To suppose that there may be a production of commodities without a demand, provided these commodities be of the right species, is as absurd as to suppose that the revenues of the several individuals composing the society may be too great for their consumption." The statement expresses certain aspects of Say's law, but it is highly questionable if it covers every point as Lambert asserts. Nonetheless, such pronouncements, in all likelihood, influenced the developers of Say's law who appeared on the scene only a generation later.

Joseph Spengler (1945) assigns much credit to Smith and the Physiocrats for having laid the foundation of Say's law. He (1945, p. 331) argues, "Say's law may be derived from Smith's even as it may be inferred from the physiocratic writings, and it would have been deduced from one or the other had Say never written." However, the "contribution" of the Physiocrats in one key area is similar to that of mercantilists, in that the Physiocrats believed consumption plays the primary role in the economy, an idea Say vehemently opposed. In the first edition of his book Say noted that the advocates of "mercantilist tradition" and "the Physiocrats"

> consider consumption to be useful in relation to production, while it is useful only for the pleasure that it produces. A consumer offers no advantages by *that which* he consumes, but by that which he provides as a replacement; now, he can give *that* much more in replacement as he undertakes less unrewarding consumption and more reproductive consumption. (Translated and quoted by William Baumol, 1977, p. 151, italics in original)

Relying on such passages, Spengler (1945, p. 346) notes,

> Say was able, therefore, to direct two counter principles against both the physiocratic thesis that consumption is primary and Lauderdale's thesis that there could be too much saving: (a) since exchange consists essentially in bartering goods and services, the demand for goods is equivalent to their supply and increases with supply; (b) consumption is always commensurate with production, since that portion of income received which is not devoted to unproductive consumption is expended upon productive consumption. Say thus supposed what the physiocrats had implicitly denied: that an economy is always in a healthy state.[14]

It is surprising that Spengler writes "Say supposed what the physiocrats had implicitly denied: that an economy is *always* in a healthy state" (italics added).

Of course, Say knew too well the economy is *not* always in a healthy state. As noted above, in his letter to Malthus, Say set out to discover how economic downturns occur and how this "chronic disease" (as he called it) can be remedied. We shall see in the next section that Say identified instances of disequilibrium in the economy, although he attributed much of it to government policies. It would be correct to note that Say believed market forces steer the economy *towards* a healthy state.

4. The evolution of the law of markets in the nineteenth century

The first decade of the nineteenth-century witnessed the germination and even fruition of the law of markets. The earliest presentation of the law appeared in the first edition of Say's seminal book, *A Treatise on Political Economy, or the Production, Distribution, and Consumption of Wealth*, published in 1803. Passages containing elements of Say's law were scattered throughout the book. In 1804 James Mill put forth some aspects of the law of markets in his review of Lord Lauderdale's *Inquiry* and in 1805 he published his review of Say's book.[15] Hence by 1808 Mill was well-prepared to present a highly systematic analysis of the law of markets in an essay titled "Commerce Defended."[16] Say, upon reading Mill's essay, revised the presentation (but not the substance) of the law of markets and republished his book in 1814.[17] The American edition of Say's book, which is used in the present chapter, became available in 1821. In this edition, the most comprehensive analysis of the law of markets appears in chapter XV, titled "Of the Demand or Market for Products."

In the early part of the chapter, Say (1821b/1880/1964, p. 133) assigns the primary impetus for economic activities to production by enunciating the proposition that "it is production which opens a demand for products." This statement sounds like "supply creates its own demand," but Say's writings make it clear that the "demand" in the sentence is *not* for the produced goods but for "other products." Consider his statement that "a product is no sooner created, than it, from that instant, affords a market for other products to the full extent of its own value" (Ibid., p. 134). The reason is, "producers are at the same time consumers" (Ibid., p. 15); that is, producers are motivated by their own demand for goods and services.

The law of markets rests on the premise that human beings have an innate and insatiable demand for goods. Hence demand is always present and does not need to be encouraged. Moreover, producers adjust their output to the desires of consumers. As Say observes, "… all produce naturally gravitates to that place where it is most in demand …" (Ibid., p. 134). Since demand is always present, the mere supply of a good is sufficient for, and tantamount to, the creation of a *market* for the good. James Mill (1808/1997, p. 56) expresses the proposition as follows: "The production of commodities creates … a *market* for the commodities produced" (italics added). Mill's statement, similar to that of Say, sounds like "supply creates its own demand," but Mill is talking about the creation of a market, not demand. The phrase "supply creates its own demand" implies that the supply of x creates the demand for x but as Hutt (1974, p. 3) explains, "the supply of plums does not create the demand for plums." Hutt goes on to note that "What the law really asserts is that the supply of plums *constitutes* demand for whatever the supplier is destined to acquire in exchange for plums under barter, or with the money proceeds in a money economy" (italics in original). Hutt's interpretation corresponds to Say's rendition of the law of markets.

But there are other statements that remind us of "supply creates its own demand." For example, J. S. Mill (1829/2006, p. 278) notes, "Nothing is more true than that it is produce which constitutes the market for produce, and that every increase of production, if distributed without miscalculation among all kinds of produce in the proportion which private interest would dictate, creates, or rather constitutes, its own demand." Note that Mill's statement includes the condition of "without miscalculation" regarding the dictate of "private interest" – the condition is missing in Keynes' rendition of the law. However, as John Chipman (1965, p. 712) has pointed out, if one argues, "supply creates its own demand … provided, of course, that no more is produced than will be demanded," such a position "takes much of the punch out of Say's law."[18] Indeed for the law of markets to be a meaningful proposition it must embody more than, and even be different from, "supply creates its own demand." Baumol (2003, p. 35) has pointed out that Keynes' definition is "a very bad caricature that only marginally resembles any of the original and certainly leaves out the bulk of its substance." Robert Clower and Axel Leijonhufvud (1973, p. 7) characterize "supply creates its own demand" as "perhaps the most ambiguous statement that students of economics are ever asked to ponder." Nonetheless, virtually all economists including some scholars of Say's law (e.g., Sowell) have accepted Keynes' definition as the correct description of Say's law.[19]

The realization that money facilitates the exchange of goods for goods serves as a premise from which Say (1821b/1880/1964, p. 132) deduced the following crucial proposition of the law of markets:

> money is but the agent of the transfer of values. Its whole utility has consisted in conveying to your hands the value of the commodities, which your customer has sold, for the purpose of buying again from you; and the very next purchase you make, it will again convey to a third person the value of the products you may have sold to others. Otherwise, *how could it be possible that there should now be bought and sold in France five or six times as many commodities as in the miserable rein of Charles VI*? Is it not obvious, that five or six times as many commodities must have been produced, and that they must have served to purchase one or the other? (Italics added)

The italicized part of the passage is quite significant not only for the law of markets but also for the whole of classical economics; it implies that market transactions constitute the engine of economic growth, and that production drives the transactions. Embedded in Say's rhetorical question is the realization that the economy can continuously expand over a long period. This realization debunks the (fallacious) mercantilist dogma that economic transactions are a zero-sum game.[20] Say's rhetorical question also implies that production generates a purchasing power identically equal to the full value of the output and facilitates market transactions which expand the economy and wealth.

In Say's account, entrepreneurs and producers are the fountainhead of economic activities since they create new ideas and products that advance the economy. But entrepreneurs and producers occasionally misallocate resources. As Say argues (Ibid., p. 135), "the glut of particular commodities arises from its having outrun the total demand for it in one or two ways: either because it has been produced in excessive abundance, or because the production of other commodities has fallen short." Notice that either way producers are responsible for the glut. Following this analysis, Say calls attention to unsold English goods in Brazil, and argues that if Brazil had produced enough commodities of her own, Brazilians would have had sufficient purchasing power to buy the English products. England, for her part, needs to eliminate barriers against importation of Brazilian goods. He writes (Ibid., p. 136),

> I would not be misunderstood to maintain in this chapter, that one product can not be raised in too great abundance, in relation to all others; but merely that nothing is more favourable to the demand of one product, than the supply of another; that the import of English manufactures into Brazil would cease to be excessive and be rapidly absorbed, did Brazil produce on her side returns sufficiently ample; to which end it would be necessary that the legislative bodies of either country should consent, the one to free production, the other to free importation.

Say is assuming Brazilians have the will to buy the imported British goods but they lack the purchasing power. He identifies a disequilibrium outcome, which he attributes to institutional barriers in Brazil against free markets ("free production") and in England against free trade.

Quite significantly, in the year 1814 when Say's revised book was published, Thomas Robert Malthus (1766–1834) and David Ricardo exchanged letters that shed much light on the issue of "power" versus "will" to purchase. On 11 September 1814 Malthus wrote to Ricardo:

> Effectual demand consists of two elements the *power* and the *will* to purchase. The power to purchase may perhaps be represented correctly by the produce of the country whether small or great; but the will to purchase will always be the greatest, the smaller is the produce compared with the population, and the smaller is the produce compared with the population, and the more scantily the wants of the society are supplied. When capital is abundant it is not easy to find new objects sufficiently in demand.... I by no means think that the power to purchase necessarily involves a proportionate will to purchase; and I cannot agree with Mr. Mill ... that in reference to a nation, supply can never exceed demand. A nation must certainly have the power of purchasing

> all that it produces, but I can easily conceive it not to have the will.... You have never I think taken sufficiently into consideration the wants and tastes of mankind that determines prices. (The letter is in Ricardo, 1951/2004, Vol. VI, pp. 131–132, italics in original.)

On 16 September 1814, Ricardo replied,

> We agree that effectual demand consists of two elements, the *power* and the *will* to purchase, but I think the will is very seldom wanting where the power exists, – for the desire of accumulation will occasion demand just as effectually as a desire to consume; it will only change the objects on which the demand will exercise itself. If you think that with an increase of capital men will become indifferent both to consumption and accumulation, then you are correct in opposing Mr. Mill's idea, that in reference to a nation, supply can never exceed demand, – but does not an increase of capital beget an increased inclination for luxuries of all description, and tho' it appears natural that the desire of accumulation should decrease with an increase of capital, and diminished profits, it appears equally probable that consumption will increase in the same ratio.... I consider the wants and tastes of mankind unlimited. (Ibid., pp. 134–135, italics in original)

The letters reveal irreconcilable differences between Ricardo and Malthus. To Ricardo (as well as to Say) people always have the "will" but may lack the "power" to purchase while to Malthus people may have the power to purchase but not necessarily the will. Siding with Ricardo, John Ramsay McCulloch (1789–1864), an ardent supporter and expounder of Say's law (1864/1965, p. 146) wrote,

> Malthus has justly stated that the demand for a commodity depends "on the *will* combined with the *power* to purchase it," that is, on the power to furnish an equivalent for it. But who ever heard of a want of *will* to purchase.... The power to purchase is the real desideratum. It is the inability to furnish equivalents for the products necessary to supply our wants, "that makes calamity of so long life." (Italics in original)

This analysis implies that to end a recession and commence an economic recovery production (not consumption) should be encouraged, which is the central policy implication of Say's law. We shall return to the policy implications of the law in a later section.

Say presents the following four (in his words) "important conclusions" in the last part of the chapter. First, "in every community the more numerous are the producers, and more various their production, the more prompt, numerous, and extensive are the markets for those production; and ... the more profitable are they to the producers ..." (1821b/1880/1964, p. 137). Of course profitability requires that businesses produce goods for which consumers are likely to have a demand. However, this obvious and seemingly trivial statement portends a problem for market economies since (as pointed out before) entrepreneurs at times misread consumers' demand and produce the wrong goods and disrupt the smooth operation of the market and even cause a recession. We will return to this crucial point when we introduce the contributions of James Mill and David Ricardo.

Say's second conclusion is that "each individual is interested in the general prosperity of all, and that the success of one branch of industry promotes that of all the others" (Ibid., p. 137). This conclusion is reminiscent of Hume's argument in his 1758 essay "Of the Jealousy of Trade" that we covered in chapter two of the present work. Recall, Hume argued that the prosperity of a nation spills over to other nations. Say applies Hume's argument to industries within a nation and transactions among individuals. Say's third conclusion is as follows: "it is no injury to the internal and national industry and production to buy and import commodities from abroad; for nothing can be bought from strangers, except with native products, which find a vent in this external traffic" (Ibid., p. 139). We have already encountered this principle in the writings of Smith and Say himself. It supports free trade in the context of Say's law by stipulating that a country acquires foreign goods in exchange for her own goods.

The fourth and final conclusion constitutes the culmination of Say's law and deduces its policy implication. He (Ibid., p. 139) writes,

> the encouragement of mere consumption is no benefit to commerce; for the difficulty lies in supplying the means, not in stimulating the desire of consumption; and we have seen that production alone, furnishes those means. Thus *it is the aim of good government to stimulate production, and of bad government to encourage consumption.*
>
> For the same reason that the creation of a new product is the opening of a new market for other products, *the consumption or destruction of a product* is the stoppage of a vent for them. (Italics added)

Quite significantly, Say is advancing an argument *not* in favor of laissez-faire but against stimulating consumption; he would support policies such as lower taxes on business firms and even public spending on infrastructure, provided that they "stimulate production."

Say places "the consumption" of a product in the same level as its "destruction." James Mill, too, exhibits disdain for consumption. He (1821/1844, p. 226) begins his analysis of Say's law in *Elements of Political Economy* with the following argument:

> Everything, which is produced, belongs to somebody, and is destined by the owners to some use. There are however, but two sorts of use: that for immediate enjoyment, and that for ultimate profit. To use for ultimate profit, is to consume productively. To use for immediate enjoyment, is to consume unproductively.

Say's and Mill's characterization of consumption is puzzling because it dismisses the mutual relationship between production and consumption. If consumption is increased through, say, a *permanent* reduction in income tax or sales tax, then ultimately in response to higher demand production will increase. The disdain that both Say and Mill display for consumption goes against the following argument that Smith (1776/1981, p. 748) presents in the *Wealth of Nations*:

> *The increase of demand*, besides, though in the beginning it may sometimes raise the price of goods, never fails to lower it in the long run. It *encourages production*, thereby increases the competition of the producers, who, in order to undersell one another, have recourse to new division of labour and new improvements of arts, which might never otherwise have been thought of. (Italics added)

Despite the fact that the founders of Say's law made countless references to Smith in their writings, they ignored this passage. Perhaps the reason is that the dictum "The increase of demand … encourages production" is irreconcilable with Say's law. The case of Ricardo is particularly surprising, for he made over fifty references to the *Wealth of Nations* in his *Principles of Political Economy and Taxation*, many of which were critical of Smith's economics, but he did not refer to this passage. If the developers of Say's law had heeded Smith's wisdom on the role of demand and adopted a balanced approach towards production and consumption, the law of markets would have likely garnered more traction in the economics profession. Let's now turn to James Mill whose contribution to the development of Say's law proved decisive and even indispensable.

Mill's main intent is to dispel the fear of "over-production." He begins his analysis of Say's law in "Commerce Defended" with the observation that people save in order to earn profits in the future. He (1808/1997, p. 52) then notes, "That part, however, which is destined for future profit, is just as completely consumed, as that which is destined for immediate gratification." He further (Ibid., p. 56) writes, "The *Economistes* [sic] and their disciples express great apprehension lest capital should increase too fast, lest the production of commodities should be too rapid." But Mill (Ibid., p. 56) assures his readers that there is no ground for such apprehension because "The production of commodities creates, and is the one and universal cause which creates a market for the commodities produced." Mill (Ibid., p. 56) further notes that it is "the collective means of payments which exist in the whole nation that constitute the entire market of the nation." Moreover, "if a nation's power of purchasing is exactly measured by its annual produce, as it undoubtedly is; the more you increase the annual produce, the more by that very act you extend the national market, the power of purchasing and the actual purchases of the nation." Hence Mill (Ibid.) deduces that "a nation can never be naturally overstocked either with capital or with commodities; as the very operation of capital makes a vent for its produce." For this proposition to hold "All that here ever be requisite is that the *goods should be adapted to one another*; that is to say, that every man who has goods to dispose of should always find all those different sorts of goods with which he wishes to supply himself in return" (Ibid., p. 57, italics added). In chapter IV of his book *Elements of Political*

Economy (1821/1844), Mill elaborates on what he means by "adaptation" (the italicized phrase in the quote above) and the consequences of maladaptation. He (Ibid., pp. 234–235) writes,

> Let us next suppose, that this exact adaptation to one another of the parts of demand and supply is disturbed; let us suppose that, the demand for cloth remaining the same, the supply of it is considerably increased: there will of course be a glut of cloth, because there has been no increase of demand. But to the very same amount there must of necessity be a deficiency of other things; for the additional quantity of cloth, which has been made, could be made by one means only, by withdrawing capital from the production of other commodities and thereby lessening the quantity produced.

Mill goes on to explain that the operation of the price mechanism will eliminate the glut of any commodity. He (Ibid., p. 235) writes,

> The commodity, which happens to be in superabundance, declines in price; the commodity, which is defective in quantity rises … the lowness of the price, in the article which is superabundant, soon removes, by the diminution of profits, a portion of capital from that line of production: The highness of price, in the article which is scarce, invites a quantity of capital to that branch of production, till profits are equalized, that is, till the demand and supply are adapted to one another.[21]

In "Commerce Defended," Mill analyzes "foreign commerce" in the context of the law of markets. He states (1808/1997, p. 58), "The intention of [foreign commerce] is not to furnish a vent for the produce of the industry of the country, because that industry always furnishes a vent for itself." This statement counters Smith's "vent-for-surplus" argument. Smith (1776/1981, p. 372) had stated, "When the produce of any particular branch of industry exceeds what the demand of the country requires, the surplus must be sent abroad and exchanged for something for which there is a demand at home."[22] Mill, while criticizing the "vent-for-surplus" argument, apparently does not realize that his statement, "industry always furnishes a vent for itself," contradicts Say's observation (noted above) that the British goods had remained unsold in Brazil. Say blames Brazil's lack of purchasing power on insufficient production. But regardless of the reason, Say's observation demonstrates that, contrary to Mill's claim, an industry may fail to furnish a vent for itself. Mill (1808/1997, p. 58) goes on to point out that

> The intention of [foreign commerce] is to exchange a part of our own commodities for a part of the commodities which we prefer to our own of some other nation.… Its use and advantage is to promote a better distribution, division and application of labour of the country than would otherwise take place, and by consequence to render it more productive.

This passage reiterates the insight of several thinkers including Henty Martyn and Adam Smith (as noted in chapter two of the present work) that international trade is an exchange of our goods with those of other nations. This exchange, Mill (1808/1997, p. 58) notes, improves the allocation of resources, which is what international trade is fundamentally about, a crucial point that is still not understood by many policymakers.

Mill credits Smith for having been the first thinker to illustrate "that important doctrine ... that a progression is necessary in national affairs to render the circumstances of the great body of the people in any degree comfortable, our humanity, as well as our patriotism, will become deeply interested in the doctrine of parsimony" (Ibid., p. 59). Mill goes on to argue that economic growth is necessary to advance the living standards of "the laboring classes." He ends his analysis of the law of markets with these words: "Were the doctrine that it [the augmentation of capital] can increase too fast, as great a truth as it is an absurdity, the experience of all the nations on earth proves to us, that of all possible calamities this would be the least to be feared" (Ibid., pp. 59–60).

If Say and James Mill are the primary developers of the law of markets, David Ricardo and J. S. Mill qualify as its most ardent defenders and expounders. In *The Principles of Political Economy and Taxation*, Ricardo (1817/1996, p. 14) praises Say for having "succeeded in placing the science in a more logical and more instructive order; and has enriched it by several discussions, original, accurate, and profound." In a footnote (Ibid.) he writes that chapter XV of Say's book (the same chapter we reviewed above) "contains ... some very important principles." In chapter XXI of his own book, Ricardo (Ibid., p. 201) notes, "M. Say has ... most satisfactorily shown that there is no amount of capital which may not be employed, because a demand is only limited by production." He (Ibid., p. 202) reiterates the proposition that "Productions are always bought by productions, or by services; money is the only medium by which the exchange is effected."

In one of his correspondences with Malthus, Ricardo (1951/2004, Vol. VI, p. 148) writes,

> Mr. Say ... supports ... the doctrine that demand is regulated by production. Demand is always an exchange of one commodity for another. The shoemaker when he exchanges his shoes for bread has an effective demand for bread.... And if his shoes are not in demand it shews that ... he has not used his capital and his labour in the manufacture of the commodity required by the society; – more caution will enable him to correct his error in his future production.

The first part of the passage is a succinct restatement of some aspects of the law of markets already enunciated by Say. But the second part is different from, although not contradictory to, what Say had previously said. According to Say, the solution to a partial glut is to produce more of other goods while Ricardo calls for making less of the overproduced good. The chasm between them surfaces in a letter from Ricardo to Malthus in which he refers to Say and Robert Torrens (1780–1764).

Torrens had published an article in *Edinburgh Review* in 1819 in which he had sounded just like Say by writing that "a glut is an increase in the supply of a particular class of commodities, unaccompanied by a corresponding increase in the supply of those other commodities which should serve as their equivalents" (quoted in Chipman, 1965, p. 714). In his letter to Malthus, Ricardo (1951/2004, Vol. VIII, pp. 227–228) writes,

> They [Say and Torrens] appear to think that stagnation in commerce arises from a counter set of commodities not being produced with which the commodities on sale to be purchased, and they seem to infer that the evil will not be removed till such other commodities are in the market. But surely the true remedy is in regulating future production, – if there is a glut of one commodity produce less of that and more of another but do not let the glut continue till the producer chuses to produce the commodity which is wanted. I am not convinced by anything Say says of me – he does not understand me…

Although on this issue Ricardo disagrees with Say, he completely agrees with him on a central proposition of the law of markets – i.e., demand deficiency is not the cause of gluts. Ricardo writes, "Mistakes maybe made, and commodities not suited to the demand may be produced – of these there may be a glut; they may not sell at their usual price; but then this is owing to the mistake, and not to the want of demand for productions" (Ibid., Vol. II, pp. 304–306). Ricardo then asks if a producer cannot sell his output, "what does it prove? that he has not adapted his means well to his end, and he has miscalculated … it is at all times the bad adaptation of the commodities produced to the wants of mankind which is the specific evil, and not the abundance of commodities" (Ibid.). The notion of "bad adaptation," as we saw above, had already appeared in James Mill's "Commerce Defended."[23] On another occasion Ricardo (Ibid., Vol. IV, p. 345) notes, "When markets are dispersed and competition active great mistakes are made in the application of capital to the production of particular commodities, but this only proves the great risk of miscalculation, it does not impugn the general principle that if there were no mistakes there would be no glut." William Blake (Ibid., Vol. IV, p. 345) responded to Ricardo by writing, "This case therefore if founded does impugn the general principle. It shews that there may be more of every thing than is wanted – unless new tastes are introduced." McCulloch (1845, pp. 21–22) defended Mill and Ricardo as follows:

> if market be encumbered and a difficulty be experienced in effecting sales, we may be satisfied that the fault is not in producing too much, but in producing articles which do not suit the tastes of buyers, or which we ourselves cannot consume.… A glut never originates in an increase of production; but, is in every case, a consequence of the misapplication of the ability to produce, that is, of the producers not properly adapting their means to their ends. Let this error be rectified and the glut will disappear.

While classical economists believed that the operation of the market would eventually correct such errors, they argued that miscalculations and the resultant coordination failures could lead to economic downturns. Kates (2003, pp. 7–8) has described the consequences of failing to adapt the "means" of production to the "ends" as follows:

> Recessions are due to structural problems of one kind or another. In particular, recessions occur where the structure of supply does not match the structure of demand. Recessions occur when the pattern of demand is different from the actual composition of output so that a significant proportion of the goods and services put up for sale remain unsold.
>
> Partial overproduction of individual goods and services frequently occurs within economies and can lead to general downturn in the economy. The transmission mechanism commences from a reduction in earnings in some sectors of the economy where sales have been below expectations, through to a fall in demand in other sectors and therefore to a wholesale downturn in activity.

This sort of recession, however, should be relatively shallow and short since as soon as businesses realize their mistakes, they will set out to correct them. Calamities such as the Great Depression of 1930s and the Great Recession of 2008–2009, even if they start off as endogenously generated recessions, are usually exacerbated by exogenous forces.[24] Such forces, according to McCulloch, include "political regulations" and, more importantly, "sudden collapse of credit." With regard to the latter, he (1864/1965, p. 158) writes,

> A contraction and consequent rise in the value of money, being usually accompanied by a sudden collapse of credit … leads sometimes to very extensive revulsions. Such changes cannot, indeed, take place without entailing the most serious losses on all who have on hand considerable stocks of produce; they are also very apt to involve those who have been carrying on their business by the aid of borrowed money in serious difficulties; and if the rise in the value of money be considerable, the influence of the shock given to industry, and the disturbance in commercial channels, may be such as materially to abridge the power of the society to make their accustomed purchases; and may thus occasion a glut of the market.

Similarly, J. S. Mill (1848/2006, p. 574) while analyzing the law of markets argues,

> From the sudden annihilation of a great mass of credit, everyone dislikes to part with ready money, and many are anxious to procure it at any sacrifice. Almost everybody therefore is a seller, and there are scarcely any buyers; so that there may really be, though only while the crisis lasts, an extreme depression of general prices, from what may be indiscriminately called a

> glut of commodities or a dearth of money. But it is a great error to suppose, with Sismondi, that *a commercial crisis is* the effect of a general excess of production. It is *simply the consequence of an excess of speculative purchases. It is not a gradual advent of low prices, but a sudden recoil from prices extravagantly high: its immediate cause is a contraction of credit, and the remedy is, not a diminution of supply, but the restoration of confidence.* (Italics added)

This is an extraordinarily important passage. Mill attributes a commercial crisis to "an excess of speculative purchases" and "sudden recoil from prices extravagantly high" caused by a "contraction of credit." In such an economy, "confidence" is eroded and the remedy lies in its "restoration." But this was not the first time Mill had written of the role of confidence in the economy. In his 1829 essay on the law of markets, he had already mentioned "a want of commercial confidence" as a cause of recessions. In his own words (1829/2006, p. 279),

> The essentials of the doctrine [i.e., the law of markets] are preserved when it is allowed that there cannot be permanent excess of production, or of accumulation; though it be at the same time admitted, that as there may be a temporary excess of any one article considered separately, so may there of commodities generally, not in consequence of over-production, but of a want of confidence.

Exogenous factors that cause economic downturns impact not only the aggregate supply but quite often also the aggregate demand. As an example, consider the recession of the early 1980s in the United States. The recession was caused by the Federal Reserve System's sharp reduction in the supply of money in order to stanch the high rate of inflation in the late 1970s. The resultant soaring interest rate (in double digits) adversely affected not only the aggregate supply by reducing investment and production but also the aggregate demand by increasing the financing cost of durable items such as homes, automobiles, and appliances. In fact the aggregate demand fell independently of the decline in aggregate supply because the higher financing cost reduced the purchasing power of all people including those who retained their jobs and maintained their incomes. Besides, the concomitant collapse in the real estate and stock markets reduced households' wealth and thus consumption.

J. S. Mill's (along with Ricardo's) endorsement of Say's law in his seminal essay in 1829 and in *Principles of Political Economy* (1848) solidified the status of the law as a central theory in economics. Mill's analysis and exposition of the law of markets remained largely unchallenged until the onset of the Great Depression and the publication of Keynes's *General Theory* in 1936.

5. The law of markets in the twentieth century

In the early part of the *General Theory*, Keynes (1936/1997, p. 18) writes, "From the time of Say and Ricardo the classical economists have taught that supply creates its own demand; – meaning by this in some significant, but not clearly defined, sense that the whole of the costs of production must necessarily be spent in the aggregate, directly or indirectly, on purchasing the product." He makes it clear that his aim is to refute Say's law which he regards as a pillar of "the classical theory." Keynes (Ibid., pp. 21–22) argues that the classical theory rests on the following assumptions:

> 1 that the real wage is equal to the marginal disutility of the existing employment;
> 2 that there is no such thing as involuntary unemployment in the strict sense;
> 3 that supply creates its own demand in the sense that the aggregate demand price is equal to the aggregate supply price for all levels of output and employment.
>
> These three assumptions, however, all amount to the same thing in the sense that they all stand and fall together, any one of them logically involving the other two.

Keynes (1936/1997, p. 26) then draws a fundamental conclusion from these assumptions:

> Say's law, that the aggregate demand price of output as a whole is equal to its aggregate supply price for all output, is equivalent to the proposition that there is no obstacle to full employment. If, however, this is not the true law relating the aggregate demand and aggregate supply functions, there is a vitally important chapter of economic theory which remains to be written and without which all discussions concerning the volume of aggregate employment are futile.

Keynes set out to write "the vitally important chapter of economic theory" and produced the *General Theory*.

Although Keynes' statement – that according to Say's law "there is no obstacle to full employment" – is correct, the presence of unemployment does not discredit the law, which was developed in order to explain why recessions occur. The law, however, stresses the ability of the economy to recover *endogenously* from structural disharmonies as long as there are no external impediments to the workings of the market. Further, the law asserts that demand cannot fail and cause a recession. This is stated in a letter (dated 9 October 1820) from Ricardo (1951/2004, VIII, p. 277) to Malthus: "The difficulty of finding employment for Capital in the countries you mention proceeds from the prejudices and obstinacy with which men persevere in their old employments, – they expect daily a change for the better, and therefore continue to produce commodities for which there is no adequate demand.... Men err in their productions, there is no deficiency of demand." That is, demand exists but the wrong goods are produced.[25] Any apparent deficiency of demand, Say's law implies, reflects a deficiency of supply. The reason, in Ricardo's words (1817/1996, p. 2010), is that "demand is only limited by production." Malthus disagreed with this view, as did Keynes a century later. Keynes struck at the heart of Say's law by arguing that not all incomes are spent in the economy:

> The psychology of the community is such that when aggregate real income is increased aggregate consumption is increased, but not by so much as income. Hence employers would make a loss if the whole of the increased employment were to be devoted to satisfying the increased demand for immediate consumption. Thus, to justify any amount of employment there must be an amount of current investment sufficient to absorb the excess of total output over what the community chooses to consume when employment is at the given level. (Keynes 1936/1997, p. 27)

Keynes (Ibid., p. 21) maintains that saving and investment are "essentially different activities" and it is fallacious to suppose "that there is a nexus which unites decisions to abstain from present consumption with decisions to provide future consumption; whereas the motives which determine the latter are not linked in any simple way with motives which determine the former." Further, he (Ibid., pp. 27–28) notes that "the amount of current investment will depend, in turn, on what we shall call inducement to invest; and inducement to invest will be found to depend on the relation between the schedule of marginal efficiency of capital and the complex of interest on loans of various maturities and risks." Thus, according to Keynes, there is no guarantee that all savings will be absorbed in the economy – an assertion tantamount to saying that the aggregate demand can fall short of the aggregate supply and trigger a recession. Keynes further argues that the economy can get stuck in equilibrium below full employment in which case no endogenous force can bring forth full employment, and hence only an exogenous boost to the aggregate demand would solve the problem.

Keynes points to a fundamental issue with respect to unemployment. As Temin and Vines (2014, p. 51) put it, "Keynes was the first to argue that involuntary unemployment represented a failure in the product market, not a failure in the labor market." Accordingly, Keynesians argue that flexibility of wages will fail to reduce unemployment in a recession since businesses refrain from hiring workers, not because wages are too high, rather because of insufficient demand for their products. Keynes stressed the short run. He (1923/1971) famously remarked, "The long run is a misleading guide. In the long run we are all dead. Economists set themselves too easy, too useless a task if in tempestuous seasons they can only tell us that when the storm is long past the ocean is flat again." All this led to the Keynesian policy prescription that when there is a recession the government must increase the aggregate demand and reduce it when inflation is high.

Nonetheless, we find some common ground between Keynes and Say. Ricardo and James Mill argued that all savings would be borrowed for spending or investment; Malthus disagreed as did Keynes a century later. But surprisingly Say sided with Malthus (thus with Keynes) against Ricardo and Mill. In a letter to Malthus, Say (1821a/1967, p. 40) wrote,

> Mr. Ricardo insists that, notwithstanding taxes and other charges, there is always as much industry as capital employed; and that all capital saved is always employed, because the interest is not suffered to be lost. On the contrary, many savings are not invested, when it is difficult to find employment form them, and many which are employed are dissipated in ill-calculated undertakings. Besides, Mr. Ricardo is completely refuted, not only by what happened to us in 1813, when the errors of Government ruined all opportunities of employing it; but by our present circumstances when capitals are quietly sleeping in the coffers of their proprietors.

This is an astonishing statement. By resorting to empirical evidence Say refutes one of the tenets of the law of markets and notes that, contrary to Ricardo's claim, "many savings are not invested." Gootzeit (2003, p. 169) comments that "'capitals quietly sleeping' suggested hoarding."[26] This argument is substantively the same as that of Keynes, presented above. However, it is wrong to conclude – as Jeff Madrick (2014, p. 55) does – that Say "more or less eventually repudiated the proposition." Although he conceded that hoarding takes place, he never drew the policy implication (as Keynes did) that the government should manage the aggregate demand.

Related to the preceding analysis is Keynes' famous statement on "animal spirits," by which he means the public perception of the state of the economy plays a crucial role in making economic decisions. He (1936/1997, pp. 161–162) notes,

> a large portion of our positive activities depend on spontaneous optimism rather than on a mathematical expectations, whether moral, hedonistic or economics. Most, probably, of our decisions to do something positive, the full consequences of which will be drawn out over many days to come, can only be taken as a result of animal spirits – of a spontaneous urge to action rather than inaction.... Thus if the animal spirits are dimmed and the spontaneous optimism falters ... enterprise will fade and die; – though fears of loss may have a basis no more reasonable than hope of profit had before.

What is striking about this passage is that Keynes' argument about faltering "spontaneous optimism" substantively resembles J. S. Mill's "want of confidence." Both sentiments operate through the same channel and have the same adverse effect on the economy. Even on the most fundamental chasm between Keynesians and the classicists, namely, the role of government when the economy is in doldrums, some common grounds are possible. For example, the two camps would likely agree on policies such as government's spending on infrastructure – although they would interpret them differently. Keynesians would regard it as a boost to the aggregate demand since more people would be hired, and their increased consumption would lift the economy, while the classicists would view it as a boost to the aggregate supply because of the increase in capital formation. Of course, Keynes advocated policies that the classicists would have fiercely opposed. For example, he (1936/1977, p. 129) argued,

> If the Treasury were to fill old bottles with banknotes, bury them at suitable depths in disused coalmines which are then filled up to the surface with town rubbish, and leave it to private enterprise on well-tried principles of *laissez-faire* to dig the notes up again (the right to do so being obtained, of course, by tendering for leases of the note-bearing territory), there need be no more unemployment and, with the help of the repercussions, the real income of the community, and its capital wealth also, would probably become a good deal greater than it actually is. It would, indeed, be more sensible to build houses and the like; but if there are political and practical difficulties in the way of this, the above would be better than nothing.

The classicists maintained that in a recession the remedy lies in creating the purchasing power, which only production can accomplish.

In the decade following the publication of Keynes' *General Theory*, several important contributions to the literature on Say's law appeared. They include Oscar Lange (1942/1970) and Donald Patinkin (1948). They both argued that Say's law is incompatible with any theory of money. Lange (1942/1970, p. 50) introduced Walras' law, which maintains that, considering all commodities, "total demand and total supply are identically equal" where money is regarded as one of the commodities. He then defined Say's law, as "total demand for commodities (exclusively of money) is identically equal to their total supply." Hence, if Say's law holds, Lange (Ibid., p. 52) argued, by Walras' law demand for money must always equal the supply of money. But this implies that there is no need for a theory of money. As Lange (Ibid., p. 66) put it, "Say's law precludes any monetary theory. The theory of money must, therefore, start with a rejection of Say's law." Patinkin (1948, p. 135) argued that "the basic postulate of the classical monetary theory is that people do not derive any utility from holding money, and consequently it does not enter the utility function." But since people do want to hold "money as a means of dealing with uncertainty," Patinkin (Ibid., p. 136) deduced, "in a monetary economy, it is impossible for Say's law to hold."

The Lange–Patinkin attack on Say's law motivated Gary Becker and William Baumol (1952) to delve deeply into the law of markets. They (1952, pp. 356–357) noticed that there are two distinct variants of Say's law, not spelled out clearly in the literature. Becker and Baumol termed the two variants "Say's Identity" and "Say's Equality." They (Ibid.) defined Say's identity as follows:

> by summing over all individuals, we see that at any set of prices the total money demand for *commodities* will be equal to the total money value of the quantity supplied of all *commodities*. It is this which Lange and Patinkin have identified with Say's Law. Because it is taken to hold no matter what the price

> structure and to distinguish it from other versions of the "Law" we shall refer to it as Say's Identity. (Italics in original)

Say's identity implies that "the quantity of money demanded, considered either as a stock or a flow, is independent of the price structure and is always equal to the quantity supplied" (Ibid., p. 357). In a later publication, Baumol (1977, p. 146) defined Say's identity as "the assertion that no one ever wants to hold money for any significant amount of time, so that, as a result, every offer (supply) of a quantity of goods automatically constitutes a demand for a bundle of some other items of equal market value." That is, the only demand for money is for transaction purposes. This version of Say's law is clearly unrealistic. In fact in his 1829 classic essay J. S. Mill rejected Say's identity in the context of what he called "superabundance of commodities." He (1829/2006, p. 277) noted,

> What they called a general superabundance, was not a superabundance of commodities relatively to commodities, but a superabundance of all commodities relatively to money. What it amounted to was, that persons in general, at that particular time, form a general expectation of being called upon *to meet sudden demands*, liked better to possess money than any other commodity. Money, consequently, was in request, and all other commodities were in comparative disrepute. In extreme cases, *money is* collected in masses, and *hoarded*; in the milder cases, people merely defer parting with their money, or coming under any new engagements to part with it. (Italics added)

The statement allows for money to be held "to meet sudden demand" and even for "hoarding" which conforms to Say's contention that, as noted above, not all savings may be invested. Mill reintroduced the same argument in the context of the quantity theory of money in his *Principles of Political economy* as follows:

> Whatever increases the amount of this portion of the money in the country, tends to raise prices. But *money hoarded* does not act on prices. Money kept in reserve by individuals *to meet contingencies* which do not occur, does not act on prices. The money in the coffers of the Bank, or retained as a reserve by private bankers, does not act on prices until drawn out, nor even then unless drawn out to be expended in commodities. (1948/2006, pp. 514–515, italics added)

Note that for Mill money may be demanded for three purposes: transaction, hoarding, and contingencies. Again this is a rejection of Say's identity. Joseph Schumpeter (1954/1994, p. 619) rightly argues that the identity version "should not be called Say's law." Yet, it is the identity version that Lange and Patinkin interpreted as Say's law and attacked. Schumpeter (Ibid., pp. 619–620) further notes that this "identity or tautology was ludicrously created by Say for the express purpose of making his law unassailable.... What could not be sold except at a loss does not constitute production in the economic sense any more so than overproduction is excluded by definition! The professional world has laughed at him ever since." But this is an unfair characterization because as we have seen, Say did accept the reality of hoarding. Despite the harsh indictment, Schumpeter praises Say for having introduced the law of markets (as quoted in the epigraph to this chapter) and refers to Say's law as "neither trivial nor unimportant" (Ibid., p. 617). Hollander (1979) in two places (pages 512 and 513) notes that Ricardo "adhered to that version of the law of markets labelled 'Say's Equality.'" Perhaps only James Mill believed in (a mild version of) Say's identity.

Baumol (1977, p. 146) defines the second variant, i.e., Say's equality, as "the possibility of (brief) periods of disequilibrium during which the total demand for goods may fall short of the total supply, but … there exist reliable equilibrating forces that must soon bring the two together." The impetus behind Say's equality is the conviction that the market system is inherently stable and will restore full employment provided that prices are flexible.

Since Say's equality maintains that all markets gravitate towards equilibrium, it has a palpable affinity with the neoclassical interpretation of the invisible-hand theory (i.e., general equilibrium), explained in chapter one of the present work. But each proposition focuses on a different aspect of the market. The invisible hand concerns the spontaneous emergence of economic order through the endogenous coordination of countless transactions whereas Say's equality operates within the economic framework that has already emerged through the invisible-hand process. The invisible hand stresses processes such as decentralized division of labor across business units, utilization of knowledge dispersed among individuals, and the impossibility of macro-economic planning. But central to Say's equality are the notions of production, saving, investment, consumption, shortage, surplus, and hoarding – which only tangentially, if at all, enter into the analytical framework of the invisible hand. Yet the above contrasts pale compared with a philosophical chasm between Smith and Say. Evelyn Forget (2001), a scholar of Say, has argued that Say believed in only a limited version of the invisible-hand proposition. She (2001, p. 194) writes,

> Jean-Baptiste Say, while clearly aware of the writings of Smith … builds a coherent social analysis that accepts, to some extent, the idea of spontaneous order within the context of the marketplace, but emphatically rejects the idea that social institutions evolve and develop as an unplanned response to the uncoordinated behavior of many discrete and self-interested agents.

Forget (Ibid., p. 195) further writes, "while there is some evidence that Say was more sympathetic to Smith's system of natural liberty at the end of his life than he was in 1803 … he never fully adopts Smith's analysis." The starkest contrast between the two leading classical economists lies in the extent to which they believed people can be trusted to shape their own lives. According to Forget (Ibid.), Say operated on the premise that "individuals cannot be expected to determine their own [interests] correctly." Say's ideas on this point reflect the French intellectual tradition that regarded the ordinary human beings as incapable of making the right decisions.[27] Forget (Ibid., p. 200) further writes, "Say believed that administrators and teachers would know an individual's true interests better than the individual herself." In contrast, Smith in the tradition of the Scottish Enlightenment trusted people to pursue their own interests even though he believed in the fallibility of human beings. He (1776/1981, pp. 530–531) wrote,

> The man who employs either his labour or his stock in a greater variety of ways than his situation renders necessary, can never hurt his neighbour by underselling him. He may hurt himself, and generally does so. Jack of all trades will never be rich. But the law ought always to trust people with the care of their own interest, as in their local situations they must generally be able to judge better of it than the legislator can do.

Strikingly, on this crucial aspect of classical economics, Say's views are fundamentally different from those of Smith, and even more strikingly Say is on the same side as Keynes is! Recall from chapter one, Keynes, in his Sidney Ball lecture titled "The End of Laissez-Faire" (1924/1926, p. 8), argued, "It is *not* a correct deduction from the principle of economics that enlightened self-interest always operates in the public interest. Nor is it true that self-interest generally *is* enlightened; more often individuals acting separately to promote their own ends are too ignorant or too weak to attain even these" (italics in original). It is hardly believable that on such a core aspect of classical economics, Say is closer to Keynes than to Smith!

6. A final note

According to the law of markets, producers (i.e., entrepreneurs), while playing the primary role in the market, occasionally misread the market signals and make mistakes that derail the economy. But the law also maintains that price flexibility guarantees the system corrects itself. This self-correction character of the market raises certain questions. For example, did the founders of Say's law allow for any regulation of markets? Further, did they advocate activist policies by the government during a recession or a hands-off approach even though the recession might last for years? Concerning the first question, Arie Arnon (2011, chapter three) has argued that both Hume and Smith adopted an invisible-hand approach towards money and banking. While the assertion is correct about Hume, Smith's position on regulation is complicated. As noted in chapter one, classical economists including Smith and Ricardo recognized the tendency for overshooting in certain sectors of the economy, particularly the financial sector, and recommended some regulation. For example, in the context of regulating the financial sector, Smith (1776/1981, p. 324) noted, "Such regulations may, no doubt, be considered as in some respects a violation of natural liberty. But those exertions of the natural liberty of a few individuals, which might endanger the security of the whole society, are, and ought to be, restrained by the laws of all governments, of the most free as well as of the most despotical." Arnon (2011, p. 44) argues this quote represents an exception rather than the rule and that Smith's "general argument on money and banking is that of laissez-faire." Of course Smith's position rests firmly on the principle of natural liberty. But we saw in chapter one that Smith allowed for myriad interventions in the economy. With regard to the currency market David Laidler (1991, p. 39) notes, "The classical economists were clear that the regulation of the *currency* was the responsibility of government and provided an important exception to *laissez-faire* principles" (italics in original). In chapter one we also quoted Ricardo recommending certain regulations in the financial sector.

Concerning the second question on whether in a recession government should pursue policies to commence a recovery, let's recall Say's maxim, "it is the aim of good government to stimulate production, and of bad government to encourage consumption." Hence, Say would support policies that boost the aggregate supply but not the aggregate demand. A relevant question that has gained much traction lately in the wake of the Great Recession of 2008–2009 is whether massive government spending along with the resultant large budget deficits and seemingly unsustainable national debt hinder or advance economic recovery. Keynesians argue that since in a recession the economy may get stuck in underemployment equilibrium, even if the budget deficit is already large, it is necessary for the government to increase spending to move the economy towards full employment. But economists are divided on this issue. Some argue that if the government's budget deficit is large, economic recovery may require a decrease in government spending (i.e., austerity) rather than an increase.[28] Kates (2012) has argued austerity is consistent with Say's law and will lead to economic recovery. Jeff Madrick, a fierce critic of Say's law and austerity, notes (2014, p. 45) that "Say's law made a comeback after the Great Recession" and is the primary reason for the volatile European economy and the lackluster recovery in the U.S.[29] Whether Say's law ever made a comeback and – if it did – is responsible for the slow and haphazard recovery remains controversial.

Appendix: components of the law of markets

This appendix provides the propositions underlying the law of markets, as presented by Andrew Skinner (1967), William Baumol (1977) and Steven Kates (2003).

A1. Andrew Skinner

Skinner (1967, p. 162) condenses the law of markets in the following four propositions.

> 1 The law strictly so called establishes a necessary relationship between production and the level of purchasing power.

This is the basic proposition of the law of markets. Its veracity can be shown by noting that the "income created as a result of the production of commodities provides an equivalent which can be used in order to purchase commodities" (Skinner, 1967, p. 164). A corollary of the proposition is that higher levels of income generate higher levels of purchasing power. Skinner's second proposition is as follows.

> 2 Say assumed that the level of effective demand would be co-extensive with the level of purchasing power.

This proposition is tantamount to saying that effective demand depends on production since production generates the income/purchasing power which in turn determines the level of demand. Skinner's third proposition is the following.

> 3 Given the above assumption it was then possible for Say and James Mill to hold that there would be no tendency for a fall to take place in the level of activity.

This proposition is closely related to the preceding proposition and rests on the argument that savings return to the economy as investment. Skinner's final proposition is as follows.

> 4 However, since this last point depends not on the wording of the law, but on an assumption, it is evident that Say could and did, quite consistently with his statement of the law, recognise the *possibility* of a fall in the level of activity. Such a case will obtain wherever the assumed equality between purchasing power and effective demand does not hold good. (Italics in original)

This proposition has received the least attention in the literature because "while Say and the Mills recognized the possibility of contraction in the level of activity, they did not regard this as a probable case and thus did not give the problem any great emphasis" (Skinner, 1967, p. 166). Perhaps this was a position that Say held at some point. Recall that in a letter to Malthus, Say (1821a/1967, p. 40) admitted the reality of hoarding. See section five above.

A2. William Baumol

Since his 1952 paper with Becker, Baumol has made several contributions to the literature on Say's law. His 1977 paper, which we have already cited and quoted, is a highly important contribution to both the history and the theory of Say's law. A helpful feature of Baumol's paper is the inclusion of long passages from the first edition of Say's 1803 book and Mill's 1808 essay. His analysis led him to express the law of markets in the following seven propositions. As we shall see shortly, Baumol's first two propositions are very similar to those of Skinner.

> *Say's First Proposition*. A community's purchasing power (effective demand) is limited by and is equal to its output, because production provides the means by which outputs can be purchased. (p. 147, italics in original)

> *Say's Second Proposition.* Expenditure increases when output rises. (p. 147, italics in original)

> *Say's Third Proposition.* A given investment expenditure is a far more effective stimulant to the wealth of an economy than an equal amount of consumption. (p. 149, italics in original)

The third proposition has a significant policy implication because, as we saw before, according to the law of markets consumption cannot stimulate the economy. This remains a contentious and central issue respecting effective policies whenever the economy experiences a downturn.

> *Say's Fourth Proposition.* Over the centuries the community will always find demands for increased outputs, even for increases that are enormous. (p. 152, italics in original)

This proposition is a corollary of the first two propositions. As we already noted, Say observed that the level of consumption had substantially increased over the past few centuries, which he attributed to more production. The idea is that no society should ever be concerned with overproduction because "it is production which opens a demand for products" (Say, 1821b/1880/1964, p. 133). But as explained in section four above, this "demand" is for other "products."[30]

> *Say's Sixth Proposition.* Production of goods rather than the supply of money is the primary determinant of demand. Money facilitates commerce but does not determine the amounts of goods that are exchanged. (p. 154, italics in original)

Say expressed this notion as follows: "it is not the abundance of money but the abundance of other products that facilitates sales" (quoted in Baumol, 1977, p. 148).

> *Say's Seventh Proposition.* Any glut in the market for a good must involve relative underproduction of some other commodity, or commodities, and the mobility of capital out of the area with excess supply and into industries whose products are insufficient to meet demand will tend rapidly to eliminate the overproduction. (p. 154, italics in original)

This proposition is clearly laid out in James Mill's *Elements of Political Economy* (1821/1844, pp. 234–235) where he writes:

> … let us suppose that, the demand for cloth remaining the same, the supply of it is considerably increased; there will of course be a glut of cloth, because there has been no increase in demand. But to the very same amount there must of necessity be a deficiency of other things; for the additional quantity of cloth, which has been made, could be made by one means only, by

> withdrawing capital from the production of other commodities and thereby lessening the quantity produced.

James Mill (along with Say, Ricardo, and J.S. Mill) maintains that the reallocation of capital from the overproduced to the underproduced goods takes place *endogenously* in the economy. This is explained below in the next proposition.

> … the eighth (and for our purposes the last) of Say's eight propositions is Say's Law itself. Apparently this takes the form of a type of Say's equality, i.e., supply and demand are always equated by a rapid and powerful equilibration mechanism. (p. 159)

A3. Steven Kates

Kates edited a book on the law of markets in 2003 to mark the 200th anniversary publication of Say's first edition that launched the proposition which bears its name. In a fairly lengthy introduction to the book Kates (2003, pp. 7–8) presented the following bullet points as the components of the law of markets.

- Recessions are never due to demand deficiency. An economy can never produce more than its members would be willing or able to buy. A general glut (i.e. general overproduction) is therefore impossible. Neither high levels of saving nor the redirection of resources into higher levels of capital formation cause recessions to occur.
- Demand is constituted by supply. Aggregate demand is not independent of aggregate production but is identical with it. A community's purchasing power is constituted by its value added.
- The process involved in purchase and sale is the conversion of one's own goods or services into money and then the re-conversion of the money one has received back into other goods and services. There is no implication of a barter economy. Money is intrinsic to the processes involved.
- Recessions are common and result in high levels of involuntary employment.
- Recessions are due to structural problems of one kind or another. In particular, recessions occur where the structure of supply does not match the structure of demand. Recessions occur when the pattern of demand is different from the actual composition of output so that a significant proportion of the goods and services put up for sale remains unsold.
- Partial overproduction of individual goods and services frequently occurs within economies and can lead to a general downturn in the economy. The transmission mechanism commences from a reduction in earnings in some sectors of the economy where sales have been below expectations, through to a fall in demand in other sectors and therefore to a wholesale downturn in activity.
- Monetary factors, most notably a contraction of credit, can also be and often are an important cause of recession. Even where monetary instability has not

been the originating cause of recession, monetary factors will often deepen a recession brought on for other reasons.

- Because recessions are not due to a failure of demand, practical solutions to recession do not encompass increased levels of public spending. While such expenditure may provide some limited benefit if spending is concentrated on value adding goods and services, such expenditure is merely a palliative rather than a cure.

Notes

1 Economic historians have written voluminously and continue to write on why the West pulled ahead of the rest of the world and why the Industrial Revolution took place in England, and not elsewhere. For recent scholarship on these questions, see Niall Ferguson (2011) and Joe Mokyr (2009).
2 See William Easterly (2013, p. 288).
3 See Maddison (2001/2002, pp. 28, 126).
4 The countries are England, Holland, Italy, Spain, Sweden, and Portugal.
5 On this point, see Thomas Sowell's entry on Say's law in the *New Palgrave* (1987, p. 289).
6 Keynes (1883–1946) adopted (directly or indirectly, we do not know) the term "Say's law" from Fred Taylor (1855–1932) who coined it in a 1909 paper and used it in a text-book in 1921. For Keynes' adoption of the term, see Steven Kates (1998, p. 148). Kates (Ibid., p. 151) suggests that Keynes did not cite Taylor as the originator of the term because unlike Keynes, Taylor saw "no inconsistency between acceptance of Say's Law, recognition of the existence of depression and advocacy of public works. Keynes would thus not have found in Taylor support for his attacks on classical economic theory."
7 In reference to the law of markets, J. S. Mill (1848/2006, p. 576) writes, "the merit of having placed this most important point in its true light, belongs principally, on the continent, to the judicious J. B. Say, and in this country to Mr. Mill …"
8 For example, Paul Krugman (2014, p. 42) notes that in the recession of 2008–09 Say's law made a "comeback." Richard Posner (2010) argues that the deep recession of 2008–09 proves Say's law is a fallacious proposition. In particular, see chapter eight of his book. Jeff Madrick (2014, chapter two) says the U.S. economy has not been growing fast enough in the aftermath of the recession of 2008–09 because President "Obama may not have known that he subscribed to Say's law or that it was a foundation for economists' attacking the deficit." We return to this issue at the end of the chapter.
9 See the Appendix for the list of the components of Say's law put forth by the other scholars.
10 This is a theme in Barnard Mandeville's *Fable of the Bees* (1714) which we covered in chapter one in the context of the invisible-hand proposition.
11 That Keynes sided with mercantilists is clear from the following passage in the *General Theory* (1936/1997, p. 210): "AN [sic] act of individual saving means – so to speak – a decision not to have dinner to-day. But it does *not* necessitate a decision to have dinner or to buy a pair of boots a week hence or a year hence or to consume any specified thing at any specified date. Thus it depresses the business of preparing to-day's dinner without stimulating the business of making ready for some future act of consumption. It is not a substitution of future consumption-demand for present consumption-demand, – it is a net diminution of such demand" (italics in original).
12 Baumol (1977) has translated and provided many passages from the first edition of Say's book that was published in 1803. One of the passages is this: "When the exchanges have been completed it will be found that one has paid for products with products" (Baumol, 1977, p. 148).

13 Tucker is known to historians of economic ideas for his correspondences with David Hume on the impact of international trade on the economy. The exchanges between them is known as the "rich country–poor country" controversy and covered in Istvan Hont (2005) and Bruce Elmslie (1995).

14 In the literature on Say's law, saving is called "productive consumption" while consumption of goods and services is called "unproductive consumption."

15 See Samuel Hollander (1979, p. 73).

16 "Commerce Defended" is a lengthy essay which includes much more than the law of markets.

17 Evelyn Forget (1993, p. 123) has pointed out that Say published his revised book in 1814 even though he had completed the revision much earlier. This was owing to the fact that in France "freedom of the press did not exist, and no publisher was prepared to bring out another edition of" Say's book before 1814.

18 Chipman makes his statement while analyzing Ricardo's position. But of course it equally applies to Mill's.

19 Clower and Axel Leijonhufvud (1973), based on earlier works by Clower, introduce a proposition which they label "Say's principle" and define it as "*the net value of an individual's planned trades is identically zero*" (p. 2, italics in original). This definition, the authors believe, should replace "supply creates its own demand." They (Ibid., p. 10) argues that unlike Keynes' definition, Say's principle "is entirely consistent with the existence of large-scale unemployment." The principle "is also consistent with indefinite persistence of unemployment on a large-scale, for it involves no assumptions and yields no implications about the dynamic adjustment behavior of the economic system." Say's principle may be a sensible proposition but its utility is not spelled out, which perhaps explains why, despite the notable reputation of the authors, most scholars of Say's law with the exception of Hutt (1974) and Kates (1998) do not even cite it in their works.

20 In a footnote, Say (1821b/1880/1964, p. 138) chastises Voltaire for repeating the erroneous mercantilist view that "it is clearly impossible for one country to gain, except by the loss of another." Say correctly refers to it as "false reasoning."

21 Mill's analysis of market operation in this quote is considerably similar to Smith's analysis in chapter VII of Book I of the *Wealth of Nations*.

22 Ricardo (1817/2006, p. 202) quotes Smith's passage and expresses his disagreement with it.

23 Mill in his *Elements of Political Economy* (1921/1965, p. 241) also blames gluts on what he calls "miscalculation." Such miscalculations abound in the economy. The following example is from James Brickley *et al.* (2004, p. 67). In the late 1970s General Electric made substantial investment in developing small appliances based on the data showing "houses and families were shrinking." From these data GE inferred that the demand for small appliances should rise. But despite the smaller families the size of kitchens was actually getting larger and households "wanted larger refrigerators … General Electric wasted a lot of time and money designing smaller appliances."

24 As discussed in the next chapter on the quantity theory of money, Milton Freidman and Anna Schwartz (1963) argue that the Federal Reserve System's failure to prevent a significant decline in the money supply turned an ordinary recession in 1929 into the Great Depression of the 1930s. Joseph Stiglitz, who *rejects* the notion that markets are efficient, stable, and self-correcting (2014, p. 334), nonetheless, in his list of possible causes of the recession of 2008–2009, includes (2009) a sharp reduction in the interest rate engineered by the Federal Reserve System that inadvertently led to the housing bubble and, when burst, exacerbated the recession. Without the housing bubble the recession, even if it still happened, would not have been as severe as it turned out to be.

25 In the year 1837 Sismonde de Sismondi complained, "industrialists … pile up products on the markets.… Production continues to grow at an incalculable speed. Has the moment not yet come, or is it not imminent when we will have to say: this is too much?" (Quoted in Evelyn Forget, 2003, p. 58).

26 As we shall see shortly, J. S. Mill, too, accepted the reality of hoarding.

27 François Quesnay (1694–1774) a leading figure in the physiocratic school of economics in France is a representative of this French tradition. Say must have been thoroughly familiar with Quesnay's views and in all likelihood he came under his sway. On Quesnay's view on this point, see Easterly (2013, pp. 335–337).

28 Empirical works have not settled this issue. See Dellas and Dirk Niepelt (2014), Benjamin Born *et al.* (2015), and Alesina *et al.* (2015). These authors have not been able to substantiate the Keynesian stance by examining the data.

29 As we noted in the introduction to this chapter, Krugman (2014, p. 42) also remarked that Say's law made a comeback during the Great Recession.

30 The title of Baumol's paper is, "Say's (at least) Eight Laws…" but he actually listed only seven, as he acknowledged in a later paper (Baumol, 2003, p. 35). He does not present a fifth proposition.

Bibliography

Alesina, Alberto, Omar Barbiero, Carlo Favero, Francesco Giavazzi, and Matteo Paradisi (2015), "Austerity in 2009–2013," *NBER Working Paper* No. w20827.

Arnon, Arie (2011), *Monetary Theory and Policy from Hume and Smith to Wicksell*, Cambridge, UK: Cambridge University Press.

Baumol, William J. (1977), "Say's (at Least) Eight Laws, or What Say and James Mill May Really Have Meant," *Economica* 44, pp. 145–162.

Baumol, William J. (1999), "Retrospectives: Say's Law," *Journal of Economic Perspectives* 13, 1, pp. 195–204.

Baumol, William J. (2003), "Say's Law and More Recent Macro Literature: Some Afterthoughts," in *Two Hundred Years of Say's Law*, Ed. by Steven Kates, Cheltenham, UK: Edward Elgar, pp. 34–38.

Becker, Gary and William Baumol (1952), "The Classical Economic Theory: The Outcome of the Discussion," *Economica* 19, pp. 355–376.

Blaug, Mark (1997), "Say's Law of Markets: What Did It Mean and Why Should We Care?" *Eastern Economic Journal* 23, 2, pp. 231–235.

Born, Benjamin, Gernot Muller and Johannes Pfeifer (2015), "Does Austerity Pay Off?" *CEPR Discussion Paper* No. DP10425.

Brickley, James (2004), *Managerial Economics and Organizational Architecture*, New York, NY: McGraw-Hill Irwin.

Chipman, John (1965), "A Survey of the Theory of International Trade: Part 2, The Neo-Classical Theory," *Econometrica* 33, 4, October, pp. 685–760.

Clower, Robert and Axel Leijonhufvud (1973), "Say's Principle, What It Means and Doesn't Mean," *International Economic Review* 4, pp. 1–16.

Dellas, Harris and Dirk Niepelt (2014), "Austerity," *CEPR Discussion Paper* No. DP10315.

Easterly, William (2013), *The Tyranny of Experts: Economists, Dictators, and the Forgotten Rights of the Poor*, New York, NY: Basic Books.

Eichengreen, Barry (2015), *Hall of Mirrors*, Oxford, UK: Oxford University Press.

Elmslie, Bruce (1995), "Retrospective: The Convergence Debate between David Hume and Josiah Tucker," *Journal of Economic Perspectives* 9, 4, pp. 207–216.

Eltis, Walter (2005), "Money and General Gluts: The Analysis of Say, Malthus, and Ricardo," *History of Political Economy* 37, 4, pp. 661–689.

Ferguson, Niall (2011), *Civilization: The West and the Rest*, New York, NY: Penguin Books.

Forget, Evelyn (1993), "J.-B Say and Adam Smith: An Essay in the Transmission of Ideas," *The Canadian Journal of Economics* 26, 1, February, pp. 121–133.

Forget, Evelyn (2001), "Jean-Baptiste Say and Spontaneous Order," *History of Political Economy* 33, 2, pp. 193–318.

Forget, Evelyn (2003), "Jean-Baptiste Say and the Law of Markets: Entrepreneurial Decision-Making in the Real World," in *Two Hundred Years of Say's Law*, Ed. by Steven Kates, 2003, Cheltenham, UK: Edward Elgar, pp. 50–66.

Fouquet, Roger and Stephen Broadberry (2015), "Seven Centuries of European Economic Growth and Decline," *Journal of Economic Perspectives* 29, 4, pp. 227–244.

Freidman, Milton and Anna Schwartz (1963), *A Monetary History of the United States, 1867–1960*, Princeton, NJ: Princeton University Press.

Gootzeit, Michael (2003), "Savings, Hoarding and Say's Law," in *Two Hundred Years of Say's Law*, Ed. by Steven Kates, Cheltenham, UK: Edward Elgar, pp. 168–185.

Hollander, Samuel (1979), *The Economics of David Ricardo*, Toronto, CAN and Buffalo, NY: University of Toronto Press.

Hont, Istavan (2005), *Jealousy of Trade: International Competition and the Nation-State in Historical Perspective*, Cambridge, MA: The Belknap Press of Harvard University Press.

Hutt, W.H. (1974), *A Rehabilitation of Say's Law*, Athens, OH: Ohio University Press.

Kates, Steven (1998), *Say's Law and the Keynesian Revolution: How Macroeconomics Lost Its Way*, Cheltenham, UK: Edward Elgar.

Kates, Steven (2003), *Two Hundred Years of Say's Law*, Cheltenham, UK: Edward Elgar.

Kates, Steven (2012), "Alesina and the Keynesians: Austerity and Say's Law," *Atlantic Economic Journal* 40, pp. 401–415.

Keynes, John Maynard (1923/1971), *A Tract on Monetary Reform: The Collected Writings of John Maynard Keynes*, Volume IV, London, UK: MacMillan St. Martin's Press.

Keynes, John Maynard (1924/1926), 'The End of Laissez Faire' in J. M. Keynes, *Essays in Persuasion*, London: Palgrave-Macmillan.

Keynes, John Maynard (1936/1997), *The General Theory of Employment, Interest, and Money*, Amherst, NY: Prometheus Books.

Krugman, Paul (2014), "Why Weren't Alarm Bells Ringing?" *New York Review of Books*, October 23 issue. Accessed January 2016 from www.nybooks.com/articles/archives/2014/oct/23/why-werent-alarm-bells-ringing.

Laidler, David (1991), *The Golden Age of the Quantity Theory*, Princeton, NJ: Princeton University Press.

Lambert, Paul (1956), "The Law of Markets prior to J.-B. Say and the Say-Malthus Debate," *International Economic Papers* 6.

Lange, Oscar (1942/1970), "Say's Law: A Restatement and Criticism," in *Papers in Economics and Sociology*, Ed. by Oskar Lange, Oxford, UK: Pregamon Press, pp. 49–68.

Maddison, Angus (2001/2002), *The World Economy: A Millennial Perspective*, OECD: Development Centre Studies.

Madrick, Jeff (2014), *Seven Bad Ideas: How Mainstream Economists Have Damaged America and the World*, New York, NY: Alfred A. Knopf.

Mandeville, Bernard (1714/1924), *The Fable of the Bees: Private Vices, Publick Benefits*, Oxford: The Clarendon Press.

McCulloch, John Ramsay (1845), *The Literature of Political Economy*, London, UK: Longmans, Brown, Green, and Longmans.

McCulloch, John Ramsay (1864/1965), *The Principles of Political Economy*, 5th edition, New York, NY: Augustus M. Kelley.

Mill, James (1808/1997), "Commerce Defended," in *Free Trade: 1793–1886, Early Sources in Economics*, Volume I, Ed. by Lars Magnusson, London, UK and New York, NY: Routledge, pp. 21–98.

Mill, James (1821/1844), *Elements of Political Economy*, 3rd edition, New York, NY: Augustus M. Kelley, Booksellers.

Mill, John Stuart (1829/2006), "On the Influence of Consumption on Production," in Volume 4 of *Collected Works of John Stuart Mill*, Ed. by J. M. Robson, Toronto, CAN: University of Toronto Press, pp. 262–379.

Mill, John Stuart (1848/2006), *Principles of Political Economy*, Collected Works of John Stuart Mill, Indianapolis, IN: Liberty Fund.

Mokyr, Joel (2009), *The Enlightened Economy*, New Haven, CT and London, UK: Yale University Press.

Patinkin, Don (1948), "Relative Prices, Say's Law, and the Demand for Money," *Econometrica* 16, pp. 135–154.

Posner, Richard (2010), *The Crisis of Capitalist Democracy*, Cambridge, MA: Harvard University Press.

Ricardo, David (1817/1996), *Principles of Political Economy and Taxation*, Great Mind Series, Amherst, NY: Prometheus Books.

Ricardo, David (1951/2004), *The Works and Correspondence of David Ricardo*, Volumes I through XI, Ed. by Pier Sraffa, Cambridge, UK: Cambridge University Press.

Robbins, Lionel (1953), *The Theory of Economic Policy in English Classical Political Economy*, New York, NY: St. Martin Press.

Say, Jean-Baptiste (1803/1827), *A Treatise on Political Economy*, 3rd edition, Philadelphia, PA: John Griggs.

Say, Jean Baptiste (1821a/1967), *Letters to Mr. Malthus on Various Subjects of Political Economy; Particularly on the Causes of the General Stagnation of Commerce*, New York, NY: Augustus M. Kelley.

Say, Jean Baptiste (1821b/1880/1964), *A Treatise on Political Economy*, New York, NY: Augustus M. Kelley.

Schumpeter, Joseph A. (1954/1994), *History of Economic Analysis*, New York, NY: Oxford University Press.

Skinner, Andrew (1967), "Say's Law: Origins and Content," *Economica* 34, 134, pp. 153–166.

Smith, Adam (1776/1981), *An Inquiry into the Nature and Causes of the Wealth of Nations*, Indianapolis, IN: Liberty Fund.

Sowell, Thomas (1972), *Say's Law: An Historical Analysis*, Princeton, NJ, Princeton University Press.

Sowell, Thomas (1987), "Say's Law," in *The New Palgrave: A Dictionary of Economics*, Ed. by John Eatwell, Murray Milgate, and Peter Newman. Vol. 4, pp. 249–251.

Sowell, Thomas (2006), *On Classical Economics*, New Haven, CT and London, UK: Yale University Press.

Spengler, Joseph (1945), "The Physiocrats and Say's Law of Markets. II," *Journal of Political Economy* 53, 4, December, pp. 317–347.

Stiglitz, Joseph (2009), "Capitalist Fools," Vanity Fair, January 2009, Reprinted in Stiglitz (2015), *The Great Divide*, New York, NY: W.W. Norton & Co, pp. 40–48.

Stiglitz, Joseph (2014), "The Lessons of the North Atlantic Crisis for Economic Theory and Policy," in *What Have We Learned*, Ed. by George Akerlof, Olivier Blanchard, David Romer, and Joseph Stiglitz, Cambridge, MA: The MIT Press.

Sweezy, Paul (1947/1960), "Keynes, the Economist," in *The New Economics: Keynes' Influence on Theory and Public Policy*, Ed. by Seymour Harris, London, UK: Dennis Dobson, pp. 102–109.

Temin, Peter and David Vines (2014), *Keynes: Useful Economics for the World Economy*, Cambridge, MA: The MIT Press.

4 The quantity theory of money

"One thing is certain: the quantity theory of money will continue to generate agreement, controversy, repudiation, and scientific analysis, and will continue to play a role in government policy during the next century as it has in the past three." (Milton Friedman, 1987, p. 19)

Chapter contents

1. Introduction

According to the quantity theory of money, the volume of money is the primary determinant of the price level. Mark Blaug (1995, p. 28) has put it this way: "There is absolutely no doubt that the quantity theory of money is, and always has been, a theory of the determination of the general price level." However, during the transition period, i.e., between a *change* in the supply of money and its impact on prices, money can and often does affect the economy's output. This means money with respect to output is neutral in the long-run but non-neutral in the short-run. In the long-run, output depends on real factors including population, physical capital, and technology while whatever the level of money supply happens to be, the quantity theory asserts, prices ultimately will adjust to it. In 1752 David Hume (1711–1776) laid down these two properties of the quantity theory in an essay titled "Of Money." He (1752a/1955, pp. 37–38) wrote,

> though the high price of commodities be a necessary consequence of the encrease of gold and silver, yet it follows not immediately upon that encrease; but some time is required before the money circulates through the whole state, and makes its effect be felt on all ranks of people. At first no alteration is perceived; by degrees the price rises, first of one commodity, then of another; till the whole specie which is in the kingdom. In my opinion, it is only in this interval or intermediate situation, between the acquisition of money and rise of prices, that the encreasing quantity of gold and silver is favourable to the industry.

In a later section we shall delve into the writings of Hume; here, it suffices to note that this passage establishes the proposition of causality; that is, a change in the money supply is the casual factor and precedes the change in the level of prices. Hume also affirms the proposition of proportionality; that is, a change in the money supply leads to a proportional change in the level of prices. He (1752a/1955, p. 33) writes, "If we consider any one kingdom by itself, it is evident, that the greater or less plenty of money is of no consequence; since the prices of commodities are always proportioned to the plenty of money…" Hume reiterates the proposition of proportionality in another essay titled, "Of the Balance of Trade." In this latter essay Hume (1752b/1955, p. 68) argues that "We fancy, because an individual would be much richer, were his stock of money doubled, that the same good effect would follow were the money of everyone encreased; not considering, that this would raise as much the price of every commodity, and reduce every man, to the same condition as before." In modern terms, real income remains the same even though the nominal income has doubled.

Although the insight into the effects of money on the economy predates Hume by at least two centuries and only a generation before him, John Locke (1632–1704) had authored a lengthy treatise much of which focused on the quantity theory, Hume's writings in the middle of the eighteenth century have been most influential for the subsequent evolution of the theory. This chapter describes and analyzes the historical development of the quantity theory of money since it was first articulated in the sixteenth century. We will also study the application of the quantity theory in various economic episodes, in particular the periods of economic upheavals including the Great Depression of the 1930s and the Great Recession of 2008–2009. While this latter episode is still unfolding, sufficient time has elapsed for an assessment in light of the quantity theory of money.

In the minds of many thinkers, the Great Depression of the 1930s discredited the tenets of classical economics including the quantity theory of money. John Maynard Keynes reinforced the prevailing sentiment and convinced a lot of people that the quantity theory is an unreliable guide for policy formulation. In fact an inseparable part of the history of the quantity theory of money in the twentieth century is Keynes' critical writings. In addition to reviewing Keynes' analysis of the quantity theory, we will present Milton Friedman's scholarly efforts that played the central role in restoring the theory's credibility.

2. The quantity theory of money before David Hume

In 1576 the French scholar Jean Bodin published a treatise in which he argued the rising prices in the middle of the sixteenth century were caused by several factors including the flow of gold and silver from the Americas into Europe. Because of this observation, Joseph Schumpeter (1954/1995, p. 31) writes that Bodin "is universally voted as the 'discoverer' of the Quantity Theory of Money." However, Hugo Hegeland (1951, pp. 7–14) mentions several thinkers who prior to Bodin had related rising prices to an increase in the quantity of species. They include Chia Yi, a disciple of Confucius; the Greek historian Xenophon; Julius Paulus, a lawyer in ancient Rome; Nicole Oresme, a fourteenth-century scholar; and most famously Nicholas Copernicus (1473–1543). These thinkers generally don't receive much credit because they expressed their understanding of the quantity theory of money less clearly than Bodin did. In this group of thinkers Copernicus stands out because he had designed monetary reforms including that of Prussia in 1519 even though he was an astronomer. Additionally, his writings on the quantity theory are the least obscure as compared to those of the others. In 1526 he wrote,

> Money loses its value above all when it is increased too much, for example, when too great a quantity of silver has been transformed into money, so that men will strive to attain bullion rather than the denominator. Money will lose all its 'dignity' when it cannot any longer buy as much silver as it contains, and when it will be profitable to melt it down. The only remedy, then, is not to coin money any more until it has restored its equilibrium and regained a higher value than bullion. (Quoted in Hegeland, 1951, p. 14)

Hegeland (Ibid.) refers to this passage as "peculiar, because it says that the value of money can *sink below* the value of the quantity of metal contained ... making it profitable to melt the coins and to pay with bullion. So if the metal in question does not appear as coins, its value will increase!" (italics in original). Although Copernicus understood the relationship between money and prices, he did not articulate it as well as Bodin would do fifty years later. But he prepared the path for Bodin and others.[1]

The next major thinker in the history of the quantity theory is John Locke. He presented his views in 1691 in a lengthy response (reads like a treatise) to Josiah Child, who had proposed in 1688 that the maximum interest rate be reduced from six to four percent. In the early part of the treatise, Locke (1691/1963, p. 14) rejected "conquest" as a means of acquiring wealth, and argued that "Trade, then, is necessary to the production of riches, and money necessary to the carrying on of trade." Since the institution of central banking did not exist at that time, trade surplus served as the main, if not the only, source of increasing the supply of money. Thus Locke espoused mercantilist views such as "our growing rich or poor depends not at all upon our borrowing upon interest, or not; but only, which is greater or less, our importation or exportation of consumable commodities"

(Ibid., p. 15). Moreover, he (Ibid., p. 20) argued, "We may trade, and be busy, and grow poor by it, unless we regulate our expenses. So that ... money is brought into England by nothing but spending here less of foreign commodities than what we carry to market can pay for..."

Locke practiced what he preached. Walter Eltis (1995, p. 23) notes that as "a Member of the Board of Trade ... Locke... ran a very interventionist industrial policy.... He protected British woollen industry from Irish competition, but sought none the less to give Ireland something by subsidizing the start-up of an Irish linen industry." Locke, unlike some other mercantilists, did not regard money as wealth, but his advocacy for protectionist policies and trade surplus as a means of creating riches casts doubts on his understanding of the complexity of the economy. As we saw in chapter two, David Hume showed why the mercantilists' position is unsustainable, and Adam Smith exposed the fallacy of their argument.[2] Locke's attempt to maintain the necessary level of money supply in Britain led him to oppose Child's proposal that the interest rate be reduced. He (1691/1963, p. 29) argued, "we may see what injury the lowering of interest is like to do us, by hindering trade, when it shall either make the foreigner call home his money, or your own people backward to lend, the reward not being judged proportionable to the risque." If the money supply declines, he (Ibid., pp. 70–71) argued, landowners will be the first to be impacted

> because money failing, and falling short, people have not so much money as formerly to lay out, and so less money is brought to market, by which the price of things must necessarily fall. The labourer feels it next; for when the landholder's rent falls, he must either bate the labourer's wages, or not employ, or not pay him; which either way makes him feel the want of money. The merchant feels it last, for though he sells less, and at a lower rate, he buys also our native commodities, which he exports at a lower rate too, and will be sure to leave our native commodities unbought, upon the hands of the farmer or manufacturer, rather than export them to a market which will not afford him returns with profit.
>
> If one-third of the money employed in trade were locked up, or gone out of England, must not the landholders necessarily receive one-third less for their goods, and consequently rents fall; a less quantity of money by one-third being to be distributed amongst an equal number of receivers?

Locke's analysis amounts to the non-neutrality of money because, he argued, changes in the supply of money affect the real sector of the economy in addition to affecting prices. He (Ibid., p. 49) makes this point more clearly and explicitly in the following passage:

> Supposing then, that we had now in England half as much money as we had seven years ago, and yet we had still as much yearly product of commodities, as many hands to work them, and as many brokers to distribute them, as before; and that the rest of the world we trade with had as much money as

> they had before … it is certain, that either half our rents should not be paid, half our commodities not be vented, and half our labourers not employed, and so half the trade be clearly lost; or else, that every one of these must receive but half the money for their commodities and labour they did before, and but half so much as our neighbours do receive, for the same labour, and the same natural product at the same time. Such a state of poverty as this, though it will make no scarcity of our native commodities amongst us, yet it will have these ill consequences.

Thus Locke argued that halving the money supply will proportionally lower output (hence employment) or prices (hence wages and rent) or conceivably and alternatively will lower both output and prices. Locke's treatise prepared the path for several thinkers in the eighteenth century.

3. Richard Cantillon, Montesquieu, and David Hume

According to Richard Cantillon (1680–1734), by the 1730s the basic concept of the quantity theory had become a commonly accepted doctrine.[3] He (1755/2010, p. 147) writes, "Everybody agrees that the abundance of money, or an increase in its use in exchange, raises the price of everything." Part two of the *Essai*, titled "Money and Interest," offers an extensive analysis of the quantity theory. In particular, almost the entire chapters six, seven, and eight focus on the impact of the quantity of money on prices and the transmission mechanism. Cantillon (Ibid., p. 148) takes an issue with Locke because

> Mr. Locke lays it down as a fundamental maxim that the quantity of goods in proportion to the quantity of money is a regulator of market prices. … he has clearly seen that abundance of money makes everything more expensive, but he has not considered how this happens. The great difficulty of this question consists in knowing in what way and in what proportion the increase of money raises the price of things.

Cantillon (Ibid.) further notes that a rise in the velocity of money has the same effect on the economy as an increase in the money supply.

Cantillon (Ibid.) argues that the main channel through which money affects prices is consumption: "an increase of hard money in a state will cause a corresponding increase in consumption and this will gradually produce increased prices." He (Ibid., p. 149) goes on to say that rents and wages will also rise. However, he rejects the proportionality proposition of the quantity theory. He (Ibid., p. 157) writes,

> an increase in actual money in a state always causes an increase in consumption and a routine of greater expenditures. But the higher prices caused by this money does not affect all commodities and merchandise equally. Prices do not rise proportionally to the quantity of money, unless what has been added

> continues in the same circulation channels as before. In other words, those who offered one ounce of silver in the market would be the same and only ones to offer two ounces when the amount of money in circulation is doubled, and that is hardly the case.

Cantillon warns against what he (Ibid., pp. 149–150) calls "overabundance of money," for it leads to higher prices and wages as well as importation of goods and hence exportation of money. Here Cantillon espouses a Mercantilist fallacy. He says the money that "will necessarily go aboard to pay for the imports … will gradually impoverish the state and make it, in a way, dependent on foreigners to whom it is obliged to send money …" Cantillon also loathes the purchase of luxury items from abroad to the point that he (Ibid., p. 167) argues "the Roman Empire declined through the loss of money before losing its estates. That is what luxury brought about, and what it always will bring about in similar circumstances." This is a puzzling statement since the downfall of a nation hinges on many variables and is far more complicated than consuming a certain category of goods.[4] As we saw in chapter two of the present work, both Hume and Smith wrote extensively to refute such mercantilist dogmas. Hume's enunciation of the quantity theory, in particular, as we shall see shortly, intended to demonstrate that the quantity of money is irrelevant to the operation of the economy.

The famed French philosopher Montesquieu (1689–1755) published his influential book *The Spirit of the Laws* in 1748 (i.e., before Cantillon's *Essai* came out) but he had likely read the *Essai* because, along with Smith and Hume, he belonged to the intellectual circle in which the *Essai* had been disseminated before publication. *The Spirit of the Laws* is not a work on economics, but in book XXII Montesquieu discusses various aspects of money including the effects of money on prices. Since book XXII covers nineteen topics in thirty-five pages, the analysis of each topic is quite short. Nonetheless, we will review it here because Montesquieu presents a clear statement of the quantity theory, which – as we shall see shortly – elicited a response from Hume. Quite possibly the correspondence between the two philosophers motivated Hume to author his classic essays on money, interest, and the balance of payment.

Montesquieu asserts the proportionality aspect of the quantity theory. He (1748/1900, p. 456) writes, "If, since the discovery of Indies, gold and silver have increased in Europe in the proportion of one to twenty, the price of provisions and merchandise must have been enhanced in the proportion of one to twenty." His next sentence is quite significant for the evolution of the quantity theory: "But if, on the other hand, the quantity of merchandise has increased as one to two – it necessarily follows that the price of this merchandise and provisions, having been raised in proportion of one to twenty, and fallen in proportion of one to two – it necessarily follows, I say, that the proportion is only one to ten." If we assume the velocity of money remains constant, Montesquieu's statement qualifies as a statement of "the equation of exchange" that Irving Fisher popularized in 1911. (We shall explain Fisher's contribution in a later section.) Montesquieu (Ibid., pp. 456–457) continues, "The quantity of goods and merchandise increases by an augmentation of commerce, the augmentation of commerce [sic] by an augmentation of the specie which successively arrives, and by new communications with freshly discovered countries and seas, which furnish us with new commodities and new merchandise." Montesquieu articulated the quantity theory, albeit quite briefly, more clearly and concisely than anyone before him including John Locke.

In 1749, one year after the publication of *The Spirit of the Laws*, Hume wrote a letter to Montesquieu regarding several issues in the book including the effect of money on prices. A part of the letter reads:

> The abundance of gold and silver in a state is very advantageous to it, if one considers the neighboring states, because those foreigners will exchange for it their goods and labour; but, *in respect to domestic commerce, this abundance of gold and silver is of no advantage whatever*; on the contrary, it raises the cost of labour and hinders exportation; paper has the same inconveniences as coined money, and none of its advantages. (Hume, 1749/1955, p. 188, italics added)

The italicized statement, as we shall see shortly, is central to Hume's quantity theory of money. Following the above passage, Hume (Ibid.) notes,

> It appears that we are, in England, too much concerned about the balance of trade. It is difficult for a loss of balance to reach the point where it will do considerable harm to a nation. If half the money in England were suddenly destroyed, labour and goods would suddenly become so cheap that there would suddenly attract to us the money of all our neighbours. If half the money which is in England were suddenly doubled, goods would suddenly become more expensive, imports would rise to the disadvantage of exports and our money would be spread among all our neighbours.

This passage lays out Hume's "specie-flow mechanism" which we briefly reviewed in chapter two. It maintains that trade deficit is not sustainable since the resultant outflow of money causes prices to fall, leading to less import and more exports. Nor is trade surplus sustainable because, Hume argues, the reverse process would shrink the surplus. Further, in an open economy the quantity of money "must rise and fall in proportion to the goods and labour contained in each state" (Ibid., p. 189). The strength of Hume's argument rests on his ability to employ a general equilibrium method of analysis in which prices, trade flows, and the money supply in an economy are connected to those in other economies through a self-adjusting international trading and financial system. Further, these variables are endogenous. In the essay "Of the Balance of Trade" he adds a new dimension to his analysis. He (1752b/1955, ft. p. 64) writes "When we import more goods than we export, the exchange turns against us, and this becomes a new encouragement to exports …" Again, trade deficit should not concern us, for it causes the currency to depreciate and the depreciation increases exports.

Hume's letter contains the seeds of his thought on the quantity theory of money, which he laid out in the essay "Of Money" – quite possibly the most significant contribution to classical monetary economics. Hume begins by clarifying the role of money in the economy. He (1752a/1955, p. 33) writes that money "is none of the wheels of trade: It is the oil which renders the motion of the wheels more smooth and easy." Thus,

> money is nothing but the representative of labour and commodities, and serves only as a method of rating and estimating them. Where coin is in greater plenty; as a greater quantity of it is required to represent the same quantity of goods; it can have no effect, either good or bad, taking a nation within itself; any more than it would make an alteration on a merchant's books … (Ibid., p. 37)

Accordingly, money is neutral because "it can have no effect, either good or bad." But Hume continues,

> notwithstanding this conclusion, which must be allowed just, it is certain, that, since the discovery of the mines in AMERICA, industry has encreased in all nations of EUROPE, except in the possessors of those mines.… Accordingly we find, that, in every kingdom into which money begins to flow in greater abundance than formerly, every thing takes a new face: labour and industry gain life; the merchant becomes more enterprising, the manufacturer more diligent and skillful, and even the farmer follows his plough with greater alacrity and attention. (Ibid.)

According to this passage money is non-neutral because the flow of money does have real and beneficial effects. The apparent "contradiction" is repeated a few more times. For example, two pages later, Hume (Ibid., p. 39) notes, "it is of no manner of consequence, with regard to the domestic happiness of a state, whether money be in a greater or less quantity." But he (Ibid.) then adds, "the good policy of the magistrate consists only in keeping it [i.e., money], if possible, still increasing; because, by that means, he keeps alive a spirit of industry in the nation, and increases the stock of labour, in which consists all real power and riches." Similarly, at the end of the essay "Of the Balance of Trade" he (1752b/1955, p. 77) writes, "a government has great reason to preserve with care its people and its manufactures. Its money, it may safely trust to the course of human affairs, without fear or jealousy." He (Ibid.) then continues, "Or if it ever give attention to this latter circumstance, it ought only to be so far as it [money] affects the former [manufactures]." The gist of these passages can be summed up as follows: if the quantity of money is increased to stimulate the economy, the effect will be temporary and will eventually become ineffective. As Eugene Rotwein (1955, p. lxiv), the editor of Hume's "Writings on Economics" notes in the introduction, "Seeking to preserve the quantity theory, he has supposed that the beneficial effects of any monetary expansion would ultimately be transitory, or that the net effect of the process would be a pure price increase."

The crux of Hume's argument is that "The absolute quantity of the precious metals is a matter of great indifference" (1752a/1955, p. 46). Hegeland goes as far as saying that the proposition that "the *quantity* of money is irrelevant" is the "essence of the quantity theory" (1951, p. 41, italics original). He also notes, "The real issue is not what will happen *if* the quantity of money is increased, but that the actual quantity of money has no significance, since prices are always in proportion to the amount of money. Very few have realized this distinction, but Hume is one of them" (Ibid., p. 35, italics in original). Hume's quantity theory of money aimed to refute the mercantilist position by noting that "the want of money can never injure any state within itself: For men and commodities are the real strength of any community" (1752a/1955, p. 45).[5]

4. Adam Smith, David Ricardo, and John Stuart Mill

In a lecture in 1766, Smith referred to Hume's monetary theory. He (1982, p. 507) said,

> Mr. Hume published some essays shewing … very ingeniously that money must always bear[s] a certain proportion to the quantity of commodities in every country, that wherever money is accumulated beyond the proportion of commodities in any country the price of goods will necessarily rise, that this country will be undersold at the forreign market and consequently the money must depart into other nations; but on the contrary whenever the quantity of money falls below the proportion of goods the price of goods diminishes, the country undersells others in forreign marketts and consequently money returns in great plenty. Thus money and goods will keep near about a certain level in every country. Mr. Hume's reasoning is exceedingly ingenious. He seems to have gone a little into the notion that public opulence consists in money, which was considered above.

Given this passage in which Smith praises "Hume's reasoning," one would expect the specie-flow mechanism to have been incorporated into the *Wealth of Nations*, but it is not.[6] However, Smith does make a reference to Hume's quantity theory of money. He (1776/1981, pp. 325–326) writes,

> The increase of paper money, it has been said, by augmenting the quantity, and consequently diminishing the value of the whole currency, necessarily augments the money price of commodities. But as the quantity of gold and silver, which is taken from the currency, is always equal to the quantity of paper which is added to it, paper money does not necessarily increase the quantity of the whole currency. From the beginning of the last century to the present time, provisions never were cheaper in Scotland than in 1759, though, from the circulation of ten and five shilling bank notes, there was then more paper money in the country than at present. The proportion between the price of provisions in Scotland and that in England is the same now as before the

> great multiplication of banking companies in Scotland. Corn is, upon most occasions, fully as cheap in England as in France; though there is a great deal of paper money in England, and scarce any in France. In 1751 and in 1752, when Mr. Hume published his Political Discourses, and soon after the great multiplication of paper money in Scotland, there was a very sensible rise in the price of provisions, owing, probably, to the badness of the seasons, and not to the multiplication of paper money.

This passage appears to reject the quantity theory, but note that Smith is speaking against, not the link between money supply and the general price level, but the link between money supply and the price of a single item such as food. In fact in the following statements he reaffirms two propositions of the quantity theory: "The most abundant mines either of the precious metals or of the precious stones could add little to the wealth of the world. A produce of which the value is principally derived from its scarcity, is necessarily degraded by its abundance" (1776/1981, p. 192). This statement, which declares money is not wealth, belongs in the same category as Hume's dictum that the quantity of money is of no consequence to the economy.[7] Moreover, concerning the flow of gold and silver into Europe, which Bodin had used as the backdrop to make his statement on the quantity theory, Smith (Ibid., pp. 49–50) writes, "The discovery of the abundant mines of America reduced, in the sixteenth century, the value of gold and silver in Europe to about a third of what it had been before."

Nonetheless, Smith does not exhibit much interest in the quantity theory of money. A likely reason is that he adhered to "the real bills doctrine." Thomas Humphrey (1982, p. 3) defines this doctrine as "a rule purporting to gear money to production via the short-term commercial bill of exchange, thereby ensuring that output generates its own means of purchase and money adapts passively to the legitimate needs of trade." Thus the real bill doctrine renders the supply of money endogenous and as a result diminishes the significance of the quantity theory of money. As Arie Arnon (2011, p. 166) has noted, "Smith argued that the demand for means of payments (money) creates its own supply, so that demand and supply are always equal."[8] The real bill doctrine guided the thinking of many economists throughout the nineteenth century and, as we shall see, it even guided the Federal Reserve System in the 1930s in conducting monetary policy.

In the era of classical economics under consideration in this section, we present the views of two more seminal thinkers on the quantity theory, namely David Ricardo and John Stuart Mill though many other thinkers (including Jean-Baptiste Say, James Mill, and Henry Thornton) also wrote on the quantity theory.

Ricardo's earliest articulation of the quantity theory of money appeared in a lengthy essay titled, "The High Price of Bullion, A Proof of the Depreciation of Bank Notes," published in 1810 and republished in 1811 with an appendix. In this essay Ricardo cites John Locke and David Hume but relies heavily on the writings of Adam Smith and quotes him extensively. Throughout the essay he argues against mercantilists' position on money. He (2004, Vol. III, p. 53) writes,

> If the quantity of gold and silver in the world employed as money were exceedingly small, or abundantly great, it would not in the least affect the propositions in which they would be divided among the different nations – the variation in their quantity would have produced no other effect than to make the commodities for which they were exchanged comparatively dear or cheap. *The smaller quantity of money would perform the functions of a circulating medium, as well as the larger. Ten millions would be as effectual for the purpose as one hundred million.*" (Italics added)

The italicized sentence reaffirms what we called above "the crux of Hume's argument," namely the level of money supply is irrelevant to the operation of the economy. Ricardo (Ibid., pp. 54–55) argues that whether "a mine of gold were discovered" and "brought into circulation" or "a bank were established, such as the Bank of England, with the power of issuing its notes for a circulating medium; after a large amount had been issued either by way of loan to merchants, or by advances to government, thereby adding considerably to the sum of the currency.... The circulating medium would be lowered in value, and goods would experience a proportionate rise." He further argues against controls on the flow of currency. He (Ibid., p. 55) writes, "The exportation of the specie may at all times be safely left to the discretion of individuals; it will not be exported more than any other commodity, unless its exportation should be advantageous to the country." This statement is reminiscent of the argument at the end of Hume's essay "Of the Balance of Trade" where (as quoted before) Hume (1752b/1955, p. 77) writes, "a government has great reason to preserve with care its people and its manufactures. Its money, it may safely trust to the course of human affairs, without fear or jealousy."

Ricardo's view regarding the impact of money on output evolved from dismissal (even rejection) to mild acceptance. His firm reliance on Say's equality led him to assume that the economy is either in full employment or endogenously gravitating towards it. Given this assumption, he regarded any impact that money may exert on output as transitory and unworthy of attention. Recall, in the essay "Of Money" Hume argues that an increase in the money supply is beneficial to the industry, albeit temporarily. Ricardo refers to this argument as, "An erroneous view of Mr. Hume" (2004, Vol. V, p. 524). In the following passage he gives the impression that the money supply affects only the price level and hence it is neutral with respect to output regardless of the period. He (Ibid., Vol. III, p. 90) writes,

> If the mines cease to supply the annual consumption of the precious metals, money will become more valuable, and a smaller quantity will be employed as a circulating medium. The diminution in the quantity will be proportioned to the increase of its value. In like manner, if new mines be discovered, the value of the precious metals will be reduced, and an increased quantity used in the circulation; so that in either case the relative value of the precious

> metals will be reduced, and an increased quantity used in circulation; so that in either case the relative value of money, to the commodities which it circulates, will continue as before.

However, Ricardo's later writings come close to admitting the non-neutrality of money with respect to output. For example, he (1817/1996, p. 206) writes, "If, by the discovery of a new mine, by the abuses of banking, or by any other cause, the quantity of money be greatly increased, its ultimate effect is to raise the prices of commodities in proportion to increased quantity of money; but there is probably always an interval during which some effect is produced on the rate of interest." Here one would expect Ricardo to have argued that the lower interest rate would increase investment, but he does not because – quite possibly – he firmly believes any change in the interest rate is temporary. In a later work he writes, "Reduction or Increase of the Quantity of Money always ultimately raises or lowers the Price of Commodities; when this is effected, the Rate of Interest will be precisely the same as before; it is only during the Interval, that is, before the Prices are settled at the new Rate, that the Rate of Interest is either raised or lowered" (2004, Vol. V, p. 445). Moreover, "If the Bank had doubled its circulation, it still would have no permanent effect upon the value of money. If such a thing had taken place, the general level of interest would be restored in less than six months. … when that amount of circulation was afloat, the rate of interest would find its wholesome and natural level" (Ibid., p. 222). Ricardo (Ibid., p. 346) argues that ultimately the interest rate "is regulated by the demand and supply, in the same way as any other commodity; but the demand and supply itself is again regulated by the rate of profit to be made on capital. … the market rate of interest for money depends on the proportion between the borrower and the lender of capital, without reference to the quantity or value of the currency by which the transactions of the country are carried on." Ricardo's argument on the determination of the interest rate represents the classical position, which – as we saw in chapter three – Keynes opposed.

Ricardo further argues that since an increase in the money supply causes prices to rise faster than wages, profits and output will increase in the economy. But he says this is temporary. Here is the whole argument:

> There is but one way in which an increase of money no matter how it be introduced into the society, can augment riches, viz at the expence of the wages of labour; till the wages of labour have found their level with the increased prices which the commodities will have experienced, there will be so much additional revenue to the manufacturer and farmer they will obtain an increased price for their commodities, and can whilst wages do not increase employ an additional number of hands, so that the real riches of the country will be somewhat augmented. A productive labourer will produce something more than before relatively to his consumption, but this can be only of momentary duration. (Ibid., Vol. III, pp. 318–319)

In another occasion Ricardo (Ibid., Vol. VI, pp. 16–17) elaborates on the above analysis as follows:

> There appears to me only one way in which any addition would be made to the Capital of a country in consequence of an addition of money; it would be this. Till the wages of labour had found their new level with the altered value of money, the situation of the labourer would be relatively worse; he would produce more relatively to that which he consumed, or rather he would be obliged to consume less. The manufacturer would be enabled to employ more labourers as he would receive an additional price for his commodities; he might therefore add to his real capital till the rise in the wages of labour placed him in his proper sphere. In this interval some trifling addition would have been made to the Capital of the community.

Ricardo further argues that an increase in the money supply will redistribute income without adding to the output. In his words, "The increase of money in my opinion can have no other effect than raising the prices of commodities. By such means some members of the community are enriched at the expence of others; there is a mere transfer of property, but no creation" (Ibid., p. 16). The following passage identifies the beneficiaries and losers when prices rise and the value of money declines owing to monetary expansion:

> Depreciation of money may be beneficial because it generally favours that class who are disposed to accumulate, – but I should say that it augmented riches by diminishing happiness, that it was advantageous only by occasioning a great pressure on the laboring classes and on those who lived on fixed incomes. (Ibid., p. 233)

Ricardo occasionally refers to the velocity of money. For example, he uses it in a statement that almost a century later came to be known as the equation of exchange. He (Ibid., Vol. III, p. 311) writes, "May we not as before put the mass of commodities of all sorts on one side of the line, – and the amount of money multiplied by the rapidity of its circulation on the other? Is not this in all cases the regulator of prices?" This is of course a description of the equation of exchange to which we will return below.

Several chapters of John Stuart Mill's *Principles of Political Economy* analyze the functions of money and its impact on the economy. In particular, he discusses the quantity theory of money in chapters VIII and IX of Book III. Mill regards money itself as a "good" as well as a counterpoise to goods that get transacted in the marketplace. He (1848/2006, p. 509) writes, "In point of fact, money is bought and sold like other things, whenever other things are bought and sold *for* money. Whoever sells corn, or tallow, or cotton, buys money. Whoever buys bread, or wine, or clothes, sells money to the dealers in those articles." Thus "the supply of money … is all the money in *circulation* at the time."

(It will soon become clear why Mill italicizes "circulation.") And "the demand for money … consists of all the goods offered for sale" (Ibid.). From this introduction Mill moves to a discussion on the quantity theory and invokes Hume's hypothetical example of sudden increase in the supply of money, and writes, "If the whole money in circulation was doubled, prices would be doubled. If it was only increased one-fourth, prices would rise one-fourth" (Ibid., p. 511). He stresses the point that the increase in price applies, not to every single item, but to the average or general price level.

According to Mill, the money that matters to the economy is the money in *circulation*, by which he means the money actually used in transactions. As we noted in the previous chapter, as early as 1829 Mill had been aware that money might be demanded for cautionary and/or hoarding purposes and not just for transactions. Nineteen years later, he (1848/2006, pp. 514–515) wrote,

> Whatever may be the quantity of money in the country, only that part of it will affect prices, which goes into the market of commodities, and is there actually exchanged against goods. Whatever increases the amount of this portion of the money in the country, tends to raise prices. But money hoarded does not act on prices. Money kept in reserve by individuals to meet contingencies which do not occur, does not act on prices. The money in the coffers of the Bank, or retained as a reserve by private bankers, does not act on prices until drawn out, nor even then unless drawn out to be expended in commodities.

Mill's expression of the quantity theory is as follows: "the quantity of money in circulation, is equal to the money value of all the goods sold, divided by the number which expresses the rapidity of circulation" (Ibid., p. 513).[9] This is the equation of exchange that Ricardo had also expressed in words and, as we shall see in the next section, Alfred Marshall in 1871 translated into mathematics.

Mill's analysis of the quantity theory in his *Principles* is reminiscent of his 1829 essay on Say's law in that he left for posterity a methodical and thorough description of a central theory in economics. Mill considered the quantity theory to be the foundation of monetary economics. He (Ibid., p. 514) wrote, "That an increase of the quantity of money raises prices, and a diminution lowers them, is the most elementary proposition in the theory of currency, and without it we should have no key to any of the others."

5. Alfred Marshall, Irving Fisher, and Knut Wicksell

In 1871, two years before Mill died, Alfred Marshall wrote an important piece on the quantity theory titled, "Essay on Money."[10] In this essay Marshall based his analysis of the quantity theory on Mill's theoretical framework in chapters VIII and IX of the *Principles of Political Economy* that we just reviewed.

Here Marshall introduced a mathematical version of Mill's (and Ricardo's) statement on the equation of exchange. To that end, he imagined an island where shells are used as a medium of exchange. He (1871/1975, p. 169) then wrote, "If there are a million shells in the island and each shell changes hands fifty times in the course of the year; it is then obvious that the whole of the transactions in which goods are exchanged for shells are together represented in value by fifty million shells." Next he (Ibid., pp. 169–170) expressed the theory in mathematical terms as follows:

> Let … P represent the value of the whole of the transactions in the course of the year in which goods are exchanged for shells. Let m represent the number of shells in the island, n the average times each shell changes hands, v the value of each shell. Then our statement becomes
>
> $n \times m \times v$ equals P
>
> (where × stands for 'multiplied into') therefore
>
> $$v \textit{ equals } \frac{P}{n \times m}$$

Accordingly, "It follows that if P increases, while no other change takes place, v will increase; and that if n increases while no other change takes place v will decrease" (Ibid., p. 170). This equation, which Marshall called "the ordinary statement of the theory of money," constitutes the foundation of what has come to be known as the Cambridge Cash-Balance approach to the quantity theory. According to David Laidler (1991, p. 59), "The contrast between Cambridge and other neoclassical versions of the quantity theory … lies in the fact that the traditional quantity theorists, including Fisher, put velocity, and transmission velocity at that, at the heart of their analysis, while the Cambridge economists *abandoned this concept*" (italics in original). Laidler (Ibid.) further notes that Marshall stressed what later, under Keynes' influence, came to be known as "demand for a stock of real balances."

In 1899 Marshall appeared before the Committee on Indian Currency. While responding to the Committee's questions, he (1926, pp. 267) laid out the quantity theory of money as follows:

> prices vary directly with the volume of currency, if other things are equal; but other things are constantly changing. This so called "quantity theory of the value of money" … has been the cause of much controversy; but it has never been seriously denied by anyone who has taken it as a whole, and has not stopped short, omitting the words "other things being equal.

Marshall then proceeded to explicate the Cambridge approach. He (Ibid., pp. 267–277) argued, "The fact is that in every state of society there is some fraction of their income which people find it worth while to keep in the form of currency; it may be a fifth, or a tenth, or a twentieth. A large command of resources in the form of currency renders their business easy and smooth …" The Cambridge approach is usually expressed by an equation such as "M = kPy where M is the stock of money in circulation, k is the desired cash balance ratio of the nominal money supply to nominal income, P is the price level of the national product, and y is real national income or the national product valued at constant prices" (Humphrey, 1974, p. 13). Note that in this analysis the velocity of money, an indispensable component of the quantity theory of money, is not explicitly mentioned.[11] Marshall was of course well aware of the vital role of the velocity of money in the quantity theory – he included it in his equation we presented above.

As noted before, Marshall regarded the quantity theory of money as the proposition that "prices vary directly with the volume of currency" provided that the condition "other things being equal" holds. To Marshall (1926, p. 21), this "conditioning clause … is of overwhelming importance and requires careful attention." Hence, if other things change, then the relationship between money and prices may not hold. This analysis relates to the proposition that money is neutral in the long-run but non-neutral in the short-run. Marshall's stance on the long-run neutrality of money is the same as that of other thinkers we have noted above, and for the short-run, his argument is similar to Ricardo's. Recall, Ricardo (2004, Vol. VI, pp. 16–17) had argued that if prices rise, businesses in the short-run will earn higher profits because wages rise more slowly than prices. The higher amount of profits will entice businesses to increase output, albeit temporarily. Marshall (1922/1960, p. 18) explains the process this way:

> Salaries and wages … generally retain their nominal value more or less fixed, in spite of trade fluctuations; they can seldom be changed without much friction and worry and loss of time. And for the very reason that their nominal or money value is fixed, their real value varies, and varies in the wrong direction. It falls when prices are rising, and the purchasing power of money is falling; so that the employer pays smaller real salaries and wages than usual at the very time when his profits are largest in other ways, and is thus prompted to over-estimate his strength, and engage in ventures which he will not be able to pull through after the tide begins to turn.

Notice, the impact of money on the economy is temporary since wages will sooner or later catch up with the rise in prices, at which point money can no longer affect output; that is, money becomes neutral in the long-run.[12] To demonstrate how an increase in the money supply leads to higher prices, Marshall (1922/1960, p. 256) considers an open economy that experiences "an influx of a good deal of bullion …" He then identifies two impacts. The first one is the familiar transmission mechanism: an increase in the money supply leads to lower interest rate and higher amount of lending, which causes prices to rise because borrowers use the loan to purchase goods.[13] The second impact of an increase in the money supply is that people develop expectation about rising prices before any inflation actually occurs. He (Ibid.) notes,

> Further, the influx of bullion will have caused people to expect a rise of prices, and, therefore, to be more inclined to borrow for speculative investments.... The increased demand for loans will meet the increased supply half way; and, after a time, may outrun it, causing a rise in the rate of discount. But, as this rise will be merely an incident in a series of changes which put more command over capital in the hands of speculative investors, it will go with an increased demand for goods and a continued rise of prices.

This expectation of future inflation owing to a rise in money supply has been fully incorporated into modern macroeconomic models.

J. K. Whitaker, the editor of Marshall's "Early Economic Writings" in which the "Essay on Money" is published, comments in a footnote on Marshall's equation ("$n \times m \times v$ equals P"). Whitaker (1975, p. 170) writes, "It should be noted that value is expressed in terms of goods, so that the usual Fisher equation $MV = PT$ is expressed in Marshall's notations as $mn = (1/v)\ P$. It is evident that Marshall's P must stand for the volume of transactions despite being ambiguously defined as 'the value of the whole of transactions." In Fisher's equation, M is the money supply, V the velocity of money, P is the price level, and T is the total transactions in the economy. Irving Fisher introduced the equation ($MV = PT$) in his influential book titled, *The Purchasing Power of Money* (1911). The equation qualifies as his most enduring legacy even though he did not develop it.[14] In the preface of the book, Fisher (1911/1963, p. ix) informs his readers that he wrote the book because "the evils of a variable monetary standard are among the most serious economic evils with which civilization has to deal," and he further notes that "I have proposed, very tentatively, a remedy for the evils of monetary instability. But the time is not yet ripe for the acceptance of any working plan." This motive is reminiscent of that of J.-B. Say for developing the law of markets. Both Say and Fisher set out to discover the means by which the economy can be stabilized.

Fisher (1911/1963, p. 24) presents the algebraic form of the equation of exchange as $E = MV$, where E is "the amount of money expended for goods in a given community during a given year," M represents "the average amount of money," and V denotes "the velocity of circulation." According to Fisher, E is the summation of the product of the quantity of goods produced (denoted by Q) in an economy and their respective prices (denoted by p). Thus he (Ibid., p. 26) writes, "$MV = \Sigma\, pQ$." Fisher then uses this identity to express what he calls (Ibid., pp. 26–27) "three theorems":

1 If V and Q's remain invariable while M varies in any ratio, ... either the p's will all vary in that ratio or else some p's will vary more than in that ratio and others enough less to compensate and maintain the same average.

2 If M and the Q's remain invariable while V varies in any ratio, … the p's will all vary in the same ratio or else some will vary more and others enough less to compensate.
3 If M and V will remain invariable, … if the Q's all vary in a given ratio, either p's must all vary in the inverse ratio or else some of them will vary more and others enough less to compensate.

Fisher (Ibid., p, 27) proceeds to "further simplify the right side by writing it in the form PT where P is the weighted average of all the p's, and T is the sum of all the Q's." Hence Fisher presents the equation of exchange as $MV = PT$. But he adds two variables $M'V'$ to the left-hand side where M' is "the total deposits subject to transfer by check; and V' the average velocity of its circulation" (Ibid., p. 48). Thus, the expanded version of Fisher's equation is $MV + M'V' = \Sigma\ pQ = PT$. Following a lengthy elaboration and analysis, Fisher (Ibid., pp. 156 – 157) writes,

> the equation of exchange, of itself, asserts no causal relations between quantity of money and price level, any more than it asserts a causal relation between any other two factors, yet, when we take into account conditions known quite apart from that equation, viz., that a change in M produces a proportional change in M', and no changes in V, V', or the Q's, there is no possible escape from the conclusion that a change in the quantity of money (M) must *normally* cause a proportional change in the price level (the p's). (Italics added)

Fisher repeats the same argument several times and on one occasion he explains what he means by his statement. He (Ibid., p. 320) notes, "the qualifying adverb 'normally' is inserted in the formulation in order to provide for the transitional periods or credit cycles."

Fisher (Ibid., p. 157) notes that "the equation of exchange is, if we choose, a mere 'truism,' based on the equivalence, in all purchases, of the money or checks expended, on the one hand, and what they buy, on the other …" Moreover, the equation of exchange "is an exact law of proportion, as exact and fundamental in economic science as the exact law of proportion between pressure and density of gases in physics, assuming temperature to remain the same" (Ibid., p. 320). This is a reference to Boyle's law, which states that if temperature is held constant the pressure and volume of a gas are inversely correlated. But such a strict view of economic relationships led Fisher down the wrong path concerning the stock market crash and the Great Depression in 1929. Laidler (2011, p. 21) notes that "Fisher attributed the past and future prosperity of the American economy to" several factors including price stability. Laidler (Ibid., p. 22) further writes that Fisher "since 1911," the year he published his book on the quantity theory, "had touted successful price level stabilization as virtually sufficient in itself to guarantee the continuation of overall prosperity. The quantity theory as he had come to understand it thus let Fisher down badly" because he interpreted the stability of prices in the 1920s as the reason that the economic boom would continue. The complexity of the economy, as argued in chapter one of the present work, should caution the economists who believe in the predictability of future events based on the laws of economics.

The fact remains that to Fisher the quantity theory was a full-fledged scientific proposition. To reinforce his point, he (1911/1963, pp. 320–321) ventured into epistemology and argued,

> Only those who fail to grasp the significance of what a scientific law really is fail to see the significance and importance of the quantitative law of money. A scientific law is not a formulation of statistics or history. It is a formulation of what holds true under given conditions. It is by making such allowances that we have pursued our study of the last ten centuries in the rough and of the last decade and a half in detail. In each case we found the facts in accord with the principles previously formulated.

Concerning the statistical analysis of the quantity theory, Fisher warned that one must take account of all the variables in the equation of exchange. As an example of an empirical work that ignores this principle, he cited and criticized S. McLean Hardy who in 1895 had published a paper titled, "The Quantity Theory of Money and Prices, 1860–1891. An Inductive Study." Hardy analyzed in meticulous details the evolution of price level and the supply of money in the United States over the period 1860–1891, and did not find much support for the quantity theory. One of Hardy's findings is that "Prices have fallen phenomenally since 1865, taking the period as a whole" while "The volume of circulating medium" has moved "quite the opposite of what might be expected" (Hardy, 1895, p. 157). Moreover, "From 1865 to 1891 a decrease in price of 57 per cent is contrasted with an increase in currency of 124 per cent" and "Exclusive of the three years from 1862 to 1865, the volume of money and prices move in exactly opposite directions. From the latter year on, while prices fall, the money in circulation is steadily increasing" (Ibid.). Finally, Hardy (Ibid., p. 160) concluded,

> so far as the history of prices in the United States throws any light upon the quantity theory, it appears: (1) that that [sic] dogma, in its general theoretical form, is inapplicable as an explanation for this given set of actual conditions, (2) that so far as it may be at all valid, its influence in determining the level of prices is of far less importance than is commonly supposed, (3) that prices, from 1861 to 1891, were fixed in the main by other causes than the quantity of that kind of money which was in circulation during those years.

In his criticism of this work, Fisher argued that a reliable empirical investigation requires much more than looking at the time-series evolution of two variables. He (1911/1963, p. 277) noted, "Most … writers who have attempted to test the quantity theory statistically seem to have been animated by a desire not to give it a fair test, but to disprove it. They have carefully avoided taking account of any factors except money and prices. It is not to be wondered at that they find little statistical correlation between these two factors."

Consequently, Fisher's own empirical analysis takes account of all the variables in the equation of exchange. He noted that in the equation ($MV + M'V' = PT$) the price level (P) "is really dependent on the five other factors in the equation …" (Ibid., p. 291). Fisher computed the predicted values of P from the formula $(MV + M'V') / T$, and compared it with the actual values of P over the sample period 1896–1909. He (Ibid., p. 292) aimed to find out "whether the magnitudes as calculated will actually fulfill approximately the equation of exchange." The time-series graphs of the predicted values and the actual values of P appear to be highly correlated. Fisher (Ibid., pp. 294–295) argued that

> The proper method of applying a coefficient of correlation to successive data appears to be to calculate the coefficient, not for raw figures, but for their successive year-to-year ratios. In other words, we tabulate and compare the ratios of each year's P to the preceding year's P and of each year's $(MV + M'V') / T$ to the preceding year's $(MV + M'V') / T$. … the results of this method shows a coefficient of correlation of 57 per cent. … This figure, 57 per cent, is a moderately high coefficient of correlation. We may conclude, therefore, that the "quantity theory" is statistically verified to a high degree of correlation.

Fisher (Ibid., p. 291) admitted that "there are possible errors in all the magnitudes M, M', V, V', T, and such errors, should they exist, would be registered cumulatively in P." Nonetheless, from the correlation coefficient, i.e., 0.57, he infers that the quantity theory "is statistically verified." Fisher's method is valid, but if the measurement errors are significant, we cannot be certain that his empirical findings are reliable. To validate Fisher's result, the same method should be applied to data in various time periods and, ideally, in other countries as well. I am unaware of any such extension of Fisher's work.

Despite the tremendous intellectual accomplishments, the quantity theory has remained a controversial proposition. One reason for the controversy is that many thinkers throughout history have doubted its empirical validity even though they all have agreed that the equation of exchange is necessarily true. A prominent example is Knut Wicksell (1851–1926). Wicksell (1915/1962, p. 144) calls the equation of exchange an "axiom," but for this axiom to hold in the real world, as Marshall had stressed, all else must remain constant. The problem is that, Wicksell argues, the *ceteris paribus* condition is almost always violated. He (Ibid., pp. 144–145) notes,

> In fact, an increase – or when it occurs, a decrease – in the volume of money always coincides with a number of other economic changes which tend to cancel out or to conceal its effects on the price level and the value of money. Population increases and production expands as a result of technical improvements, so that the amount of goods annually consumed increases not only to the same, but to an even greater extent than the increase in population. The turnover may increase to an even higher degree than production owing to the national and international division of labour and to the resulting transition from barter and payment in kind to business based on exchange and money wages.

The reality depicted in the passage should caution policymakers in the application of the quantity theory since they operate under the cloud of uncertainty. Nonetheless, Wicksell (1915/1962, p. 145) argues that using "these circumstances … as argument against the Quantity Theory" would be "almost as illogical as it would be in the case of the upward movements of a balloon to say that it disproved the validity of the law of gravity." In fact Wicksell (Ibid., p. 141) elevates the quantity theory, as Fisher does, to "real scientific importance." Wicksell has a valid point when he says any theory holds true in reality only under certain conditions. He (Ibid., p. 160) criticizes "The advocates of the Quantity Theory" for making "the mistake of postulating their assumptions instead of clearly proving them." In particular, Wicksell argues that the assumption of constant velocity of money is true only in a pure cash economy. In this regard, Laidler (1993, p. 170) notes, Wicksell "postulated that a modern banking system had capacity to render the velocity of currency a passive variable in the face of real shocks." Laidler (Ibid., p. 172) also notes that by 1915, when Wicksell published *Lectures on Political Economy*, he "did soften his stance" but "he did not abandon also the theoretical position that the quantity theory was inherently irrelevant to the 'pure credit' economy." Nonetheless, Wicksell (1898/1965, p. 181) maintains that "If the Quantity Theory is false – or to the extent it is false – there is so far available only one false theory of money, and no true theory."

As noted in the preceding chapter (on the law of markets), Oscar Lange (1942/1970) and Don Patinkin (1948) had argued that any monetary theory is incompatible with Say's law. Wicksell (1915/1962, p. 159) advances a similar argument. He notes that according to the quantity theory an increase in money supply will lead to higher prices, but this can happen only if the demand for goods exceeds the supply. The law of markets, however, does not permit the demand to exceed the supply "because" Wicksell (Ibid., p. 159) reminds his readers, "we have accustomed ourselves, with J. B. Say, to regard goods themselves as reciprocally constituting and limiting the demand for each other. And indeed *ultimately* they do so" (italics in original). Wicksell (Ibid., pp. 159–160) goes on to say that "Any theory of money worthy of the name must be able to show how and why the monetary or pecuniary demand for goods exceeds or falls short of the supply of goods in given conditions." Perhaps this explains why the leading modern quantity theorists such as Milton Friedman have largely ignored Say's law of markets. But, as noted in the preceding chapter, it is Say's identity version of Say's law that cannot be reconciled with any theory of money; Say's equality is compatible with the quantity theory.[15]

Wicksell may not view the quantity theory as perfect, but he (Ibid., p. 167) writes, "there is no doubt that large and continuous issues of paper money lead to a corresponding fall in the value of the paper money, which, as might be expected, is in exact accordance with the Principles of Quantity Theory." He presents, as evidence, the example of "the Republic of Colombia in South America, whose government in 1855–1905, and especially during the Civil War in 1899–1902, issued constantly increasing quantities of inconvertible paper money, which fell progressively in value." Such examples abound in recent history from the German hyperinflation following World War I to a number of countries around the world in the twentieth century that experienced considerable depreciation of their currency owing to substantial expansion of money supply.[16]

According to Arnon (2011, p. 345), although "the analysis" of the quantity theory "traditionally addressed the relationship between the quantity of money and prices, he [Wicksell] thought that the analysis should move to explain the link between interest [sic] and prices." In the tradition of classical economics, Wicksell spoke of "the natural rate of interest" and "the market rate of interest." The natural rate of interest, he said, "is determined outside the financial sphere, by conditions in the production sphere … by the marginal product of capital, or as the real profit rate in production" (Ibid., p. 352). Starting with an equilibrium condition in which the two interest rates are equal, a monetary expansion would cause the market rate of interest to fall below the natural rate and initiate a process that leads to rising prices. This "cumulative process will only come to an end when" the two interest rates become equal to one another (Ibid.). Hence prices rise when the market interest rate falls. In fact Wicksell argues, when prices are rising, "banks' rate of interest" should be increased, and if they are falling, the rate should be reduced. Arnon (2011, p. 357) calls this policy response, "Wicksell's rule." This rule is the same as the policy implication of the quantity theory for fighting price inflation and deflation because raising the interest rate (when there is inflation) is tantamount to lowering the money supply, and reducing the interest rate (when there is deflation) is tantamount to incresing the money supply. As noted in chapter three, the Federal Reserve System in 1979 lowered the money supply to stanch inflation. But this monetary contraction caused the interest rate to soar to double-digit numbers.

Finally, given the foregoing analysis, unsurprisingly Wicksell has been difficult to pin down on whether he was a quantity theorist. In a paper on Wicksell, which we cited above, Laidler delved into the question, and gave us this answer: "Only sometimes, and not when he was writing the contributions that, as it was to turn out, were to matter" (Laidler, 1993, p. 172).

6. John Maynard Keynes and Milton Friedman

In 1911 John Maynard Keynes published a review of Fisher's book, *The Purchasing Power of Money*. In his review Keynes (1911, p. 394) both praised Fisher for its "extreme lucidity and brilliance of statement" and criticized him, among other things, for exaggerating "the fixity of the ratio between bank reserves and bank deposits" and also "the fixity of the ratio between cash transactions and cheque transactions." But Keynes raised no objection to the quantity theory of money as a valid, and in Fisher's view a scientific, proposition. Nonetheless, his writings on the quantity theory eventually evolved from a lukewarm acceptance in his 1923 book *A Tract on Monetary Reform* to serious skepticism in his 1930 book *A Treatise on Money* to outright rejection in the *General Theory* in 1936. In *A Tract on Monetary Reform*, Keynes (1923/1971, pp. 37–38) made a reference to the quantity theory and provided a standard definition for it. In *A Treatise on Money* he presented a thorough analysis of the quantity theory (particularly in chapter 14 of the first volume) while making it clear that he thought the quantity theory is bereft of explanatory power and is unreliable as a guide for policy. He (1930/1971, p. 146) further questioned the empirical validity of the quantity theory when he noted, "The course of events in Great Britain between 1890 and 1896 has always seemed to be one which the old-fashioned quantity theory was ill calculated to explain." He (Ibid., pp. 146–147) went on to argue

> Between 1890 and 1896 Sauerbeck's whole sale index fell about 18 per cent, and the *Economist*'s about 14 percent.... Yet if we look into the figures it seems somewhat preposterous to ascribe this decline to a shortage of gold – at least so far as Great Britain was concerned. Between 1890 and 1896 the total stock of gold in the Bank of England was doubled, and the bank's reserves were nearly trebled, and its deposits nearly doubled.... In short, the period was marked by an extreme abundance of gold and an extreme case of credit. At the same time trade was stagnant, employment bad and prices falling.

While Keynes' criticism of the quantity theory in his *A Treatise on Money* is largely empirical, in the *General Theory* he challenged its theoretical foundation. He (1936/1997, p. 296) enunciated the quantity theory as follows: "So long as there is unemployment, *employment* will change in the same proportion as the quantity of money; and when there is full employment, *prices* will change in the same proportion as the quantity of money" (italics in original). Keynes argued that the quantity theory, as defined above, rests on two assumptions: "(1) that all unemployed resources are homogenous and interchangeable in their efficiency to produce what is wanted, and (2) that the factors of production entering into marginal cost are content with the same money wage-unit, so long as there is any unemployment" (Ibid., p. 295). He (Ibid., p. 296) then noted,

> Having, however, satisfied tradition by introducing a sufficient number of simplifying assumptions to enable us to enunciate a Quantity Theory of Money, let us now consider the possible complications which will in fact influence events:
>
> 1 Effective demand will not change in exact proportion to the quantity of money.
> 2 Since resources are not homogeneous, there will be diminishing, and not constant, returns as employment gradually increases.
> 3 Since resources are not interchangeable, some commodities will reach a condition of inelastic supply whilst there are still unemployed resources available for the production of other commodities.
> 4 The wage-unit will tend to rise, before full employment has been reached.
> 5 The remunerations of the factors entering into marginal cost will not all change in the same proportion.

Following this list of five "complications," Keynes (Ibid.) wrote,

> Thus we must first consider the effect of changes in the quantity of money on the quantity of effective demand; and the increase in effective demand will, generally speaking, spend itself partly in increasing the quantity of employment and partly in raising the level of prices. Thus instead of constant prices in conditions of unemployment, and of prices rising in proportion to the quantity of money in conditions of full employment, we have in fact a condition of prices rising gradually as employment increases. The Theory of Prices, that is to say, the analysis of the relation between changes in the quantity of money and changes in the price-level with a view to determining the elasticity of prices in response to changes in the quantity of money, must, therefore, direct itself to the five complicating factors set forth above.

In Keynes' view, the transmission mechanism involves three stages:

> The primary effect of a change in the quantity of money on the quantity of effective demand is through its influence on the rate of interest. If this were the only reaction, the quantitative effect could be derived from the three elements – (a) the schedule of liquidity-preference which tells us by how much the rate of interest will have to fall in order that the new money may be absorbed by willing holders, (b) the schedule of marginal efficiencies which tells us by how much a given fall in the rate of interest will increase investment, and (c) the investment multiplier which tells us by how much a given increase in investment will increase effective demand as a whole. (Ibid., p. 298)

He (Ibid.) further noted that this analysis "presents a deceptive simplicity, if we forget that the three elements (a), (b) and (c) are themselves partly dependent on the complicating factors (2), (3), (4) and (5) …" He (Ibid., p. 299) went on to say, "There is no reason to expect that" the velocity of money will remain constant when the money supply changes. Hence Keynes argued against the effectiveness and reliability of the transmission mechanism.

Keynes (Ibid., p. 207) believed that at a sufficiently low interest rate "liquidity-preference may become virtually absolute in the sense that almost everyone prefers cash to holding a debt which yields so low a rate of interest."[17] In such a scenario, additional supply of money fails to lower the interest rate and monetary policy becomes ineffective. And even if the interest rate does fall, business investment will rise only if there exists adequate and effective demand in the economy. If the additional supply of money fails to boost consumption and investment, then it will get hoarded and the velocity of money falls. This means in the equation of exchange ($MV = PT$) any increase in M elicits a corresponding decrease in V, so that the left-hand side of the equation remains constant, as a result of which the right-hand side remains constant as well. Hence, M fails to influence the economy, represented by P and T. The inescapable conclusion is that monetary policy is an unreliable policy tool.

Keynes (Ibid., p. 209) struck at the heart of the quantity theory by arguing that

> For the purpose of the real world it is a great fault in the Quantity Theory that it does not distinguish between changes in prices which are a function of changes in output, and those which are a function of changes in the wage-unit. The explanation of this omission is, perhaps, to be found in the assumptions that *there is no propensity to hoard and that there is always full employment.* (Italics added)

Keynes' statement that the quantity theory rests on "the assumptions that there is no propensity to hoard and that there is always full employment" is at best puzzling and at worst erroneous. As we saw in chapter three on Say's law, classical economists, to varying degrees, did recognize the reality of hoarding, and never assumed that "there is always full employment." Indeed beginning with Say, they set out to uncover the roots of commercial crisis. What they did argue is that if prices are flexible the economy endogenously will *gravitate* towards full employment.

In the second half of the twentieth century, Milton Friedman's theoretical and empirical works countered Keynes and rescued the quantity theory. In a fairly sophisticated essay titled, "The Quantity Theory of Money – A Restatement" published in 1956, Friedman demonstrated theoretically as well as empirically the utility and relevance of the quantity theory of money. He (1956, p. 3) began his essay by noting that "the quantity theory of money is a term evocative of a general approach rather than a label for a well-defined theory." Freidman (Ibid., p. 4) directed the attention of the scholars to the subtle and crucial proposition that "The quantity theory is in the first instance a theory of the *demand* for money. It is not a theory of output, or of money income, or of the price level" (italics in original). This led him to declare that a quantity theorist is someone who "accepts the empirical hypothesis that the demand for money is highly stable – more stable than functions such as the consumption function that are offered as alternative key relations" (Ibid., p. 16). If the demand for money is shown to be unstable then the velocity of money will be behaving capriciously, undermining the reliability of monetary policy as an effective policy tool. Hence, much has been done empirically on the stability of demand for money. In his essay, Friedman (1956, pp. 17–20) cites evidence that largely supports the proposition that the demand for money is stable. Laidler (1966) examined the stability of money demand with respect to the interest rate, and later summarized and reported the results in his 1977 book, *The Demand for Money*. Laidler (1977, p. 133) notes that "in the United States over the period 1892–1960 … the elasticity of demand for money M_2, with respect to the short rate of interest, appears to have varied between roughly –0.12 and –0.15 and, with respect to the long rate of interest, between –0.2 and –0.6. (If M_1 is used instead, the relevant elasticities are –0.17 to –0.20 and –0.5 to –0.8, respectively.)"

These elasticities indicate that, contrary to Keynes' hypothesis, the relationship between the interest rate and the money demand, as Laidler (Ibid.) points out, is "remarkably well determined."

Empirical studies generally find a stable money demand function until around the late 1970s to the early 1980s. The ensuing instability since the 1980s seems to have resulted from new financial instruments and regulations that were introduced in the 1970s. In a recent work, titled "On the Stability of Money Demand," Robert Lucas Jr. and Juan Pablo Nicolini (2015, p. 2) examine "Long standing empirical relations connecting monetary aggregates like M1 and M2 and the monetary base to movements in prices and interest rates" in the United States over the period 1915–2012. They show the relations were fairly stable from 1915 to the 1980s. Then the relations, as they put it, "began to deteriorate." Lucas and Nicolini find that this breakdown coincides with, and can be explained by, the changes in regulatory structure of the banking system. The regulatory changes resulted in "another monetary asset, money market deposit accounts (MMDAs), as a third important means of payment along side currency and demand deposit" (Ibid., p. 3). Lucas and Nicolini (Ibid.) show that the inclusion of MMDAs in the calculation of money demand restores its stability over the years since the 1980s. This finding reaffirms the confidence of the quantity theorists such as Lucas himself in the validity of the quantity theory of money.[18]

In their highly influential book, *A Monetary History of the United States, 1867–1960*, a remarkable historical and statistical work, Friedman and Anna Schwartz (1963) find much validation for the implications of the quantity theory. They (1963, p. 676) summarize their findings as follows:

1 Changes in the behavior of the money stock have been closely associated with changes in economic activity, money income, and prices.
2 The interrelation between monetary and economic change has been highly stable.
3 Monetary changes have often had an independent origin; they have not been simply a reflection of changes in economic activity.
4 In monetary matters, appearances are deceiving; the important relationships are often precisely the reverse of those that strike the eye.

Friedman and Schwartz elaborate on each of the four findings quoted above. For example, they (Ibid., p. 677) note that, during the sample period 1867–1960, "there have been six periods of severe economic contraction that produced widespread distress and unemployment.... Each of those severe contractions was accompanied by an appreciable decline in the stock of money, the most severe decline accompanying the 1929–33 contraction." They document that in the early 1930s the money supply fell by one-third, and argue that the Federal Reserve's failure to prevent the contraction turned an ordinary recession into the Great Depression. Barry Eichengreen (2015) recounts in detail the historical events surrounding the Great Depression, and he, too, indicts the Federal Reserve for the calamity. He (2015, p. 2) notes,

> Central Bankers, for their part, were in thrall to the real bill doctrine, the idea that they should provide only as much credit as was required for the legitimate needs of business. They supplied more credit when business was expanding and less when it slumped, accentuating booms and busts. Neglecting their responsibility for financial stability, they failed to intervene as lenders of the last resort. The result was cascading bank failures, starving business of credit. Prices were allowed to collapse, rendering debts unmanageable.

Eichengreen (Ibid.) goes on to point out that in 2008 when it became clear the economy was experiencing a financial crisis, the Federal Reserve avoided the errors of the central bankers in 1929–1930 and responded "with expansionary monetary and financial policies." Moreover,

> As a result of this very different response, unemployment in the United States peaked at 10 percent in 2010. Though this was still disturbingly high, it was far below the catastrophic 25 percent scaled in the Great Depression. Failed banks numbered in the hundreds, not thousands. Financial dislocations were widespread, but the complete and utter collapse of financial markets seen in the 1930s was successfully averted. (Ibid., p. 2)

The fact that the Federal Reserve in 2008, by drawing on the lessons of the Great Depression which Freidman and Schwartz had uncovered, managed to avert another depression is a testament to the indispensability and utility of historical and empirical analysis.

In 1968 Freidman authored an essay, titled "Money: Quantity Theory," for *International Encyclopedia of the Social Sciences*. In the essay, Friedman first presents a lengthy theoretical analysis of the quantity theory of money and then cites empirical evidence, largely based on his book with Schwartz. For example, he (1968/1973, pp. 58, 60) notes,

> Every contraction has been accompanied by an absolute decline in the stock of money, and the severity of contraction has been roughly the same order as the size of the decline in the stock of money. Although changes in the rate of growth of the stock of money have to some extent reflected the contemporaneous course of business, on many occasions they have quite clearly been the result of independent forces, such as the deliberate decisions of monetary authorities. The clearest examples are probably the wartime increases and the decreases from 1920 to 1921, 1929 to 1933 and 1937 to 1938.

Throughout his long scholarly career, Freidman repeated such findings to stress the importance of the proper conduct of monetary policy.

In 1987 Friedman wrote an expanded version of his 1968 essay for *The New Palgrave, A Dictionary of Economics*. This entry, titled "Quantity Theory of Money," is an important contribution to the literature on monetary theory. Here we find a comprehensive analysis of both theory and evidence concerning the quantity theory.

Below I will present a few of Friedman's crucial points in the essay. At the beginning of the section on "Empirical Evidence" he (1987, p. 15) writes,

> There is perhaps no empirical regularity among economic phenomena that is based on so much evidence for so wide a range of circumstances as the connection between substantial change in the quantity of money and in the level of prices. There are few if any instances in which a substantial change in the quantity of money per unit of output has occurred without a substantive change in the level of prices in the same direction. Conversely, there are few if any instances in which a substantial change in the level of prices has occurred without a substantial change in the quantity of money per unit of output in the same direction.

The historical evidence that Freidman presents in connection with the above quote in support of the quantity theory of money, in my view, is more compelling than the evidence based on econometric studies which he also cites. Econometric studies are quite useful and indeed indispensable in estimating a model's parameters. But they are often susceptible to the methodology, the model, and the sample size and period while historical records are relatively immune from such sensitivity and hence rest on a more solid ground.

One of the central conclusions in the essay is Friedman's famous pronouncement that "*inflation is always and everywhere a monetary phenomenon* in the sense that it is and can be produced only by a more rapid increase in the quantity theory than in output" (Ibid., p. 17, italics in original). This conclusion, deduced from the theory and validated by evidence (as Friedman documents), led the proponents of the quantity theory to predict high rates of inflation following the Fed's expansionary policy in the wake of the Great Recession of 2008–2009. For example, the prominent monetary economist Allan Meltzer has criticized the Federal Reserve System for, in his words, "excessive money growth." In a *Wall Street Journal* piece (6 May 2014), while quoting Friedman's dictum ("inflation is always and everywhere a monetary phenomenon"), Meltzer warns, "Inflation is in our future."[19] But should not "our future" have arrived by now – after eight years of monetary expansion? If money growth has been excessive, as Meltzer says, why is inflation at this writing (early 2016) subdued? In a conference paper on the *Monetary History* of Friedman and Schwartz, Laidler (2013, p. 16) addresses the same question and writes,

> As to all those warnings about the inflationary threat implicit in the growth of the Fed's balance sheet during 2009 and after, it is surely a key element, not only of the *Monetary History's* specific thesis about the Great Contraction, but also of monetarist doctrine in general, that the critical monetary aggregate is some appropriate measure of the money supply and not the monetary base. It is hard to believe that some monetarist critics of recent Fed policy not least that institution's historian, Allan Meltzer forgot this, but apparently they did, if only for a while.

For inflation to occur, there needs to be an increase, not just in *monetary base* (currency in circulation plus commercial banks' reserves held by the central bank), but in the *money supply* (currency in circulation plus demand deposits and even additionally some other forms of monetary assets). In the aftermath of the Great Recession, it was the monetary base, rather than money supply, that rose dramatically.

Another explanation for the subdued inflation rate despite the unprecedented increase in Fed's balance sheet is offered by William Cline (2015, p. 6) who found that

> from the end of 2007 to the end of 2008 the money multiplier fell by half (from 14), and it continued to fall much further (to 4) by the end of 2014. So *a collapse in the money multiplier has offset a sharp rise in the money base attributable to quantitative easing and the buildup of large excess reserves*.
>
> Because of the collapse in the money multiplier, the surge in Federal Reserve assets has not translated into corresponding surge in broad money. (Italics in original)

This finding does not undermine the quantity theory of money; rather, it points to the complex interrelation and interaction between monetary assets and the economy as well as the possibility of a large forecast error when one considers the impact of these assets on output or on prices. To further explore the question as to why inflation has remained low since 2008, let's turn to a conclusion that Friedman (1987, p. 17) notes in his essay,

> *In the short-run, which may be as long as three to ten years, monetary changes affect primarily output*. Over decades, on the other hand … the rate of monetary growth affects primarily prices. What happens to output depends on real factors: the enterprise, ingenuity and industry of the people; the extent of thrift; the structure of industry and government; the relations among nations, and so on. (Italics added)

Accordingly, the economy might still (in 2016) be in the short-run, and hence "monetary changes affect primarily output." This implies, notwithstanding Cline's finding, a high rate of inflation may still materialize, although it seems unlikely. Of course, it can be argued, as Keynesians generally do, the quantity theory of money is a flawed proposition and therefore the issue regarding money supply (or monetary base) and inflation is moot. But Friedman's conclusion that the short-run may be as long as three to ten years implies that if the economy is operating below full potential, an increase in the money supply (in any form) will have a greater impact on output than on prices. Hence, the absence of inflation perhaps indicates that the U.S. economy has not yet reached its potential.[20] However, even if (or when) the economy reaches its potential, with the proper management of the money supply the Federal Reserve might well avert any future inflation.

7. A final note

While empirical analysis can ostensibly validate or discredit economic theories, one must be wary of such results. We already noted in chapter two on the theory of comparative advantage the difficulty one encounters in empirical analysis of economic theories. In addition to the challenges common to all empirical works in economics, the quantity theory of money presents its own specific challenges since its components are macroeconomic variables (aggregates and averages) that encompass the whole economy.

Although the quantity theory of money has been compared to the laws of physics, economic data are subject to more measurement error and uncertainty than those in natural sciences. Additionally, the possibility always exists for any economic variable to behave in an unexpected manner. Consider that Freidman surprised a lot of people in 2003 when he told Simon London (2003), the *Financial Times* reporter, "The use of quantity of money as a target has not been a success ... I am not sure I would as of today push it as hard as I once did." While some writers (e.g., George Gilder, 2015) misinterpreted Friedman's statement as a repudiation of the quantity theory of money, Friedman's statement amounts to admitting that the economy is far more complex than he had realized. One's expectations and predictions of economic outcomes are always subject to error, often substantial error. Friedman was neither the first nor the last economist to be disappointed with a certain expectation or prediction.[21]

The quantity theory poses a serious challenge to the practitioners of monetary policy: how to apply the theoretical apparatus of the quantity theory of money in an economy that is always evolving and no one knows (indeed no one can know – at least not for sure) how economic variables would react to monetary changes. This challenge can never be fully overcome, for uncertainties are inherent in the market economic system, but the study of history will help. A student of economic theory should be a student of history as well.

Notes

1 Many books mention several thinkers including Barnard Davanzati, Luis Molina, and Geminiano Montanari as early thinkers who understood the relationship between money supply and prices.

2 Nonetheless, Locke is rightfully regarded as one of the greatest and most influential thinkers in political theory. He profoundly influenced the Founding Fathers of the United States.

3 Cantillon, an Irish native who migrated to France, wrote only one book, known as the *Essai*, between the years 1730 and 1734. The book's title is translated as *An Essay on Economic Theory*. It was published posthumously in 1755.

4 Interested readers may consult *Why Nations Fail* by Daron Acemoglu and James Robinson (2012).

5 Hume authored a third essay titled "Of Interest" also published in 1752. But we will not cover it here except for quoting from the first paragraph which sums up the gist of the essay. He (1752c/1955, p. 47) writes, "Lowness of interest is generally ascribed to plenty of money. But money, however, plentiful has no other effect, *if fixed*, than to raise the price of labour" (italics in original).

6 Jacob Viner (1937, p. 87) refers to this absence as "One of the mysteries of the history of economic thought."

7 Irving Fisher (1911/1963, p. 14) has placed Smith on a long list of economic thinkers (including Locke, Hume, and Ricardo) who had accepted the quantity theory.

8 In chapter two of Book II of the *Wealth of Nations* Smith coined the phrase "real bill" and provided the rationale for the doctrine. He (WN, p. 304) wrote, "When a bank discounts to a merchant a real bill of exchange drawn by a real creditor upon a real debtor, and which, as soon as it becomes due, is really paid by that debtor, it only advances to him a part of the value which he would otherwise be obliged to keep by him unemployed and in ready money for answering occasional demands. The payment of the bill, when it becomes due, replaces to the bank the value of what it had advanced, together with the interest. The coffers of the bank, so far as its dealings are confined to such customers, resemble a water pond, from which, though a stream is continually running out, yet another is continually running in, fully equal to that which runs out; so that, without any further care or attention, the pond keeps always equally, or very near equally full. Little or no expence can ever be necessary for replenishing the coffers of such a bank."

9 Mill disliked the term "the rapidity circulation," and suggested "the efficiency of money." But the term was later changed to "the velocity of money."

10 I thank David Laildler for pointing out to me that this essay was not published until J. K. Whitaker (1975) included it in his compilation of Marshall's early writings on economics.

11 Arthur Pigou (1917) published an important paper on the quantity theory in which he laid out his version of the Cambridge cash balance equation. In particular, see pages 41–43.

12 Although Marshall's argument is similar to Ricardo's, he attached more importance to the effect of money on output than Ricardo did.

13 Marshall's passage on this point is as follows: "an influx of a good deal of bullion into the city is likely to lower the rate of discount. This does not increase the amount of capital, in the strictest sense of the word: It does not increase the amount of building materials, machinery, etc. But it does increase the amount of command over capital which is in the hands of those whose business it is to lend to speculative enterprise. Having this extra supply, lenders lower still more the rate, which they charge for loans; and they keep on lowering it till a point is reached at which the demand will carry off the larger supply. When this has been done, there is more capital in the hands of speculative investors, who come on the markets for goods as buyers, and so raise prices." (Ibid., p. 256)

14 Fisher (Ibid., pp. 24–25) notes that "the algebraic statement of the equation of exchange was made by Simon Newcomb" in 1885, and several other scholars including Edgeworth in 1887 and Fisher himself in 1899. He also credits Mill for having stated the equation in his book (as we saw above) and points out that "Ricardo probably deserves chief credit for launching the theory."

15 For the intricacies of Say's identity and Say's equality, see chapter three of the present work. Here it suffices to note that it was in 1952 when Gary Becker and William Baumol spelled out the distinction between the two versions of Say's law.

16 Steve Hanke and Nicholas Krus (2013) document fifty-six episodes of hyperinflation in the twentieth century. The *daily* inflation rates range from 207% in Hungary in 1945–1946 to 1.38% in Taiwan in 1947.

17 Keynes, however, had no evidence for this possibility. He (Ibid.) noted, "whilst this limiting case might become practically important in future, I know of no example of it hitherto."

18 In a review article titled, "Robert E. Lucas Jr.'s Collected Papers on Monetary Theory," Thomas Sargent (2015, p. 44) quotes Lucas, "My contributions to monetary theory have been in incorporating the quantity theory of money into modern, explicitly dynamic modelling …"

19 Similarly, Arthur Laffer (*Wall Street Journal*, 11 June 2009) noted, "we can expect rapidly rising prices and much, much higher interest rates over the next four or five years."

20 The low unemployment rate in the United States (about five percent in early 2016) primarily reflects the fact that the labor force participation is historically low (lowest in 40 years) rather than the economy being close to its potential.

21 In 1943, Paul Samuelson predicted that "were the war to end suddenly within the next six months … then there would be ushered in the greatest period of unemployment and industrial dislocation which any economy has ever faced" (quoted in David Henderson, 2010, p. 1). Samuelson's misprediction rivals that of Robert Malthus on famine and death.

Bibliography

Acemoglu, Daron and James Robinson (2012), *Why Nations Fail*, New York, NY: Crown Business.

Arnon, Arie (2011), *Monetary Theory and Policy from Hume and Smith to Wicksell: Money, Credit, and the Economy*, Cambridge, UK: Cambridge University Press.

Blaug, Mark (1995), "Why Is the Quantity Theory of Money the Oldest Surviving Theory in Economics?" in *The Quantity Theory of Money: From Locke to Keynes and Friedman*, Ed. by Mark Blaug, Brookfield, VT: Edward Edgar, pp. 27–49.

Cantillon, Richard (1755/2010), *An Essay on Economic Theory*, Translated by Chantal Saucier, Ed. by Mark Thornton, Auburn, AL: Mises Institute's Website.

Cline, William (2015), "Quantity Theory of Money Redux? Will Inflation Be a Legacy of Quantitative Easing?" Peterson Institute for International Economics, *Policy Brief* Number PB15-7, May.

Eichengreen, Barry (2015), *Hall of Mirrors: The Great Depression, the Great Recession, and the Uses – and Misuses – of History*, Oxford, UK: Oxford University Press.

Eltis, Walter (1995), "John Locke, the Quantity Theory of Money and the Establishment of a Sound Currency," in *The Quantity Theory of Money: From Locke to Keynes and Friedman*, Ed. by Mark Blaug, Brookfield, VT: Edward Edgar, pp. 4–26.

Fisher, Irving (1911/1963), *The Purchasing Power of Money*, New York, NY: Augustus M. Kelley.

Friedman, Milton (1956), "The Quantity Theory of Money – A Restatement," in *Studies in the Quantity Theory of Money*, Ed. by Milton Friedman, Chicago, IL: The University of Chicago Press.

Friedman, Milton (1968/1973), "The Quantity Theory of Money," in *Money and Banking: Selected Readings*, Ed. by A. A. Walters, Ringwood, Victoria, AUS: Penguin Books, pp. 36–66. Reprinted from *International Encyclopedia of the Social Sciences*, Free Press, pp. 432–447.

Friedman, Milton (1987), "Quantity Theory of Money," in *The New Palgrave: A Dictionary of Economics*, Volume 4, Ed. by John Eatwell, Murray Milgate, and Peter Newman, pp. 3–20.

Friedman, Milton and Anna Schwartz (1963), *A Monetary History of the United States, 1867–1960*, Princeton, NJ: Princeton University Press.

Gilder, George (2015), *The 21st Century Case for Gold: A New Information Theory of Money*. Accessed January 2016 from https://americanprinciplesproject.org/economics/new-george-gilder-book-the-21st-century-case-for-gold-a-new-information-theory-of-money/.

Hanke, Steve and Nicholas Krus (2013), "World Hyperinflation," in *The Handbook of Major Events in Economic History*, Ed. by Randall Parker and Robert Whaples, London, UK: Routledge, pp. 367–377.

Hardy, S. McLean (1895), "The Quantity Theory of Money and Prices, 1860–1891," *Journal of Political Economy* 3, 2, pp. 145–168.

Hegeland, Hugo (1951), *The Quantity Theory of Money: A Critical Study of Its Historical Development and Interpretation and a Restatement*, Gotenborg, SWE: Elanders Boktryckeri Aktiebolag.

Henderson, David (2010), "Paul Samuelson's Prediction for Post World War II," *Library of Economics Liberty*. Accessed January 2016 from http://econlog.econlib.org/archives/2010/07/paul_samuelsons.html.

Hume, David (1749/1955), "Hume to Montesquieu," in *David Hume: Writings on Economics*, Ed. by Eugene Rotwein, Madison, WI: University of Wisconsin Press, pp. 187–190.

Hume, David (1752a/1955), "Of Money," in *David Hume: Writings on Economics*, Ed. by Eugene Rotwein, Madison, WI: University of Wisconsin Press, pp. 33–46.

Hume, David (1752b/1955), "Of the Balance of Trade," in *David Hume: Writings on Economics*, Ed. by Eugene Rotwein, Madison, WI: University of Wisconsin Press, pp. 60–77.

Hume, David (1752c/1955), "Of Interest," in *David Hume: Writings on Economics*, Ed. by Eugene Rotwein, Madison, WI: University of Wisconsin Press, pp. 47–59.

Humphrey, Thomas (1974), "The Quantity Theory of Money: Its Historical Evolution and Role in Policy Debates," *Economic Review*, Federal Reserve Bank of Richmond, May/June, pp. 2–19.

Humphrey, Thomas (1982), "The Real Bill Doctrine," *Economic Review*, Federal Reserve Bank of Richmond, September/October, pp. 3–13.

Keynes, John Maynard (1911), "Reviews: *The Purchasing Power of Money*," *The Economic Journal* 21, 83, pp. 393–398.

Keynes, John Maynard (1923/1971), *A Tract on Monetary Reform, The Collected Writings of John Maynard Keynes*, Volume IV, London, UK: MacMillan St. Martin's Press.

Keynes, John Maynard (1930/1971), *A Treatise on Money, The Collected Writings of John Maynard Keynes*, Volume V, London, UK: MacMillan St. Martin's Press.

Keynes, John Maynard (1936/1997), *The General Theory of Employment, Interest, and Money*, Amherst, NY: Prometheus Books.

Laffer, Arthur (2009), "Get Ready for Inflation and Higher Interest Rates," *Wall Street Journal*, June 11.

Laidler, David (1966), "The Rate of Interest and the Demand for Money – Some Empirical Evidence," *Journal of Political Economy* 74, 6, pp. 543–555.

Laidler, David (1977), *The Demand for Money: Theories and Evidence*, 2nd Edition, New York, NY: Dun-Donnelley.

Laidler, David (1991), *The Golden Age of the Quantity Theory*, Princeton, NJ: Princeton University Press.

Laidler, David (1993), "Was Wicksell a Quantity Theorist?" in *Essays in Honor of Don Patinkin*, Ed. by Haim Barkai, Stanley Fischer, and Nissan Liviatan, London, UK: The Macmillan Press LTD.

Laidler, David (2011), "Professor Fisher and the Quantity Theory – a Significant Encounter," unpublished manuscript, presented on October 14, 2011, at the Universite Lumiere-Lyon 2 Conference.

Laidler, David (2013), "Reassessing the Thesis of the *Monetary History*," prepared for a conference entitled *Retrospectives on the Great Depression*, Princeton University, February 15–16, 2013.

Lange, Oscar (1942/1970), "Say's Law: A Restatement and Criticism," in Papers in *Economics and Sociology*, Ed. by Oskar Lange, Oxford, UK: Pregamon Press.

Leamer, Edward (1994), "Testing Trade Theory," in *Survey in International Trade*, Ed. by David Greenaway and L. Alan Winters, Oxford, UK: Basil Balckwell, pp. 66–106.

Locke, John (1691/1963), "Some Considerations of the Consequences of the Lowering of Interest and Raising the Value of Money," in *The Works of John Locke*, Volume V, London, UK: Scientia Verlag Aalen.

London, Simon (2003), "Lunch with Milton Friedman," *Financial Times*, June 28.

Lucas Jr., Robert and Juan Pablo Nicolini (2015), "On the Stability of Money Demand," Federal Reserve Bank of Minneapolis Research Department Working Paper 718.

Marshall, Alfred (1871/1975), "Essay on Money," in *The Early Economic Writings of Alfred Marshall, 1867–1890*, Volume 1, Ed. and Introduced by J. K. Whitaker, New York, NY: The Free Press, pp. 164–177.

Marshall, Alfred (1922/1960), *Money Credit and Commerce*, New York, NY: Augustus M. Kelley.

Marshall, Alfred (1926), *Official Papers of Alfred Marshall*, Ed. by John Maynard Keynes. London, UK: Macmillan.

Meltzer, Allan (2014), "How the Fed Fuels the Coming Inflation," *Wall Street Journal*, May 6.

Mill, John Stuart (1848/2006), *Principles of Political Economy*, Collected Works of John Stuart Mill, Indianapolis, IN: Liberty Fund.

Montesquieu, de Baron (1748/1900), *The Spirit of the Laws*, Translated by Thomas Nugent, Revised by J.V. Prichard, Volume II, New York, NY: D. Appleton and Company.

Patinkin, Don (1948), "Relative Prices, Say's Law, and the Demand for Money," *Econometrica* 16, pp. 135–154.

Pigou, Arthur (1917), "The Value of Money," *Quarterly Journal of Economics* 32, 1, pp. 38–65.

Ricardo, David (1817/1996), *Principles of Political Economy and Taxation*, Great Mind Series, Amherst, NY: Prometheus Books.

Ricardo, David (2004), *The Works and Correspondence of David Ricardo*, Ed. by Pier Sraffa, Volumes I through XI, Cambridge, UK: Cambridge University Press.

Rotwein, Eugene (1955), *David Hume: Writings on Economics*, Madison, WI: University of Wisconsin Press.

Sargent, Thomas J. (2015), "Robert E. Lucas Jr.'s Collected Papers on Monetary Theory," *Journal of Economic Literatures* 53, 1, pp. 43–64.

Schumpeter, Joseph A. (1954/1995), *History of Economic Analysis*, New York, NY: Oxford University Press.

Smith, Adam (1776/1981), *An Inquiry into the Nature and Causes of the Wealth of Nations*, Indianapolis, IN: Liberty Fund.

Smith, Adam (1982), *Lectures on Jurisprudence*, Indianapolis, IN: Liberty Fund.

Viner, Jacob (1937/1975), *Studies in the Theory of International Trade*, New York, NY: Augustus M. Kelley Publishers.

Whitaker, J.K. (1975), *The Early Economic Writings of Alfred Marshall, 1867–1890*, Volume 1, New York, NY: The Free Press.

Wicksell, Knut (1898/1965), *Interest and Prices*, New York, NY: A. M. Kelley.

Wicksell, Knut (1915/1962), *Lectures on Political Economy*, London, UK: Routledge & Kegan Paul LTD.

Index

For Product Safety Concerns and Information please contact our EU
representative GPSR@taylorandfrancis.com
Taylor & Francis Verlag GmbH, Kaufingerstraße 24, 80331 München, Germany

www.ingramcontent.com/pod-product-compliance
Ingram Content Group UK Ltd.
Pitfield, Milton Keynes, MK11 3LW, UK
UKHW020955180425
457613UK00019B/694